my soul waits

Solace for the Lonely
from the Psalms

Marva J. Dawn

AUTHOR OF *Keeping the Sabbath Wholly*

IVP Books

An imprint of InterVarsity Press
Downers Grove, Illinois

InterVarsity Press
P.O. Box 1400, Downers Grove, IL 60515-1426
World Wide Web: www.ivpress.com
E-mail: email@ivpress.com

InterVarsity Press® is the book-publishing division of InterVarsity Christian Fellowship/USA®, a student movement active on campus at hundreds of universities, colleges and schools of nursing in the United States of America, and a member movement of the International Fellowship of Evangelical Students. For information about local and regional activities, write Public Relations Dept., InterVarsity Christian Fellowship/USA, 6400 Schroeder Rd., P.O. Box 7895, Madison, WI 53707-7895, or visit the IVCF website at <www.intervarsity.org>.

Design: Cindy Kiple
Images: empty beach: Rupert Mardon/Getty Images
*   leaf: Zachary Stigler/iStockphoto*

ISBN 978-0-8308-3443-3

Printed in the United States of America ∞

Library of Congress Cataloging-in-Publication Data

Dawn, Marva J.
   [I'm lonely, Lord—how long?]
   My soul waits: solace for the lonely from the Psalms / Marva J. Dawn.
      p. cm.
   Originally published: I'm lonely, Lord—how long? Grand Rapids, Mich.: William B. Eerdmans Pub. Co., c1998. Includes bibliographical references. ISBN 978-0-8308-3443-3 (pbk.: alk. paper)
   1. Bible. O.T. Psalms—Meditations. 2. Loneliness—Religious aspects—Christianity—Meditations. I. Title.
   BS1430.54.D39 2007
   242'.5—dc22
                                                          2007016689

P 22 21 20 19 18 17 16 15   14 13 12 11 10 9 8 7 6 5 4 3 2

Y 25 24 23 22 21 20 19 18 17 16 15 14 13 12 11 10 09 08

To Nancy,
whose prayers helped this book to come into existence,
whose life enfolded everyone around her in the love of God,
whose battle against leukemia was also a means for glorifying God.

And in memory of my godson, Joshua Daniel Critchett
(September 22, 1979—July 28, 1997)

and of Tim Bigelow,
whose profoundly spiritual friendship was deeply comforting
(July 29, 1944—May 1, 2006)

"Precious in the sight of the LORD
is the death of those faithful to him."

Contents

Preface

This is not a scholarly book, though it is based on theological and literary research. Rather, this is a very personal book—not so much as autobiography, but because faith requires our whole selves. These chapters came not merely from intellectual work but from life—seemingly unendurable loneliness that demands to know if God is really here with me, with you, when our lives are afflicted with sorrows and sufferings. When dark clouds of doubt rolled in immense waves over me in black nights of despair, I wrestled and wondered if I was totally alone. Does God care? Is God here?

We need the Christian community and the Scriptures to bring God's presence to us. I first wrote this book to bring the healing presence of God's Word through the Word-shaped community to those who suffer from various kinds of loneliness, and for people who minister to them (their families, friends, pastors, fellow members in churches)—and I wrote out of my own heartache.

I no longer experience that profound anguish, so I hesitated when it was suggested that this book be reprinted. Yet many have said that the book was helpful in sorrowing times, and the truth of the Psalms abides forever; therefore, I offer these studies and these accounts again, only somewhat revised so that they still carry the authenticity of the yearning emptiness which all of us feel at times and in which some of us seem to be drowning in our worst times. May these chapters bring healing to you if you are in the throes of loneliness pres-

ently, or may they bring you grace and new tools for comforting if
you are caring for someone in that place.

Because this book is theology out of narrative, a basic sketch of my
life will bring more sense to the pieces of these chapters. I was born
a fighter. I grew up in a family that reacted to financial struggles, to
the pressures of teaching, and to the rigors of administering a large
parochial school with hard work. My parents modeled the good fight
of faith. My learning to contend in faith was positive, but difficulties
have arisen when I've foolishly thought I could, by virtue of my own
power and intellect, control the circumstances of life.

The faith developed through my childhood sustained me when, at
the age of sixteen, I watched my little world crash. I couldn't recover
from a seemingly mild case of measles at the end of my sophomore
year. Formerly a star athlete, I increasingly lost weight and strength
and, by Christmas of that year, was reduced to a mere skeleton of my
former self. The measles virus had destroyed my pancreas, necessi-
tating a lifelong battle against escalating complications of diabetes,
but these also bring me closer to God as succeeding health crashes
repeatedly test and strengthen my fight of faith.

Following my graduation from high school, I went first to a Lutheran teachers college, where I majored in English and theology and
minored in secondary education and church music, and then to the
University of Idaho in Moscow for graduate work in English—fully
intending to go on to England to get a Ph.D. and return to teach in a
Lutheran college somewhere. But two major events interrupted those
plans.

Because of my double major in college, I was given the privilege of
creating and teaching a course at Idaho on Literature of the Bible, and
thereby discovered that my real love in life was teaching the Scriptures. I also met a man there who became my husband after I finished
the M.A. program. We remained in Moscow after we married, and I
enjoyed immensely my work in a congregation's educational and mu-

sic programs and my responsibility for that parish's campus ministry at the University of Idaho and Washington State University.

When my husband's new job brought a move, I found it terribly difficult to leave the work that gave such happiness. Although I had a hard time finding myself in the transition, once again the old fighting instinct took over. I went back to school to study theology, and eventually began to work as part of the staff of a Lutheran church while finishing my M.Div. in New Testament. Once again my work was a delight; once again my life was ripped apart—this time by a crash more severe than any health problem: my husband left me and married one of the members of the youth group we led. This time there were no intellectual answers, no power to cope with the devastation. I fought the hurt and despair by pouring myself into my work.

The grace of God rescued me at that time through the founding of Christians Equipped for Ministry (CEM). Under the care of seven persons on the board of directors, this corporation has enabled me to work for the last twenty-eight years as a freelance theologian, writing books and formerly leading congregational, youth, and women's retreats, and now (after finishing a Th.M. in Old Testament and a Ph.D. in Christian Ethics and the Scriptures) speaking primarily at seminaries and clergy conferences.

In the early days of CEM, almost a year after my husband left me, God miraculously provided the finances for me to buy an old three-story house. It had room for my housemate Julie to have an art studio on the top floor and for me to have my study and CEM office in the basement, in addition to five bedrooms to give us space for ministering to women in crisis. CEM hired a director for that EPHESUS House ministry, and we learned many valuable lessons during the months that we had guests in our home. When the director went back to school, I tried unsuccessfully to carry on that ministry along with my teaching and writing, but I soon learned the limitations of my gifts.

Julie and I searched for other ways to use our big house, and finally the Carson family of four joined us to create a Christian community. After a few years together, our household split up as I finished the first edition of this book and left for the University of Notre Dame for my Ph.D., and Julie moved elsewhere.

Up until last year, when I switched to daily bicycling, I would swim three miles a week to keep my diabetes under control. This built up strength and endurance and also provided precious time for prayer and meditation. During the days of the initial writing of this book, the discipline brought great physical, emotional, and spiritual healing.

My life, however, has been constantly characterized by struggles for health. In the last twenty-five years I've had numerous minor surgeries on my hands and feet, hundreds of laser burns for my eyes, and nine major surgeries, including a resectioning of my intestine because of an intussusception, a hysterectomy, a rebuilding of a shattered foot, three eye surgeries after retinal hemorrhages, two cancer surgeries, and a kidney transplant. I've spent countless weeks on crutches or in a wheelchair because of burns, injuries, and my shattered foot, then broken leg, and present leg brace. I perpetually battle limited vision in my good eye and hearing loss in the left ear. My intestinal nerves are dead, and their functioning has to be manufactured with a combination of four medicines. Walking is difficult because of my crippled leg, bone deterioration, and dead nerves below the knee. Periodontal problems, nerve damage from cancer surgeries, and arthritis cause perpetual pain. Every day is a struggle to balance multiple insulin injections with exercise and the effects of immunosuppressants. Some days I'm thoroughly tired of all the strain.

Now the strain is made much easier because, more than ten years after I was abandoned, God brought me the enormous gift of a loving and devoted husband, Myron Sandberg, who expends great effort, diligence, and tenderness in helping with my constant health crises.

But in the profoundly lonely days when this book was first written, my reaction to emotional and physical pain was to fight. I did research, worked on writing, got ready for the next speaking engagement, swam harder and longer.

I'm not claiming that my method of coping with problems had any great merit. In fact, it had serious flaws. But it explains the stories in the pages that follow. Now as I long to learn to believe more deeply in the God of the Scriptures as expounded on these pages, I also yearn to learn better methods for dealing with life's problems—methods of trust and rest.

When I was alone, I resorted to familiar coping patterns—fighting physical limitations with a rigorous discipline of body, pushing myself to be as capable as possible, fighting the ravages of abandonment and divorce with a solid regimen of work, seeking wholeness by serving others. But how does one fight the attacks of loneliness that work on us doubly because all the other battles have to be fought alone? I struggled with my desire to be loved and dreaded the loneliness of bus stations or airports and long hours of solitary work.

My major equipment for that fight was—and remains—the Scriptures. In the book of Psalms especially God reveals Himself[1] to us as One who cares about our pain and sustains us in it. I wanted to learn better to trust the Trinity so that, instead of trying to fight my battles alone, I could rest in the LORD's fight for me and appreciate the gifts

---

[1]As I have pondered the objections of feminists to masculine pronouns for God (because they "oppress women"), I have become convinced that their arguments are given more weight since we stopped capitalizing those pronouns and thereby lost the mystery of God's transcendence that can also be personal. Therefore, I have returned to capitalizing the pronouns to emphasize that they are meant to signify not gender, but surprising relational intimacy. Though I grew up in a somewhat patriarchal denomination, still I have always recognized the words *He, Him, His,* and *Himself* not to signify God's maleness, but to carry a sense of the ineffable, the secret yet revealed wonder of God's immanence. For further discussion see, "He, His, Him, Himself" in part one of my book *Talking the Walk: Letting Christian Language Live Again* (Grand Rapids, Mich.: Brazos Press, 2005).

He gave to free me from my loneliness.

I'm grateful to the friends who helped to bring healing to my life in those days—particularly those who allowed me to include them in the stories of this book. Also I give deepest thanks to this book's original editor, Roy M. Carlisle (at that time of Harper and Row San Francisco), who cared enough about the subject matter to be patient with me in working on it, and to all the great folks at InterVarsity Press who kindly put this book back into print. Most of all, I thank the members of the CEM board, who believed in me when I couldn't.

I'm Lonely, LORD—How Long?

How long, LORD? Will you forget me forever?
    How long will you hide your face from me?
How long must I wrestle with my thoughts
    and day after day have sorrow in my heart?
    How long will my enemy triumph over me?
Look on me and answer, LORD my God.
    Give light to my eyes, or I will sleep in death,
and my enemy will say, "I have overcome him,"
    and my foes will rejoice when I fall.
But I trust in your unfailing love;
    my heart rejoices in your salvation.
I will sing the LORD's praise,
    for he has been good to me.

PSALM 13

How long, LORD?[1] How long must I stare at this typewriter and remain blocked in my efforts to get past the failures of my own life?

---

[1] I have followed the customary practice in Bibles of capitalizing all the letters in the word LORD when the Hebrew word to be translated is the name *YHWH*, which is

An overwhelming number of us are lonely—coming out of (or maybe just beginning to go into) terrible times of rejection or crisis or fear or loss. Sometimes we are lonely for a specific reason: our spouse has recently died or left us; our children have just gone from home or have been tragically killed; we are fighting a particular battle against illness or suffering the ravages of chemotherapy; we are new in the neighborhood; our values are different from those of our colleagues; it is a Friday night, and all our other single friends have dates. Sometimes our loneliness is a general, pervasive alienation: we just don't feel as if we belong in our place of work, in our community, in our family, even in our church. Maybe we don't have anyone with whom we can share the most important dimensions of our lives.

We need good news that isn't just trite folk wisdom slapped on superficially in a meaningless attempt to help us feel better. Yet after all my preparations, translating Hebrew passages and meditating on the Psalms and gathering their words of comfort, my writing has been blocked by the very "How long?" complaint that the Scriptures intend to counteract.

In that condition we think that as soon as circumstances in our lives get put right, we can proceed. When they don't, we remain incapacitated and ask, "How long, Lord?"

In our loneliness especially, we join the psalmist in asking God if He is going to forget us forever. The original Hebrew text expresses it as wondering if God will disregard us for "an everlastingness." God seems to have dropped us out of His plans. Nothing is changing. We have been abandoned.

---

often vocalized as *Yahweh* (formerly as *Jehovah*). That is the name by which the Lord revealed Himself to Moses at the burning bush in Exodus 3:14-15. It is a term that distinguishes Him from all the neighboring false deities. He is not just a god, but He alone is the faithful covenant God, the great "I am." We need to recover the promise of the name Lord in our lonely times, to learn the glory of the Lord's constant faithfulness to His covenant and His effective deliverance of His people from all their captivities.

David, the writer of Psalm 13,[2] is gutsy and honest. We are comforted to know that he struggled with the "How long?" malady as we do. His honesty, furthermore, invites us to be real about our emotions too. When we feel that God has abandoned us, sometimes we act as though we are afraid we'll sin even more by being real with God about the vacuum we experience. God already knows how we feel, so we might as well not compound our problems by being dishonest about it.

The second "How long?" question elaborates the reason that we feel forsaken by God. The poet asks how long the LORD will hide from him His face. That First Testament[3] idiom suggests withholding one's kindness or, even more painful to the (non)recipient, withdrawing it.

When we are suffering from acute loneliness, it seems that God has pulled back His love. He doesn't seem to want us to recover. If He did, we think, He would send whomever or whatever is necessary to ease our pain and fix things up.

In the heartbreak of divorce I kept wishing that my former husband would realize his error and come back—until his wedding day forced me to bury that hope. Then I wished for anything to get rid of the memories and instinctively wondered if I could ever be truly loved by God or anyone in a way that would ease my loneliness forever. If God really loved me, couldn't He stop the sorrow and suffering?

---

[2]The book of Psalms, as it has been passed to us in the canonical tradition of Jews and Christians, lists David as the author of Psalm 13. Since these meditations on the Psalms are not intended as commentary, but as devotional helps, we don't have to debate the historical accuracy of this or any other ascription. Rather, because there are deep narrative and descriptive benefits from identifying the emotions and situations of the Psalms with a particular poet, I will throughout this book accept the titles and names associated with these poems and honor them canonically.

[3]Along with many scholars and clergypersons, I prefer to call the first three-fourths of the Bible the "First Testament" or the "Hebrew Scriptures" to avoid our culture's negative connotations of the name "*Old* Testament" and to emphasize both the consistency of God's grace for all God's people and also the continuity of God's covenants in the Bible, first with Israel and then in addition with Christians.

Whatever the reason, we've all probably felt this way at times: Why does the LORD hold back His love? Must He punish us for some reason? How long must this punishment, this hollowness when we pray, this denial of our "needs," go on?

The psalmist continues by asking how long he must continue to wrestle with his thoughts. The phrase *day after day* in the next line occurs at the end of the sentence in the Hebrew text (a place of emphasis) and could also be rendered "all the day." Some commentators suggest, then, that the expression "all the night" might be presupposed in the previous line about thought-wrestling to complete the pattern.

Our own experiences confirm such a possibility for the text. Perhaps you too have stayed awake half the night trying to plan ways to end your torment. When I was excruciatingly lonely, I could usually hide it from myself during the day by being busy with work, and I could find comfort by crying with friends who cared. But after I got into bed, I ached with the emptiness. Too many nights I turned increasingly inward to hide from the loneliness that engulfed me. I tried to manipulate life so that I could either eliminate the pain or become numb to it.

However, as the poet continues, we realize that those plans of the night don't usually work out. Though he gives no specifics, David's enemies were the ones to frustrate his plans. In fact, such anguish is caused by his enemies that David fears for his life (vv. 3-4). The canonical ascription of this poem to David lets us think of such adversaries as Saul, the Philistines, or even his son Absalom.

These days, however, our enemies are not usually people trying to harm us physically. What kinds of foes seem to triumph over us today? Who or what are they for you?

Your adversaries might be individual people—even compassionate friends who mistakenly think you should be "over" your loss by now, jealous backbiters at work, inconsiderate neighbors who harass you, envious liars spreading false rumors about you, malicious gossips who exaggerate your troubles, judgmental faultfinders blaming you for a divorce you didn't want. Perhaps your enemies are financial problems or a loss that cannot ever be replaced or the lack of a home in which to find some sense of belonging and security. Maybe your foes are various fears for the future or misery from the rejections of the past.

Whether persons, situations, or attitudes, our enemies immobilize us. We get too nervous meeting new people because we fear their rejection. We can't do things we've always done because they bring up too many painful memories—or happy memories that can't be repeated because our beloved has died. We assume we're ugly when no one asks us for a date. We worry so much about how to find enough to do to fill up all our time alone that we are unable to do anything. We do not know how to reach out to recently hired workers in our office because we feel so fragmented from our divorce. We are unable to be open to feelings because previous risks have brought too much disapproval. How long, O LORD, must we be helpless in the face of these enemies?

"But I trust in your unfailing love." After all the discouraged "How long?" questions, suddenly the psalmist is writing words of hope and victory. Is such a change really possible? On what basis can we make such a turn away from the agonies of "How long?"

The key lies in one of my favorite Hebrew words, the noun *chesedh*, which is translated "unfailing love" in Today's New International Version of Psalm 13:5. The term describes the steadfast, covenant love of the LORD, the amazing grace of His infinite kindness and compassion toward us, His people.

This word answers the first and second questions of the psalm. The unfailing steadfastness of *chesedh* tells us for sure that God has not forgotten us, not for a moment; nor will He ever.

Chesedh also answers the third "How long?" The nature of *chesedh*

is that God will never withdraw His support from us. It may seem so
when He does not grant us what we ask or take away our intermina-
ble sorrow, but His infinite wisdom and love are always present with
us and on behalf of us.

Of course, it will seem that we wrestle with our thoughts for too
long. As long as we are depending upon our own thoughts, the distress will continue. Only when we are finally reduced to the point of
helplessness, the realization that we will never be able to deal with
our loneliness or grief by ourselves, will we give in to *chesedh* and let
God bring to us the gifts of His love. When we finally let God be God-
for-us and participate in His plans willingly, we can discover the Joy
of them.

For years I have been capitalizing the word *Joy* to distinguish it
from merely human happinesses. There are times when our circumstances make happiness impossible, but we can always experience
profound Joy when we are aware that in His *chesedh* God is able to
transform even the direst of circumstances. (This will be explored
more thoroughly in chapter twelve.)

We dare not be superficial about this and say, "Oh, yes, God loves
you; therefore, you *ought* to be happy." When others dump the gospel
on us like that, not only are we not comforted, but our guilt is compounded because we believe (falsely) that Christians *should* be able to
answer that *ought* by cranking up better feelings.

The essence of the matter is that we can't experience the truth of
chesedh in the reality of our feelings until we know it first as a fact of
faith. We still wonder how long, yet deep underneath we are convinced that ultimately *chesedh* reigns because that is the way God has
always dealt with His people. The LORD, the promising "I AM," has *always* been faithful to His covenants. Surely He will not single us out
as individuals to withhold from us His *chesedh*. In that fact we can
trust, even before it has sunk into our feelings.

Sometimes it helps, the psalmist points out, to look back to the

past. The final verse says, "I will sing the LORD's praise, for he has
been good to me." Not only will we be able someday to sing because
we will have learned how He has been good to us in this situation,
but also right now we can sing because He has been good to us in
the past.

Do you remember times when you felt you couldn't go on because
the loneliness was so devastating? Then, at just the right time, God
sent His love in some personal way—a phone call or a hug from
someone special, a good book or a card that brought *chesedh* into
your consciousness, a hymn verse or Bible passage that reminded
you of God's grace. We can train our minds to turn to memories of
those times in the moments when we are tempted to ask, "How
long?" and thus be strengthened by the precious instances when the
"How long?" came crashing to a halt in the wonder of God's *chesedh*.

That is why the psalmist can say, "My heart rejoices in your salvation." The Hebrew language doesn't have past, present, or future
tense verbs as our English does. Its verbs indicate simply completed
or uncompleted action. The verb here for rejoicing is in the imperfect, or incomplete, form. We could translate it, "My heart will rejoice
in your salvation," or as in the TNIV, "My heart rejoices"—the action
is continually going on. If we are not yet experiencing Joy in God's
deliverance, we can confidently look forward to the time when we
will. Furthermore, that very assurance that His *chesedh* will not fail
us, that someday He will come through with deliverance, enables us
to rejoice even now in the meantime.

The delightful irony is that usually the change of attitude is the deliverance. As soon as we stop asking, "How long?" we are liberated
from that question's bondage. Then we can rejoice instead in the
memories of how God has been good to us or how "bountifully" He
has "dealt" with us (NASB).

That is how it was there at my desk the night I began this book. I
didn't have to stare at the typewriter until my loneliness problems

were solved. Psalm 13 freed my fingers and heart from the anguish of "How long?" and its immobility. I didn't feel alone anymore. I felt Joy in the company of those who might read this book to share with me the deep awareness that the *chesedh* of the LORD our God is great enough to warrant our trust.

For Further Meditation

The following suggestions for reflection can provide connections between the theological principles discovered in the intensive Bible study of these chapters and the daily particulars of your own discipleship. May these questions be helpful to you for letting the ideas of this chapter form who you are, for perhaps preparing for future discussion if you are using this book for study in a group, and for linking what God teaches you through the Psalms with how you respond to Him and reach out to others around you.

1. What kinds of experiences cause me to think that God has forgotten me?

2. What gifts do I think God should have given me, but hasn't?

3. When and how and why do I get futilely caught in wrestling with my own thoughts and plans?

4. Who or what are the enemies that frustrate my plans?

5. In what ways have I experienced God enabling me to triumph over those enemies?

6. What are some examples of God's *chesedh* in action in my life?

7. Am I able to rejoice in His deliverance yet? Why, or why not?

The LORD Is in Control of Time

But I trust in you, LORD;
I say, "You are my God."
My times are in your hands.

PSALM 31:14-15a

Suppose you have two groups of friends. One set is not very reliable. Just when you count on them, they let you down. If you reveal to them your deepest secrets, they either laugh at you or tell everybody else.

Your other friends are made of solid rock. You know that you can confide in them and they will be true to you, no matter what. You can count on them in any circumstance; they will stand by you or else be honest about why they can't.

To which kind of friend will you turn in a crisis? Which one will you trust?

Exactly. You will turn to the one who is trustable, the one who is worthy of your confidence. Your trusting does not depend upon how good you are at trusting, but upon your knowledge that the one on whom you lean is stable and will assuredly support you.

That is the necessary basis for this chapter's discussion of our "times." In fact, it is the basis for all of this book. The psalmist David declares that it is the LORD, *YHWH*, in whom he trusts. We must, therefore, first of all consider who *YHWH* is.

The difference between LORD, *Lord* and *lord* in most translations of the First Testament tells us which Hebrew word underlies the English rendering. If the Hebrew word is *YHWH*, then all the letters are capitalized, to signify this covenant "I AM" name for God.[1] If the word is *adonai*, Hebrew for "master" or "ruler," then only the first letter is capitalized when it refers to God, but the first letter is left lowercase when it refers to human masters. French Bibles seem to me wiser, for they translate *YHWH* as "l'Éternal" and *adonai* as "le Seigneur."

Throughout the First Testament, God continually reveals to Israel new dimensions of the meaning of His name. Then, when Jesus comes, the New Testament records that He claims the same "I AM"-ness for Himself (see John 8:58) and demonstrates in human form for all to see what the character of *YHWH* is like. He shows us the Triune God's tender love, His infinite care, His overwhelming patience and grace.

On the basis of God's thorough revelation, we can, throughout this study of His comfort for our loneliness, come back again and again to the fact that God is called by the name *YHWH*. He is the Covenant God, the One who has never broken any of His promises. He is the faithful, loving, holy, just, steadfast, compassionate, creative One,

---

[1]The original Hebrew noun was composed of these four consonants, Y H W H, which relate to the root of the verb "to be." Since the Jews honor God's name by not saying it aloud (for fear that they might blaspheme it), and since the original Hebrew manuscripts were written with only consonants and not the vowel points, scholars are not sure how to say the word. This is why it was formerly vocalized as *Jehovah*, but now is customarily written as *Yahweh*. Rather than make it readable, I will use *YHWH* in this book and hope that this will cause you to reflect upon its mystery and God's unreachable majesty. It seems to me that our postmodern times suffer from a lack of awe and reverence and "fear" for God. I put the word *fear* in quotation marks because I don't mean "terror," but I do intend a profound realization of our unworthiness before God so that we do not take God's gracious love and steadfast mercy for granted, as if we deserved it or could earn it or pay it back.

whose infinite majesty and sovereignty we can never comprehend. Yet the more we search to know who He is, the more we will be able to trust Him.

If we have learned that He is perfectly wise, then we can trust Him for His purposes in our lives. If we know Him to be unremittingly loving, then we can believe Him even when something doesn't appear to be the product of His love.

That is why in Psalm 31 David, despite the apparent triumph of his enemies, can say, with a strong Hebrew adversative pronoun, "*But I* trust in you, *YHWH*." Greatly to the contrary of how others might normally react—in fear, because of who the foes are—the poet is able to trust *YHWH* because of who *He* is.

The Hebrew verb meaning "to trust" is related to the noun for "security." We trust in *YHWH* because He alone is able to give us genuine refuge. When enemies of every sort are filling our lives with sadness or terror, it is the best of hope to remember that *YHWH* is faithful and can be trusted.

In these days of corporate downsizing and an escalating economic gap between rich and poor throughout the world, no one can trust in work or money anymore. Turmoil over personal matters or dread of terrorists leaves us feeling frightfully lonely and insecure. In the midst of doubting and searching, we must continually go back to reexamine the character of *YHWH;* again and again the Scriptures assure us that His character can be trusted. Knowing that He loves us with the compassion of a father (Psalm 103:13) or a mother (Isaiah 49:13-15) or a shepherd (Psalm 23; John 10:1-3, 11-16), we can find the security for which we long.

That is why the psalmist continues, "I say, 'You are my God.'" The Hebrew verb for "say" could be understood in either of two ways. If it is connected to the adversative that begins the verse, then the verb is an incomplete one and means that the poet is continually repeating, "You are my God." Or it could be a perfect (finished-action) verb, meaning that he has declared it pointedly and, therefore, it is a foundation for his life.

In the midst of our struggles, especially when we are mourning or dejected, we need to keep reasserting that our God is *YHWH*. Otherwise, we fall into the temptation of making idols out of security, or marriage, or companionship, or possessions, or whatever else we think we need to ease our loneliness and grief.

When I was first writing this chapter, distressing things had been piling up all day long. One of my options for how to use my big house fell through, and I wasn't sure how I would manage financially. Someone whom I'd been counseling misunderstood my words and got very angry with me without letting me clarify what I was saying. Then the mail brought extensive work with a deadline on some writing, and I didn't see how I could fit everything into my overloaded schedule. Finally, at about ten that night, I knew I needed support and telephoned a friend—but he wasn't home.

"Now, God, why did you let that happen?"—that was my first reaction. I ached for support; why, of all times, was there no answer now?

In such disappointment, we need to repeat, "*YHWH*, you are my God. I can't necessarily rely on human beings to minister to my yearnings. You are the One to whom I can always tell my grief, and you will hear."

Such times remind us that our friends are channels of God's love. Much later that night, my friend did call and sort through my discouragements with me. But God let me first remember that He alone is God so that I could understand that telephone call as another sign to me of *YHWH's* care.

The Hebrew strikingly underscores the decisiveness of the psalmist's declaration more than our English translations do; the literal phrase is, "My God—you!" Since pronouns are usually attached to other words in Hebrew, their appearance as separate entities is always especially emphatic. Also in this phrase there is no verb, which makes the point even more dramatic: "my God—YOU!" Isn't it a wonder that we can address Him with the second person singular and be in such a close relationship with Him, the God of all gods and LORD of lords?

We can also read the verb as a decisive "I said," and then it suggests a turning point in the psalmist's life and faith, some moment at which he realized that God alone is God. Sometimes we need such a dramatic point at which, reduced to helplessness, we must give up our dependence upon human resources and say, "my God—YOU!" After we have released everything into His hands, we will become more able to see His love in action and to feel His comfort in our lives.

Has there been such a major turning point for you? A decisive time when I was a teenager changed the focus and course of my life profoundly. The God I had known since childhood became intensely real to me on a stormy night in January when I argued with Him at the edge of coma and death. My wrestling with the Trinity matched the wildness of the winter clouds until I could cry from the hospital bed, "My God—YOU!"

But we forget the fact of God's relationship with us at times, especially in the despair and hurt of grieving or rejection. When these times come, we must re-sort our priorities and deal with our doubts in order to come again to this declaration: "Yes. All other gods cannot be trusted. Everything else will pass away. My God is you, *YHWH,* Covenant God!"

In that declaration we join the psalmist in putting our times back into the LORD's hands. And in such a committing of ourselves into God's care, we finally come to peace.

"In your hands" evokes images of tenderness and security. I remember a moment when my good friend Tim and I were talking through some very difficult problems. I trembled on the verge of tears, and Tim, one arm fastened to the blood tubes of his kidney dialysis machine, noticed. Immediately he held out his free hand to me, and, when I gave him mine, he enfolded it safely in both of his. The comfort and assurance of his touch gave me the courage to continue wrestling with the challenges.

It is not that God takes over our lives and controls everything arbitrarily. No, rather, in His hands He gives us the perfect freedom to be wholly ourselves, yet under His infinitely wise and loving care. He lets us choose how to spend our times, but He warns us if we go the wrong way (see Isaiah 30:20-21). He will guide us through our very own desires, which are being newly formed as we grow in faith.

When we can rest enough to trust with our times the One who is trustable, then we don't have to ask the "How long?" questions. We will be able to see that however long God allows certain processes to continue is partly the gift of His perfect wisdom.

The psalmist goes on to request that God deliver him from his enemies, since his times are in YHWH's hands. Since the plural noun *times* might suggest the diversity of our many experiences and developments, we can't become too simplistic in our demands for deliverance. We might not be delivered out of the hands of certain enemies. (For example, two surgeries failed to restore the sight of my right eye, so it remains blind.) Instead, YHWH's hand allows us to be transformed, so that the enemy cannot triumph over us (see chapter four). Our times might not be changed, but *we* will be changed in those times. Furthermore, we will become more able to see some of God's purposes in them.

When I first became a freelance theologian my professional life depended upon enough invitations for speaking engagements. Thoroughly amazing to me was the way God filled up my schedule for those first four years. Always there was plenty of work to do, yet whenever I needed time to write, there seemed to be appropriate blank spots in my calendar.

Now you might be thinking that it isn't comforting at all for you to see God's hand in my schedule if your own remains empty—or outrageously busy in fruitless ways. With you I also experienced the strain of time that seemed to be out of control. In the anguish of long sleepless nights, the darkness of sobs for grief, the confusion of a future that was a vacuum, I confess that it was frequently impossible for me to trust—even as these days the multiplicity of my physical handicaps sometimes overwhelms me with doubts.

We all are challenged by the need to grow in our ability to trust. We will sometimes fail to depend on God, because we will always be human—yet in those times the character of YHWH is all the more precious to us, because we perpetually learn afresh that He is a forgiving and affirming God, our Comforter. Just when we trust Him the least, He is the most trustable, continuing to love us with perfect mercy. Therefore, we are set free to go on, feebly trusting, but learning, by means of the Psalms, to trust Him more (see especially chapter nine).

As we study passages from the Scriptures together, we are being changed. This is the promise of the Word of YHWH: it never comes back empty but, like the rain, accomplishes the purposes for which it was sent (see Isaiah 55:10-11). God's Word is soaking into your life as you read and reread the Psalms. It is forming your character with YHWH's sweet outpouring of grace. Its watering produces the fruit of deeper trusting.

For Further Meditation

1. Who is YHWH for me? What is most important to me about His character?

2. Why can we trust YHWH?

3. At what decisive moment(s) have I said, "My God—YOU!"?

4. What things pull me away from remembering that YHWH is my God?

5. How does it feel to be in the hands of God? Why do I or do I not like that image?

6. How have I experienced God's timing in my life?

7. How do I want to be changed in my times so that I can rest in God's hands, even if the times themselves aren't changed?

God Hears My Cries of Panic

In my alarm I said,
  "I am cut off from your sight!"
Yet you heard my cry for mercy
  when I called to you for help.

PSALM 31:22

Into your hands I commit my spirit;
  redeem me, LORD, my faithful God.

PSALM 31:5

I was ugly, and I knew it. I was a junior in high school, and it was perfectly clear that I was *the* class wallflower. Five feet six inches tall, I was so ill I weighed only eighty-four pounds and had no coloring at all. I hated to look in mirrors because all I saw was a skinny gray pole—hardly a person at all. I was ugly and unwanted; that was the truth about me, I thought.

Undiagnosed illness was the problem, but I was even more wounded emotionally by my own muddled perception of reality. Consequently, the loneliness seemed to me unbearable.

I wouldn't have had to be lonely. Other girls who were not very pretty certainly had friends enough. My failure to see deeper truths in my life inhibited me from reaching out to others, except to trounce them in academic affairs (the old fight instinct again!), and, as a result, the alienation and estrangement grew.

How we perceive the surface reality and the deeper truths of our lives makes all the difference in the world. And that is what the psalmist discusses in these two disjointed verses from Psalm 31. As you remember from the last chapter, Psalm 31 speaks about our times being in God's hands. The whole context of this psalm describes the poet feeling oppressed by his enemies and needing to claim YHWH as his God and the basis for trust. (At this point you might want to reread the entire psalm to put this chapter's discussion in context.)

Just before his closing injunction to all his listeners, the poet summarizes his troubles. Then, because he remembers how his God rescued him, he urges us, too, to love YHWH, to be strong, and to take heart as we hope in Him. Since in our loneliness and grief or troubles of whatever kind we would like to follow that prescription, we want to pay careful attention to the poet's basis for such an exhortation.

The psalmist remembers that he had spoken hastily when he said, "I am cut off" (v. 22). His personal dismay is underscored in Hebrew by the addition of the pronoun *I*, which isn't necessary because it is already part of the verb. Thus, the phrase emphasizes, "*I myself* said in my alarm." The word the TNIV translates "alarm" comes from the verb meaning "to be in a hurry or trepidation," which here is in the idiomatic form of an infinitive together with the preposition *in*. Thus, the phrase literally says, "I myself said in-my-to-be-in-trepidation." This Hebrew idiom graphically pictures what caused the poet to think he was cut off: a state of panic.

The idiom provides a significant clue for understanding much of our loneliness. Panic prevents us from observing the truth; we think that we are cut off because, in our dread, that is the only reality we are able to see. However, dealing with our emotions more carefully might help us to assess the situation more accurately so that we can discover genuine truth.

Think with me about this healing possibility by remembering specific examples in your own experience. Two weekends before first writing this chapter while I was in Minneapolis speaking for a singles conference, a clearer perception of the truth under a surface reality gave me powerful assurance. Rereading some materials to prepare for a class on coping with divorce, I struggled again with acute emotions of abandonment—even wondering whether friends would still be there for me when I got back from this work trip. Perhaps they were tired of my deep needs and insecurities. Then I stood up and put on some hand lotion, which had been a birthday present from my friend Tim. I closed my Bible, which was marked by a bookmark that he had given me for that weekend to remind me of his prayers while I spoke. Then I put on my jacket, brightened by a brilliant pink rose appliquéd on the pocket. Yes, he had give me that rose, too, several months before. Tim's presents always reminded me of the depth of our friendship, which grew with each of our many long discussions while he was on the kidney dialysis machine.

Now I felt immeasurably strengthened for my classes and assembly speech. I could hardly wait to thank Tim again for the profundity of his friendship, apparent to me when far away. How precious is the gift of Christian community in which such friends are formed.[1] Tim's reminders had thoroughly registered.

How often we overlook the reminders of God. In our panic, we might suppose that we are cut off from God, but that is not the truth of our lives.

---

[1]For discussion on building such community, see my *Truly the Community: Romans 12 and How to Be the Church* (Grand Rapids, Mich.: Eerdmans, 1992; reissued 1997). I will occasionally footnote my other books to encourage pursuing topics more thoroughly. Since the royalties of my books are given away to educational ministries or agencies that help the poor, your extended reading will also support this aid.

The Hebrew original shows much more clearly than our English translations how violent our alarm becomes. In its basic form the verb that we render "I am cut off" means "to exterminate." It is related to the common noun for "ax," but this is the only use of the verb in the First Testament. Such a rare and violent word emphasizes that the poet's panic caused him to fear unduly that he had been obliterated from YHWH's sight, axed out of His goodness forever.

We don't usually comprehend how violent panic is to us. It robs us of the truth and causes us to overaccentuate the negatives of our observable reality. That is why we say such extreme things as "Nobody helps me," "Everybody rejects me," "I'm alone in the world," or "There isn't anyone who loves me." Into such emotional extremism, YHWH wants to bring the comfort of His loving truth.

In his summary conclusion, the psalmist remembers that God has ministered to his needs. He further recognizes the great disparity between his perceptions and the truth of his situation.

The second half of verse 22 begins in the Hebrew text with a word that the TNIV translates "yet." We could translate it "surely," but even that rendering is not strong enough. The Hebrew particle emphasizes a contrast, especially after verbs like *I said* or *I thought*, in order to express the truth, in opposition to what has been wrongly imagined. Other adversatives could be "but, indeed," or "but, in fact." In other words, after the psalmist has shown us his dread alarm and how it caused him to misunderstand extremely the details of his situation, now he will tell us, greatly to the contrary, what the truth actually is.

The poet proclaims that YHWH, true to His character, had "heard my cry for mercy when I called to [Him] for help." The Hebrew text addresses God: "You heard the voice of my supplications," or "the sound of my distress," my "lament." The word for "supplications" or "cries" is in the plural, as it is used also in Psalms 28:2, 6; 86:6; and 130:2. Looking at these psalms, too, helps us understand more thoroughly the poet's expression of anguish.

Significantly, some scholars think that the verb we translate "called" is akin to the verb that means "to deliver." That similarity enriches our comprehension of God's answer to our cries. He hears our lament and answers with a deliverance that matches our call.

Because of his strong memory of *YHWH's* rescue, the psalmist can conclude his poem with a great exhortation to his readers to love the Covenant God and to be strong because of their hope in Him. We will examine that idea in terms of one of the initial verses of the psalm.

When I first spent time meditating on this psalm, almost a year before writing this chapter, I was struck by the frequency of the word *refuge* in the first five verses. The word connotes a place of safety, a harbor, some sort of protection, and at that time I desperately needed the LORD as a refuge. I was using my home for crisis ministry then and had cared for several months for a young runaway who now was complaining about me to public crisis centers and at school because I was trying to help her find a more suitable living situation.

The morning that I studied this psalm in my devotional time, I received an irate phone call condemning me for my treatment of this girl, and it seemed to me that none of the accusations had any basis in truth. Throughout that day I reflected on the comfort of this psalm and tried to assert verse 5 with the poet, "Into your hands[, *YHWH,*] I commit my spirit." I wanted *YHWH* to be in control of the situation so that I would not react out of a spirit of hurt pride or an eagerness for vindication against my ungrateful houseguest, in whom I had invested a lot of care and money, time and prayer.

As I have studied the psalm more deeply, however, I have learned that the verb *to commit* involves more than an easy dependence arising out of desperation. It occurs here in a causative (hiphil) form of a word originally meaning "to visit at a muster (of troops)" and, therefore, connotes reviewing a matter. Thus it suggests more profoundly to give extended attention to something. When we commit our spirit into *YHWH's* hand, our action is carefully intentional, seeking thoroughly to entrust our whole being into His care. It is not a superficial handing over—and we don't take it back!

The most graphic embodiment of the true nature of such thorough commitment is given us at the point when Jesus prayed this psalm. Just as He rested His head in death and completed all that had been prophesied about Him, when He victoriously cried that everything was finished and all human debts had been paid and all evil powers defeated, then triumphantly He could say, "Father, into your hands I commit my spirit" (Luke 23:46). If God is asking for our total relinquishment into His hand, then it means death to ourselves (a topic we will explore further in later chapters).

Looking back after Jesus called out these words at the moment of His death, we New Testament believers can more thoroughly appreciate the assurance of the very next phrase in Psalm 31, which could also be translated "You have ransomed me, YHWH." Since Jesus perfectly entrusted everything into the Father's hand and fulfilled every dimension of the latter's plan, we can be confident that we are indeed redeemed. Jesus paid the price of forgiving us and submitting to us in mercy even when we killed Him, and thus He released us from prisons of sin and death, sorrow and loneliness.

Most significant to us in our present study, however, is that the poet then calls YHWH his "faithful God" or the "God of truth" (NIV). That is exactly what we need to know to be released from those four bondages: the truth about ourselves and the fidelity of God.

The truth of our relation to sin is that we are forgiven. The truth of our relation to death is that it has been overcome and we do not need to fear it.[2] The truth of our relation to sorrow is that it will never be more than we can bear. And the truth of our loneliness is that when we feel totally cut off, we have in our panic forgotten the depth of God's

---

[2]See Revelation 2:10-11 and my book *Joy in Our Weakness: A Gift of Hope from the Book of Revelation*, rev. ed. (Grand Rapids, Mich.: Eerdmans, 2002), pp. 57-62.

thorough faithfulness. He is the God of the *amen* (a Hebrew word related to the root for "truth"). *YHWH* alone is the God of reliability and stability, and His gift to us in our loneliness is the whole truth about ourselves—especially the truth that we are beloved to Him.

If I had known it then, when I struggled over my ugliness in high school, I would have realized that my appearance was not the whole story about me. The trustworthy God of faithfulness had declared His love for me, but I hadn't heard it very well.

The whole truth about us is that we are beloved to *YHWH.* We are bought out of our enslavement to any lack of self-esteem. This truth, as Jesus says, sets us free (see John 8:32). He further promises that as we continue to study His Word, we will know the truth—and that will make us free indeed (see John 8:31, 36).

For Further Meditation

1. How have I observed that my panic prevents me from accurately assessing my situation?

2. What misjudgments have made me feel cut off from *YHWH*'s sight and love?

3. How have I been enabled to discover that such perceptions were only the surface reality and not the whole truth?

4. How or through whom has *YHWH* delivered me when I cried to Him for help?

5. Am I able right now to commit my spirit thoroughly into *YHWH*'s hands? Why or why not? (How blessed we are to know that God enfolds us in mercy when we can't entrust ourselves!)

6. How does Christ's work to buy me back from prisons of pain and death affect my understanding of God's action in other dimensions of my life?

7. How does the truth about me set me free?

4

My Trust Won't Put Me to Shame

To you, O LORD, I lift up my soul;
in you I trust, O my God.
Do not let me be put to shame,
nor let my enemies triumph over me.

PSALM 25:1-2 NIV

Immediately my head was raised as if by a pulley—an automatic re-action to the sermon I had heard in chapel just a few days before. A favorite professor had commented on the Joy of this pastoral invita-tion and congregational refrain from the Lutheran liturgy: "Lift up your hearts." "We lift them up to the Lord." The privilege of that in-vitation has all too often lost its impact, especially for those who have been singing those lines since childhood.

The wondrous privilege of going to God with our desires and thanksgivings makes a shamefaced looking at the floor out of order. The pastor's challenge ought also to be, "Lift up your heads." The Scriptures frequently invite us to lift up our heads or hearts or souls or eyes in order to observe the character of *YHWH* and to see His ac-tion on our behalf.

As this chapter continues to lay the basis for understanding how God wants to comfort us in our times of loneliness, we pause to be intentional about lifting up our souls to *YHWH*. The Hebrew text of this first verse of Psalm 25 begins with the phrase "Unto you, *YHWH*." Putting this first underscores the direction. Toward *YHWH* we want to be devoting our attention and desire in the course of everyday life.

A few weeks before first writing this I had waited late at night in the hall of the kidney center in Seattle while my friend Tim went through a dialysis run. I could choose my direction—to focus on my discomfort or the privilege. To have waited miserably—hearing the moans of those patients experiencing hard runs and the resultant cramps, counting the endless minutes and hours, wishing that I could be home in my soft bed—would have prohibited the learning.

Instead, trying to help some of the patients as they finished runs or to minister to relatives and friends who waited with them stirred up great gratitude for my (at that time) healthy kidneys and for the dialysis that kept my friend Tim alive. The intricacies of God's creation and the graciousness of His protection made me long for my life to be more characterized by this direction: "Unto you, *YHWH*."

In the second phrase of the psalm, the poet lifts up to *YHWH* his soul. Sunday school lessons from childhood convinced me that the soul was some little, bitty part of me that went to heaven when I died and my body went into the ground. The Hebrew concept, used frequently in the Psalms, is much larger than that.

The word *nephesh*, first of all, signifies the living being, as in Genesis 2:7, which declares that God breathed into the man and he came alive. Derived from that first meaning is the definition "the true self, the essential part of a person." From that meaning, the word *nephesh* came to connote the seat of one's emotions and passions, one's mental acts, one's deepest self.

That sense of one's whole being or truest character seems most appropriate here in Psalm 25. We need to lift up to *YHWH* intentionally the true core of ourselves, our aspirations and desires. This interpretation is further confirmed as appropriate when we remember verse 4 from the preceding psalm, where the liturgist at the temple declares that the one who may ascend the hill of the LORD is the one "who has clean hands and a pure heart [both outside and inside purity], who does not lift up his soul to an idol" (Psalm 24:4 NIV). Instead, "unto you, YHWH," we lift up our souls.

The fact that the soul suggests our deepest self helps us specifically in times of loneliness. When we feel abandoned because God seems not to be there, we can still by an act of will lift up our inmost desires and true being to Him. We do not have to exert ourselves with frantic intensity to secure God's attention or forgiveness, but we can focus on Him with confident deliberation to receive more readily His comforting answers to our cries.

The verb is a continuing one, "I am lifting up." To direct our passions to YHWH can't be done just once, decisively, for all time. Rather, we can practice a constant discipline in our daily lives of keeping ourselves pointed toward YHWH. So many things in the world distract us, so many negative attitudes in our faith draw us away from Him, so many griefs in our days make us cry out against Him. No matter what is happening in our lives, the psalmist invites us perpetually to lift up our souls to YHWH.

An important goal for our spiritual growth is to become so directed toward the LORD that every situation is immediately turned over to Him. If we could learn instantly to refer whatever happens to His wisdom and guidance, we could faithfully practice His presence in every moment of our lives.

How can we develop such a habit? We are immensely assisted if we establish daily disciplines of prayer and Bible study and meditation. The more thoroughly we enfold ourselves in God's presence in our devotional times, the more readily He will be apparent to us in the other moments of the day.

The second verse of this psalm doubly emphasizes our relationship with God. Not only does it contain the phrase "in you," but also God is addressed as the object of trust and called "my God." In the Hebrew text the phrase "my God" is in an emphatic position, so that the relationship takes first importance. This accentuates that we trust not in an unreachable God far away and only transcendent, but in One who can also be "*my* God," the One who personally cares for you and for me and has chosen us for Himself. The constant message of the Scriptures is that God wants to relate to us. As a bumper sticker quips, "If you're not feeling close to God, guess who moved." Surely the LORD will remain our God, even more than we could ever want Him to be.

Furthermore, in the Hebrew text *trusted* is in the perfect tense here, signifying finished action. That suggests that the act of trusting in God was a point of commitment that has been decisive. Now its results still stand. In realizing that to *YHWH* we want to lift up our souls, our direction in all circumstances has been established.

This intentionality has significant implications for the way in which we read the Scriptures. We can choose to read them as Law or as Gospel, as our objectives for the day, which we *must* reach, or as our goals for the direction of our lives, the way in which we are *learning* to move.

If we read exhortations, such as to "put on compassion," as Law, we are crushed by our failure, for it is impossible for us perfectly to put on compassion. If we see those same promptings instead as Gospel invitations, then to be compassionate is our goal; it determines the direction in which we move through our days, but it is not the day's objective, which we will have failed to meet if we don't get there by tonight. Our day's objectives might include doing *acts* of compassion, like caring for a sick neighbor or giving more money or ourselves away to help the poor, but these are simply movements toward the goal of being yielded to God who forms us into compassionate people.

When we first believed in Christ and became a part of a Christian community, we became immersed in this goal in response to, and empowered by, His love: to imitate His obedient life. In each day we experience many moments characterized by His life in us, though we also often fail to let Him reign. But our direction has been set by the Gospel. In the course of living out our faith, we want to become more faithful to lift up our souls to Him.

This contrast is the same as the encouragement in Ephesians 4 to put off the old, sinful nature (v. 22) and put on the new character of Christ in us (v. 24) and the challenge to be renewed daily by the Spirit's work in our minds and lives (v. 23). The first two are decisive actions (according to the tense used in Greek), the once-and-for-all setting free of God's accepting and forgiving justification. The third is the constant process of renewal, the resultant transformational sanctification that occurs in our daily Spirit-empowered lifting up of the soul to YHWH. The two continually go hand in hand in the Scriptures, but it is helpful if we understand the difference, lest we become overwhelmed by the burden of trying to change instead of being constantly set free by God's grace at work in us to change us.

The poet's other two phrases in Psalm 25:2 are powerful arguments in his pleas to God. The first, "Do not let me be put to shame," assumes that the enemies are watching to see if his faith is grounded in truth. Moses makes the same sort of plea when he says to God, in essence, "Don't destroy Israel now. Then what would those say who wondered about your taking us out of Egypt? They will think, 'Did he take them out just to kill them?'" (see Exodus 32:11-14). Ultimately, for us to be shamed reflects back on the character of our God.

Though that might seem like blackmailing God, really we are invited by Him so to understand our relationship with Him. For us to be put to shame would mean that God cannot be trusted. Because He has demonstrated throughout history that He is thoroughly faithful, that He always keeps His promises ultimately, we can be sure He will never let that happen.

We must be careful, in our loneliness, not to misconstrue the point the poet is making here. A lonely woman cannot say, "God, you must give me a husband. If you don't, I will be put to shame since I have told others that you grant prayer requests." One of the unbiblical views going around these days is the so-called theology that we can "claim" God's action in our lives for certain material requests. Some pray, "Lord, we claim your healing," or "Lord, I claim that you have a wife for me." How can those who pray in this way be so sure that they comprehend God's perfect will?

We won't ever be put to shame for our trusting in God, but perhaps we each have felt shamed when our trust has been in our own visions for how God should work things out. Faithfully to lift up our souls to *YHWH* and to trust in Him means to believe Him for the ways in which He will guarantee that we will not be shamed.

The second phrase, "nor let my enemies triumph over me," reminds us that we do all have adversaries, which might be constantly changing. The question is not whether or not we will have them, but whether or not they will triumph over us. Our enemies can be our fears or doubts, people, circumstances, illnesses, confusions. If we are constantly lifting up our souls to *YHWH* to find His presence in the midst of these oppressions, they cannot be victorious over us.

Such is very much the case with the oppressive loneliness against which I often struggled in the days when I first wrote this book. Whenever I turned to the comfort of the Psalms and the hope of *YHWH*'s guidance, that sense of abandonment could not destroy me. When I let it have its way by neglecting my devotional disciplines or failing to believe that God was present, then the loneliness seemed to overwhelm me.

YHWH doesn't want our enemies to triumph over us. Christ made the victory sure in His own death and resurrection. What remains is for us to be more intentional about turning to the Trinity so that God can apply that victory to the particular battles of our own human lives.

For Further Meditation

1. How intentional is the lifting up of my soul? To whom or what do I primarily direct it?

2. What improvements would I like to make in my personal devotional habits and corporate worship habits to develop a more thorough lifting of my soul?

3. How can I learn to exert my will over my emotions—choosing to trust God even when I don't feel like it?

4. How do I know that *YHWH* is *my* God, even when He doesn't seem to be?

5. How does it help us to differentiate between justification and sanctification, the once-and-for-all turning around of my life into faith by God's grace and the continual turning of my soul to *YHWH* for new trust?

6. How have I seen that I am ashamed because of my own misconceptions rather than that God allows me to be shamed?

7. How have I let enemies triumph over me when I didn't need to? How could the victory of Christ over all the powers of evil become more thoroughly a part of my daily life?

5

God's Mother-Love

> *Remember, LORD, your great mercy and love,*
> *for they are from of old.*
> *Do not remember the sins of my youth*
> *and my rebellious ways;*
> *according to your love remember me,*
> *for you, LORD, are good. . . .*
> *All the ways of the LORD are loving and faithful*
> *toward those who keep the demands of his covenant.*

PSALM 25:6-7, 10

My back porch on that miserable summer afternoon was stifling and empty. I had just had a fight with my best friend and, in my fierce anger, had told her that if she didn't want to do things my way she could just go home. So she did.

I was about ten years old and the loneliest I'd ever been. Finally my remorse overcame my pride, and I raced to her house on the other side of the church building to ask her forgiveness and seek reconciliation. I knew all too well that my own sin had alienated her.

Similarly, plain old sin frequently causes our adult lonelinesses. Alienated from God and from the people around us because of our pride or temper or stupidities or prejudices, we grapple with the sin and guilt that isolate us. The pattern of Psalm 25 is instructive for our removing those obstructions so that relationships might be restored.

Verses 6 and 7a are structured chiastically in Hebrew. This means that "remember," which appears at the beginning of verse 6, is placed at the end of the initial phrase of verse 7; then the objects of those verbs both appear in the middle between them. Thus, we could literally render the phrases as follows:

> Remember your compassions, YHWH. And your
>   loving-kindnesses
>   for from long duration they (are).
> The sins of my youth and my transgressions do not remember.

The emphasis of "remember" and "do not remember" gives us hope in the face of sin. When we address God as *YHWH*, this special covenant name assures us that He will *certainly* remember His compassions. This is the character asserted in the name "I AM."

If God ever does not remember, He has, out of the fullness of His love, deliberately set something aside. The nature of God's forgiveness, the First Testament frequently persuades us, is that when He sets sins aside, He remembers them no more (see, for example, Jeremiah 31:34).

Here the psalmist asks *YHWH* to remember His "compassions." This plural Hebrew term comes from the noun meaning "womb" and therefore implies the mother-love of God. When her baby cries, a mother who has carried that child for nine months within herself, who thus is mysteriously knit to her offspring, can hardly resist picking the child up to comfort it and meet its needs.

In the same way, we are baby-helpless before God. This is one of many First Testament passages that remind us that God is beyond gender, but that the image of God is both male and female and more. Thus, we can use the human picture of a mother's womb-compassions, her unceasing mother-love, to illuminate how *YHWH* is infinitely attentive and intensely caring to answer our cries.

The psalmist is holding God to the character that He has revealed over the ages. With an idiom used frequently in the First Testament, the poet David reminds YHWH that His loving-kindnesses (a plural term here, as is *compassions*) have existed from ancient times. Truly, if YHWH has demonstrated His kindness in manifest displays of caring for Israel throughout its turbulent history, then God's character could hardly change now. Knowing that YHWH will remember, the poet can turn with confidence from his sin and hope with assurance for forgiveness.

The poet further asks YHWH to turn away from remembering those sins. The two words that he chooses for evil acts create a glaring contrast to the two terms that were the objects of YHWH's remembering. The first word, which we translate "sins," comes from the verb meaning "to miss a goal or way, to go wrong," as when a person aims for the target, but the arrow flies off into the field. Our lives are characterized by such missing of God's marks, because often we aim wrong and sometimes we slip as we shoot. Whatever the reason that we miss the target, our alienation from God produces loneliness.

We each recognize how our own selfishness causes us to miss the mark. When I am with someone who is very comforting to me, I frequently catch myself soaking up gifts with no thought at all of caring for the other's needs. Intense loneliness can come when the bond between us is marred by my concern only for myself.

The second word, which the TNIV translates "rebellious ways," is often rendered "transgressions." The term implies a deliberate defiance, the choice to step across the line into disobedient behaviors. Much of the relational alienation of young adults in our age comes because the so-called freedom to violate God's plans for genital involvement has made everyone unsure of true intimacy. If, for example, a young woman chooses to indulge in sexual intercourse outside of marriage and without the commitment that God intends to be the foundation for that gift, she will often experience the crushing loneliness of nagging doubts about whether or not her partner really loves her.[1]

The poet asks that YHWH not deal with him on the basis of these many sins of omission and commission, the slipping and the rebellion. If God were to relate to us on that basis, there would be no hope whatsoever.

The good news of the Gospel, in contrast, is that God has chosen instead to act toward us according to His *chesedh*, His loving-kindness, as seen especially in redemption from sin. Not according to our character, but according to His character of steadfast love and faithfulness, God will remember us.

Once again a poetic duplication underscores the good news. The psalmist adds a parallel phrase, which says literally in the Hebrew, "for the sake of your goodness, YHWH." The word meaning "for the sake of" reminds us that God will maintain His character. As the writer of 2 Timothy 2:13 proclaims, the Lord "cannot disown himself." His character is to be good, so that, no matter how "un-good" His people are, He will act out of that righteousness toward them, instead of reacting to their sinful rebellion and tragic failure to hit the target.

God's goodness is infinite, not only in its extent, but also in the myriads of ways that it is manifested. Most of the Psalms record dimensions of God's goodness as they recount such things as His actions toward His people (see, for example, Psalm 105), the wonders of His creation (see Psalm 104) and His constancy in forgiveness (see Psalm 103).

In the psalm before us, the poet tells us three verses later that all

---

[1]See my book *Sexual Character: Beyond Technique to Intimacy* (Grand Rapids, Mich.: Eerdmans, 1993).

the ways of *YHWH* are characterized by steadfast love and fidelity. The last word of this pair is related to the word *amen* and emphasizes the truth that *YHWH* always acts according to His attributes. The LORD's reliable faithfulness can always be trusted.

Many years ago a woman who had returned from Peace Corps service in the Pacific Islands was having a terrible time readjusting to the United States. She struggled with severe depression and, within it, an intense loneliness. As we studied the Scriptures together weekly, she began to practice the habit of repeating, when she felt overcome by waves of despair, the simple phrase, "*God* is faithful. God *is* faithful. God is *faithful!*"

With great Joy one day she brought me a present of a new box of tissues, decorated with a bow. Asked what we were celebrating, she replied, "Last weekend God and I conquered a downer all by myself." In the midst of her repetition of the fact that God is faithful, its meaning had finally sunk in, and she recognized His presence with her in that pain. That truth stopped the seemingly endless cycle of downward emotions and helped her to open her eyes to recognize newly God's presence.

An amusing addendum to her story occurred several months later when I was very discouraged about moving away from work I loved and finding my place in a new situation. Her gentle reminder, "Marva, don't forget: God is faithful," stimulated a necessary change of attitude for me.

The second part of verse 10 illustrates the importance of reading the Scriptures in their context; the addition of "toward those who keep the demands of his covenant" seems to qualify God's faithfulness, as if it were available only to those who were perfectly obedient. Such a requirement might drive us to despair and intensify our loneliness.

Notice, instead, the place of verse 10 in this context:

Verse 8: *Good and upright is the* LORD;
          therefore he instructs sinners in his ways.

This verse stresses the connection between the character of YHWH
and the availability of His instruction.

Verse 9: *He guides the humble in what is right*
          and teaches them his way.

Once again we are reminded that we learn to obey by YHWH's gracious instruction.

Verse 10: *All the ways of the* LORD *are loving and faithful*
          toward those who keep the demands of his covenant.

Verse 11: *For the sake of your name,* LORD,
          forgive my iniquity, though it is great.

After we have been reminded that our ability to "keep the demands of his covenant" has been taught us by YHWH's guidance, we
are also immediately reminded that in our great failures we are forgiven. No matter how deliberate our trespassing or how widely we
miss the mark, we can know that YHWH will forgive us for the sake
of His name—that is, He will be true to His character.

My sin against my childhood playmate had been great. Not because I was so good at repenting, but because it was in her character
to be merciful, she readily assented to my tearful plea for forgiveness.
My loneliness vanished in her grace.

Similarly, when we receive the forgiveness for our sin that YHWH
holds out to us, many kinds of loneliness are dispelled. We can return
from our alienation and find Joy in the LORD's presence. Furthermore, that restoration often gives us the freedom and courage to pursue restorations with others, as we will consider in later chapters. Because the ways of YHWH are loving and faithful, because God loves

us thoroughly as does a mother, we respond by gladly keeping the demands of His covenant.

For Further Meditation

1. Have I mistrusted God and acted as if in His infinite nature He could not deliberately *not* remember?

2. How do mothering images for God's love deepen my awareness of its presence?

3. How does the constancy of God's faithfulness over the ages give me courage for today?

4. At what moments and in what ways have I experienced God's forgiveness for all the sins of my youth? my adulthood?

5. How have I experienced God being true to His character? Why does God forgive "for the sake of" His name?

6. Is even God's venting of wrath a dimension of His loving-kindness? How?

7. How can I be set free from the worry that my inability to keep His covenant demands will prevent me from experiencing that all His ways are loving and faithful?

6

Lonely and Afflicted—but *YHWH* Releases Me from the Snare

*My eyes are ever on the L*ORD
*   for only he will release my feet from the snare.*
Turn to me and be gracious to me,
*   for I am lonely and afflicted.*
Relieve the troubles of my heart
*   and free me from my anguish.*
Look on my affliction and my distress
*   and take away all my sins.*

PSALM 25:15-18

One morning when I first wrote this book I went to the pool feeling troubled at having been misunderstood in a particular dimension of my work. I found it harder than usual to move past the first painful laps of my workout. However, because I had been using that swimming time to meditate on the Psalms, favorite passages began floating around in my brain, and consequently, my floating in the water became easier. Tension drained from my body as God's promises brought me their deep comfort. His love, in which I felt enfolded, set my mind free to think more clearly. By the time I got to Psalm 30 and spoke the words, "Weeping may remain for a night, but rejoicing comes in the morning" (v. 5), I exulted in the actual experience of that transformation.

The first line of the psalm section we are considering here challenges each of us to deepen our devotional lives. When the poet says without a verb in Hebrew, "My eyes continually to *YHWH*," he invites us to develop habits of practicing God's presence in every situation. Such habits are best rooted in specific disciplined times of Bible study and meditation and prayer.

Perhaps you need, as I do, the encouragement of the psalmist who seems to be diligent in devotional disciplines. On the morning described above I recognized that I would not have struggled against loneliness and frustration and grief so much if my eyes had been more thoroughly fixed on *YHWH*.

The TNIV translation of the next phrase, "for only he will release my feet from the snare," retains well the emphasis in the Hebrew text. The addition of the separate pronoun *he* to the *he* already included in the verb stresses uniqueness—"he indeed" or "truly he." That thrust urges us to observe more carefully how often we try to get our feet out of the net by our own strength or wisdom, our own devices and stratagems.

The case that morning was a good example. I thought I was snared by someone else's misunderstanding, but actually I was entangled in my own pride. Much of my anguish centered on my own need to clarify things, to justify myself.

When we've been the target of misunderstanding or false rumors, how much of our anguish comes out of our own need to prove ourselves in the right? If the LORD alone is the One who can get us out of our snares, then let us fix our eyes on Him in order to learn how He wants to do it. My meditation on the Psalms in the pool that day brought astonishing results.

As I contemplated the first several psalms, especially the nineteenth, they encouraged greater openness to God's instruction. Then Psalm 22, which begins with the agonizing question, "My God, my God, why have you forsaken me?" propelled into my mind other things that Jesus said when taking our place in death on the cross. Thinking about His words, "Father, forgive them, for they do not know what they are doing" (Luke 23:34), I realized that this might be true also for anyone who speaks falsely about us. We are often misunderstood because others are too burdened by their own fears or afflictions. God's method for bringing us out of the snare might be not so much for us to correct the rumors and set everybody straight, but for us to swallow our pride, forgive the ones who malign us, and seek somehow to ease their sorrows.

What sorts of snares have entrapped your feet? How can looking eagerly and consistently to YHWH bring you out of those traps? Whether others have spread the nets against us or we have tangled up ourselves, YHWH alone is the One who can bring us out successfully.

The overwhelming good news about God is that He really wants to release us. Sometimes I think that if I were the LORD, I would just leave me in some of the messes I cook up for myself. But when the poet goes on in Psalm 25 to say, "Turn to me and be gracious to me," the word *turn* strikes us with its royal reaching out.

The Hebrew word accentuates "regarding," in the sense of either caring about someone or fixing one's attention on something. Considering all our mistakes and rebellions, what right do we have to expect that God would turn to look at us? Yet He always deigns to do so; our asking reminds us that He does.

Why does a caring parent respond by looking when a little child calls out, "Watch me"? Usually the child is not doing anything extraordinary. Rather, the love of that father or mother makes room for spending time to encourage the child. In the same way the father/

mother-love of God chooses to watch us in grace.

The poet continues with a lament about his loneliness. His time of adversity included a special need for the LORD to watch with graciousness. Don't you sometimes feel that what you crave more than anything is for someone to care about the little things in your life?

This image of God's gracious regarding is especially comforting if we have lived for any length of time in a work or family situation in which we were not accepted—when the heart of someone near us has been closed to us, so that nothing that we do could ever meet with approval. When we know that we have lost even before starting, we struggle to crank up the energy to try. How released we are when we find friends who like who we are and what we do, who approve of us unconditionally, so that in their grace we have the freedom to start again and do our best!

The freedom with which the psalmist can say, "Turn to me and be gracious to me," comes from knowing that God, who has received him lovingly in the past, cannot be false to His character of covenant faithfulness. Therefore, we can with bold confidence—made more sure in the manifestation of God's love in the person of Jesus—go immediately to God and ask for His attention (see Ephesians 3:12).

"For I am lonely and afflicted," the poet despairs. This poignant Hebrew phrase could be translated "for solitary and troubled—I." The word for "solitary" signifies "the only one," an isolated individual who is friendless and a wanderer, a lonely exile. That forsakenness is often matched in the First Testament with weakness, poverty, or other destitute misery. Note also that this is another phrase that lacks a verb and concludes with an emphatic pronoun, *I*. Both devices accentuate the starkness of this state of being: to be without any human comforter in the midst of affliction.

Such statements help us remember that we are not the only ones who suffer the pain of loneliness. But even that might not be much of a comfort if it is for us an unremitting fact of life.

There is, however, another fact in our existence. The poet has been reminding us, as we despair over the lack of human comfort, that God is present with steady faithfulness to look upon us with love. We don't have to feel this fact. It is true whether we feel it or not. However, sometimes in acknowledging it as a fact we might begin to feel *YHWH*'s presence as well. Even if we don't experience it, truly God's tender regarding does enfold us.

Even when the poet's troubles are "multiplied," as the next phrase is rendered in some translations (see the NIV), the poet knows that God is able to free him from that anguish. Looking closely at his complaint might help us to understand better some of our own despair. The Hebrew phrase, which could be literally rendered "the distresses of my heart have been intensified," uses graphically descriptive words that ring true to our experience in this age of anxiety and strain. The word I translated "distresses" comes from the verb meaning "to bind, tie up, or be restricted or cramped." It is related to the word for "tight" or "narrow." Sometimes we feel that the world's troubles are hemming us in so tightly that we can't breathe.

Again, we are reminded that only *YHWH* can bring us out of the snare, for the poet turns to him to "free me from my anguish." This verb is the same word translated by the TNIV as "release" in the "snare" phrase of verse 15. The noun translated "anguish" is similar to the word for "distresses" in the preceding phrase in connoting constraints caused by pressures or anxieties.

Especially in these days of economic and time pressures, we learn that only *YHWH* can bring us out. Many of my friends who are searching for work and for some sort of security are discovering that whatever the world offers can never be sure. College presidents are telling their graduates that more than half of them will probably never find a permanent job in their chosen field; people over fifty cannot find new work when their previous position was eliminated by downsizing. As the pressures mount, the only place to find genuine release from such straits is in the comfort of knowing personally the gracious LORD who chooses to look upon us with care.

That is why the poet then appeals again to *YHWH's* tender concern for his affliction and distress. This time, however, he acknowledges another fact: by asking God to take away all his sins he implies that perhaps those same sins are the root cause of his troubles. If God will remove the source, then the poet can be freed from those symptoms of his sin.

We need to recognize continually the significant part sin plays in our adversities, but not in order to overwhelm us with guilt about our inability to be the persons we want to be. Rather, when we have a deep enough sense of our sinfulness, we will be more ready to receive the forgiveness that God freely offers. When we begin to have a more profound sense of that gracious forgiveness, we will become more able to accept ourselves. Finally, when we can accept ourselves more, we will be set free to think more clearly and to deal more decisively with our afflictions and distresses. Only when we are enfolded in *YHWH's* love do we have the power to find hope.

The psalm ends with a plea for protection and a final declaration that the poet's hope is in *YHWH*. That takes us back full circle to where we began—with the recognition that we need to learn to fix our eyes upon the LORD in order to recognize His presence and the fullness of His care in our lives. Our covenant God is turning to us to be gracious, to release us from the snares, to free us from anguish, to take away our sins. Our loneliness gets lost in the wonder of His comforting care.

For Further Meditation

1. How effective are my devotional habits for fixing my eyes on the LORD?

2. In what ways might I improve or develop them?

3. How have I seen that God's plans were better than mine for bringing my feet out of the snare?

4. How have I experienced the difference between persons looking
   upon me with grace or with disapproval?

5. How does the look of grace ease my loneliness?

6. What kinds of distresses are presently cramping my life? In which
   ones are my sins the root cause of my adversities and what can I
   do about that? (Be sure here not to come up with an answer of
   working yourself out of it. What is the answer of grace?)

7. How might I be an agent of passing on to someone I know in distress the look of grace that comes from *YHWH*?

YHWH Understands Even Betrayal

I said, "Oh, that I had the wings of a dove!
    I would fly away and be at rest.
I would flee far away
    and stay in the desert;   [Selah][1]
I would hurry to my place of shelter,
    far from the tempest and storm." . . .
If an enemy were insulting me,
    I could endure it;
if a foe were rising against me,
    I could hide.
But it is you, one like myself,
    my companion, my close friend,
with whom I once enjoyed sweet fellowship at
      the house of God,
    as we walked about among the worshipers.

PSALM 55:6-8, 12-14

At times in my loneliest years I wanted to run so far away that no rejection, anguish, or injustice could ever find me. Sometimes I felt

---

[1]The Hebrew word *Selah* is not printed in the TNIV text, except in a footnote. Since I think it is important (see below), I am including it here.

so miserable that I would have given anything simply to drop out of existence. The psalmist David longed, as we do, to escape.

We don't have to feel guilty about such yearnings to run away from everything and everyone. Psalm 55 shows us legitimate reasons for wanting to give up. What matters is how we deal with those longings; to be realistic about them is a constructive beginning.

The poet David cries out for the wings of a dove so that he might fly away and settle down to rest. His longing is born from an appalling life situation. Several verses later he laments that he wants those wings to fly away "for I see violence and strife in the city. / Day and night they prowl about on its walls; / malice and abuse are within it. / Destructive forces are at work in the city; / threats and lies never leave its streets" (vv. 9-11). He is surrounded by extensive turmoil and tumult that is out of his control.

The same is true for us. We live in an age of political deceptions and terrorist destructions, of violent gangs in the streets and escalating crimes, of grinding poverty and conspicuous consumption, of alcoholic stupors and Internet escapism, of mind-damaging drugs and soul-damaging rejection.

There is a place for righteous recoil. We can become so overwhelmed by the pain around us that it seems impossible to go on trying to be agents of change and healing. At those times our longing for retreat is prompted by a holy disquietude.

In the Garden of Gethsemane Jesus, too, was overwhelmed by the battle against evil. We cannot even begin to comprehend the anguish that He felt as He contemplated the hours ahead. Did He know that He faced separation from the Father, the very source of His guidance, comfort, and strength? How can we understand the unity and distinction of the Trinity as all of God suffered separation of God's very self, as God loved us even while we killed Him?

We cannot even begin to comprehend the intense torment of Christ's becoming sin for us (see 2 Corinthians 5:21). We know the guilt we feel when we do something wrong. How could one ever stand the enormous suffering of all the brokenness of our world, all the hardships human beings inflict on each other, all the groaning of the creation?

We dare not make it too simple for Jesus. He was God, of course, but He had laid the powers of His God-nature aside in order to live and die as a man for us. Consequently, He faced all that physical pain, emotional anguish, and spiritual separation with the fears and despairs of a human being. Yet, the writer to the Hebrews insists, He did not sin (see Hebrews 4:15).

To be horrified by the immensity of the battles or suffering before us is not to sin. What matters is what we do with that burden or sorrow. If we are feeling overwhelmed by the pain of our world or lives and pray, "My Father, if it is possible, may this cup be taken from me" or "Give me wings to fly away and escape," we have not transgressed. What causes separation from God for us is our inability to add, "Yet not as I will, but as you will" (see Matthew 26:36-44).

Are we willing in the midst of everything to believe that God is infinitely wise and gracious? Do we trust Him even when He doesn't fly us away from whatever brings us despair and believe that His mysterious purposes are, according to His patient mercy, ultimately good? Do we know that, though the powers of evil rage and cause chaos in our lives and world, Christ has triumphed over them and will someday obliterate them forever?

The poet of Psalm 55 continues with the wish to hurry away to a place of refuge and rest. He wanted to abide in the desert to be sheltered far away from the storm and tempest.

Solitude is critical for our psychic balance. Jesus often retreated from the crowds and the wounds of the world around Him. He escaped into the hills to pray, to spend time in quiet communion with His Father. It is right for us to get away for times of recuperation and strengthening in order that we might have the will to continue battling the evils against which we are struggling.

We need in our Christianity a better theology of rest. We are often so eager to serve the LORD or are so caught up in our occupations or projects that we forget to balance our work with genuine repose. Somehow we have neglected the importance of the First Testament Sabbath in our New Testament faith. The Jews worked hard for six days and rested on the seventh. They recognized the rhythms of life; they realized that we need space to be restored, to rest, to find healing.[2]

Usually in times of depression or discouragement we have trouble giving ourselves enough room to allow emotional healing. Our Christianity would be much more wholesome for ourselves and relevant for our neighbors if we could learn to take, and help others get, enough time for spiritual renewal, psychological restoration, and physical recharging.

That is the value for me not only of a weekly Sabbath rest, but also of such things as working out on the bicycle or in the swimming pool every day, taking breaks in the midst of my labor to play the piano, spending time with friends with whom I can share my struggles and find active support in a listening ear and comforting words. Is there a place in your life for fishing trips or hikes in the woods or puttering in the garden to soak up the warmth of the sunshine and the splendor of God's magnificent creation? I savor the healing of a hot cup of tea and classical music, a fire in the fireplace and a rocking chair. Whatever gives us strength provides a personally suitable escape so that we can find courage for the tasks ahead.

In fact, the very liturgy of our worship allows time for reflection and soaking up strength. At two points in Psalm 55 the word *selah*

---

[2]See my books *Keeping the Sabbath Wholly: Ceasing, Resting, Embracing, Feasting* (Grand Rapids, Mich.: Eerdmans, 1989) and *The Sense of the Call: A Sabbath Way of Life for Those Who Serve God, the Church, and the World* (Grand Rapids, Mich.: Eerdmans, 2006).

appears, a word thought by most scholars to be some sort of musical directive. Perhaps it noted a quiet pause in the reciting of the psalm or a moment during which instruments were played to give participants in the worship some time for pondering the words that had just been recited.

If this is so, then its placement between verses 7 and 8 is strategic. Having heard the poet's wish to have wings to fly away to the desert to retreat, the worshiper could contemplate the desirability of rest and its effectiveness, could partake of a reprieve apart for a moment. Then the poetry continues with the further wish that such an escape would provide a shelter from the storm and tempest, which are reported in the next three verses.

After describing all the violence and destruction that he observes in the world around him, however, the poet declares that the enemy isn't what is really causing him the most distress. If it were just an adversary, he could endure it or hide.

We often think in such a manner when we can't cope. If only this weren't the trouble, we muse, we could handle it. Wouldn't it be good, we think, if we could choose our struggles?

In this case, though, the poet continues by announcing what for many of us has also been the greatest grief of our aloneness: that it was a close friend who hurt us most deeply. We had "once enjoyed sweet fellowship at the house of God."

The day that I first read this psalm in my morning devotional time, I sat at my desk and wept, because the poem seemed to have been written just for me. So often I had thought that I could handle whatever came from an enemy, but how could one endure the pain of being betrayed by two friends—a husband and one's student in whom one had invested so much care?

Many of us have searched in vain for an answer to that question. We'll never find an explanation for the evil that causes those we love to hurt us. Yet the reality of that pain is too overwhelmingly real. "It is you," the poet says graphically in the original Hebrew, a person "sitting in the same row" or "similar to me." In other words, "You are an individual, a human being like myself, an equal." Not only that, but you are "my companion, my close friend."

Our English words don't reveal the poignancy of these Hebrew expressions. The first word for "friend" implies an intimacy often used to describe the relationship of a woman and her husband. The profound closeness that once existed with the beloved has been violated. The second comes from a verb signifying deep knowing and involving the idea of revealing or discovering. This friend is one to whom the poet has disclosed his hidden self, the most profound truths of his being. Yet this is the one who has attacked him, who has violated the covenant that knit them together (see vv. 20-21 of the psalm).

When I first wrote this chapter I had recently received rich comfort in confiding to a good friend some of my secret hopes concerning my life's work—without being laughed at. Months before I had revealed those same bits of the deepest me to someone else who had cast it all off as preposterous. I had wondered then if I could ever again trust anyone enough to share what really mattered in my life.

The poet grieves that once he had enjoyed sweet fellowship with this close friend. In fact, they had walked together with the throng of worshipers at the house of God. And now, that dear person had double-crossed him.

Similarly, some of us have drowned in the anguish of betrayal— the life-ripping, heartbreaking, soul-wrenching despair of having one that we deeply trusted destroy our lives. An office colleague maligns our character or work and dirties our reputation. A spouse leaves us for someone else, who was also a good friend. A neighbor spreads malicious rumors throughout the community. A close family member divulges personal secrets. There seems to be no way to heal such wounds. We may have forgiven the one who hurt us. The fracturing of our lives might have taken place long ago. Yet we still have occasional nightmares and frequent flashbacks to bad memories, even as we try to run away from those scenes. How do we deal with the rending torment that our lives have been broken apart by someone with whom we once worshiped?

Perhaps one of the deepest tragedies of sin in the world is that it hits us in the hardest places because it comes from the last source we would expect. We would not assume that a source of pain for us could be our churches. Yet often there we are most deeply injured. It might have been the betrayal of some Christian friend or a spouse. Sometimes it is the policies of a congregation that have been destructive to us. Many times we who are single and alone and struggling with our loneliness have been cruelly rejected by those who are supposed to be the people of God.

Then the problem of pain, for which there is no simple explanation, is compounded by the failure of the Christian community. We cannot comprehend the breaking of a marriage vow or deception or adultery or broken commitments. We are not able to cope with the seeming endlessness of grief. Sin, which we cannot understand, is more rupturing when its perpetrators call themselves people of faith.

I won't offer any superficial comfort here. Some of you reading this are suffering acute heartache right now because of betrayal by Christian people. How can we bear these incomprehensible hurts?

That is the poet's agony. That is ours. And that was the burden of Jesus. Only in that last fact can we begin to find a way to deal with the immensity of the pain.

Jesus endured everything that we do, including betrayal by one of His best friends, so that He knows our suffering (see Hebrew 4:15). Indeed, He can stand beside us in every aspect of our loneliness and understand. The next chapter will deal with the poet's answers, and then, as we study Psalm 56, we will see even more clearly how much God fathoms our woe and cares for us in the midst of it.

For Further Meditation

1. What life experiences or situations make me want to escape?

2. How does it help me to know that Jesus felt like that too?

3. What habits and practices give me rest and relief so that I can be strengthened?

4. What opportunities for "*Selah*" meditation does the worship service at my church offer?

5. What kinds of enemies *can* I handle?

6. How have I been deeply hurt by close friends? Have I forgiven them? If not, what could help me move to the point of forgiveness and reconciliation?

7. Have I been deeply hurt in my church? Have I been able to forgive? How could I be an agent of building a Christian community of reconciliation and compassion?[3]

---

[3]For suggestions, see my book *Truly the Community.*

8

Evening, Morning, and Noon, God Hears My Voice

As for me, I call to God,
and the L<small>ORD</small> *saves me.*
Evening, morning and noon
I cry out in distress,
and he hears my voice. . . .
Cast your cares on the L<small>ORD</small>
and he will sustain you;
he will never let
the righteous be shaken.

PSALM 55:16-17, 22

An old advertisement for Wind Song perfume pictured a young man wistfully imagining a lovely maiden, whose dancing figure floats across his head. The caption promises, "He can't get you out of his mind."

That caption serves as a lovely paraphrase of the well-known verses, perhaps memorized when we were children: "Casting all your care upon him; for he careth for you" (1 Peter 5:7 KJV); and "Cast your cares on the LORD and he will sustain you" (Psalm 55:22). Indeed, God cannot get us out of His mind—not that He would want to, which is the incredible part about it. *YHWH* would never want to cease caring for us.

As in many other lament psalms, the composer David moves in Psalm 55 from stating his difficulties to asserting, "As for me, I call to God." This is the response to adversity by the person of faith. As we continue to study psalms together, I pray that increasingly this will be our natural response—that the more we meditate on the Psalms and are immersed in the language of faith, the more easily we will move into prayer in our daily lives. This habit of practicing the presence of God will be our best weapon to combat all the griefs of various kinds of loneliness in our lives.

When the psalmist continues with the assurance "and the LORD saves me," he uses a Hebrew verb that is a favorite of mine. Most commonly translated "to save" or "to deliver," it more deeply signifies giving width and breadth to, or liberating. Since we considered in the previous chapter the tightening around him that the poet was experiencing, this image sets up a radical contrast. When the evils around us seem to hem us in more and more closely, the liberation of *YHWH* is a glorious giving of space—range and scope to breathe and move.

Verse 17 forms the focus for our consideration in this chapter. We must understand it thoroughly to fight a common misconception that is promoted in some prayer groups and which, I'm afraid, is destructive to our relationship with God.

The poet says graphically, "In the evening and in the morning and at middays I will complain and groan." This is a picture of a soul in dire distress and prayer, and it underscores the deep compassion and sympathy with which *YHWH* responds. The TNIV rendition, "I cry out in distress," doesn't quite capture the double-verbed intensity of the Hebrew expression. The poet is grieving and moaning, wailing with heavy hurt. He is protesting vehemently all the troubles of his life and groaning in his agony.

This line continues the emphasis in the psalm on the intense and immense sorrow of the poet, as we observed in the previous chapter. The poet helps us be potently realistic about the fierce torment suffered by those who have been betrayed by the ones they have loved most. There is no easing of that pain in any simple way. The wounds inflicted by those closest to us seem to negate any possibility of healing. In this overwhelming anguish the psalmist cries out—and so do we.

The poet does not cry out just once in a while either. He cries out morning, noon, and night. These words do not merely signify three particular times of prayer in one's day—when we arise, when we go to sleep, and before lunch—although these were specific times of prayer for the people of Israel. Rather, the poet unceasingly bemoans the constancy of his woe; he cries out continually with the severe sorrow of his suffering.

The misconception that needs to be combated is the well-intentioned advice of those who say, "Make your intercession or petition once, and then start thanking God for His answer." To be always thanking God for how He will work things out in the future for our benefit is indeed a helpful habit. We can trust our God's promise that He is active to transform circumstances to bring good out of evil. However, I resist the phoniness of merely thanking God when we are still suffering from overwhelming, unhealed wounds.

The danger of this common theology that advocates only thanking rather than continuing our complaint is that such forced gratitude puts a veneer of religiosity over our anguish and often inhibits the healing that mourning brings. When we are suffering grief, we dare not suppress it—not even with religious piety.

We must nuance this carefully, for other passages in the Scriptures (1 Thessalonians 5:18, for example) encourage us to give thanks continually *in* all things. The preposition *in* is important in that passage, for we are not commanded to give thanks *for* all circumstances.[1] I don't give thanks *for* evil, but I can certainly thank God *in* the situations of evil that I encounter because His gracious presence is with me, His mercy is sustaining, and the Christian community is always at work to overcome evil whenever possible. Such thanksgiving is a very effective tool for regaining a godly perspective on what is happening in our lives.

But the danger is that we won't adequately deal with the confusion and grief that afflict us if we don't also recognize in the Scriptures the presence of texts like this one from Psalm 55. As long as we are struggling with the pain of our existence in a sin-sick and broken world, God's grace invites us to be real about those sorrows with *YHWH*. Besides, lamenting to Him is one of the best ways to sort out our observations and determine what is really true.

In light of the confusion arising from the many varying philosophies about prayer, a student once asked me how often to pray for a particular request. As long as our mind is not settled about an issue, we might as well be honest with God and with ourselves by pouring out our feelings about it. Why compound our struggles by being phony with God?

I think this is especially important when we wrestle with loneliness and other overwhelming sadnesses that we bear in solitude. Though I often prayed about it and often also came to peace about it, I still became distraught sometimes in my many years of aloneness. The night I first wrote this chapter, I experienced such a crash.

I had spent a two-day Thanksgiving vacation with the family of one of my friends from Seattle. Though a stranger in their midst, I had felt at home in the conversations. Thanksgiving dinner was especially delightful because of the large family gathering, the fragrant aromas, the many specialities of the season. Several of us had enjoyed a long, leisurely walk in the crisp fall air. I had even been able to help

---

[1]Ephesians 5:20 similarly uses the preposition *on behalf of* rather than a simple *for*.

the family in a conversation about an issue that was tough emotionally, so I felt useful and loved.

But then I came home to an empty and very cold house. Everyone from our household community was gone for the Thanksgiving vacation. As I struggled for more than an hour to light a fire in the basement woodstove, I kept clobbering myself with logs, burning my fingers while trying to position the kindling, and inundating the study with smoke. I didn't usually have any trouble with the stove, so frustration kept mounting until I finally screamed, "God, I wish I didn't have to be alone!"

There wasn't unbearable pain in that aloneness, but the irritations accentuated the cold silence of our big house, and I mourned for the six-hundredth time that I didn't have anyone to share the rest of the holiday with me. What great relief the psalm brings us that we can in the evening and in the morning and in any other time of the day cry out our distress to God.

That freedom to be real is especially comforting because, as the poet continues, *YHWH* "hears my voice." When we complain continually to those around us, they get tired of listening and sometimes close their ears to our pleas. In contrast, *YHWH* will always listen to our cries, even if they are ascending on the same subject for the billionth time.

The TNIV translates the verb for "hearing" as a continuing state of affairs. In keeping with the faithfulness of His character, the LORD will always listen. Furthermore, if we in turn listen for His voice when we cry, we will be able to sort out our griefs, grow from them, and, in the meantime, hear His comfort and receive His strength to endure.

Perhaps Peter was thinking of verse 22 from Psalm 55 when he penned his well-known line, "Cast all your anxiety on him because he cares for you" (1 Peter 5:7). When the psalmist urges his readers to "cast your cares on the LORD," he uses a Hebrew verb that could

be translated "to throw or fling" and a noun that signifies "whatever
is given to a person." All the things that compose our existence—
including the terrible grief caused by the close friend who has turned
against us (vv. 13-14)—we are to fling upon YHWH rather than taking them upon ourselves and turning inward into depression.

This is a tremendous invitation, yet we hesitate to receive it. Furthermore, when we do accept it, sometimes we do so only momen-
tarily. Soon after throwing everything at God's feet, we pick up those
burdens again and carry them back with us into our thoughts and
lives. Why are we so unable to take YHWH at His word and thoroughly place our cares upon Him?

Part of the reason, it seems, is that we haven't learned the assurance of the escape that in the evening, in the morning and at midday
we can cry out in distress. Every time we are plagued by those same
old thoughts, we are invited to cast them back *again* upon YHWH.
When we develop that habit and turn over into His hands whatever
grieves us, upsetting thoughts will afflict us less.

It is a matter of disciplining our thoughts. Either we can turn inward and struggle with them in our own minds and spirits, or we can
cry them out to the LORD and experience His sustaining.

That is the assurance of the poet, and it is reinforced once again by
an emphatic pronoun. The Hebrew text insists, "And He Himself will
sustain you." The verb *sustain* is an elaborated form that includes
nourishing. Thus we can be sure that when God sustains us, He does
not merely prop us up. His nourishment enables us to endure. When
we cast our burdens upon the LORD, they might not go away, but we
will be able to stand them.

That word of comfort gives us an answer when we are betrayed by
those we trust or when we suffer any other similar tearing of our confidence. Since there seems to be no ultimate erasure of the scar from
such a deep wound, we find hope from the fact that in the grief of
that death we will be sustained.

Discovering this truth of support in the midst of mourning began for me a long process of healing. When I finally learned that I didn't have to "get past" the pain of betrayal, then I could, in the midst of it, rely more thoroughly on *YHWH* to sustain me in it.

The heartache is there. We cannot chase it away; we cannot deny its existence; we cannot even cope with it successfully. But we can cry out to *YHWH,* and He will hear. When we fling the burden of that hurt upon Him, He will grant the relief that enables us to bear the scar constructively. We will learn in truth to love the scar as a sign of how deeply we loved and of the suffering involved in bearing the cost of loving. It is a sign that links us to Jesus, who paid the ultimate price of costly loving.

Yet the poet offers an additional word of assurance beyond this. The TNIV presents a revision of the NIV that better captures the sense of the original Hebrew text and makes the final phrase of verse 22 fit more completely into the context as we have discovered it. Rather than "he will never let the righteous fall," the TNIV says, "he will never let the righteous be shaken," by which the Hebrew also stresses the sense of "forever." We can't say that the righteous will never fall; we have all experienced falling. But the point is that such falling will never last a whole lifetime.

The Hebrew text begins with the word *not,* followed by the phrases *will He give* and *to forever*—"*Not* forever will He give us over to the shaking." The final word indicates the negation of security and comes from a verb meaning "to totter or slip." When we are rattled by the experiences of our lives, the LORD will not let us be battered by them indefinitely.

God does not push us, but He always cares for us when the brokennesses of life cause us to fall. Our covenant God will not let us be trampled in the dust when we are down. The more we learn to cast our cares on Him, the more we will experience His sustaining to keep us from falling or to hasten our recovery.

The key lies in the evening, morning and noontime crying out to YHWH. Peter's expression of casting our cares on Him continues with "because he cares for you" (1 Peter 5:7). God watches over everything that concerns us. All the little details of our lives, even the most minor of falls, are noticed by His infinitely loving and caring eyes. He can't get us out of His mind. When we call upon Him all the time—morning, noon and night—then we can't get Him out of ours either.

For Further Meditation

1. What is the importance of thanksgiving when I am suffering?
2. In what ways has YHWH liberated me lately and given me plenty of space?
3. What is the value for me of crying out to YHWH whenever I am feeling distress?
4. How do I know that God will hear?
5. What does it mean to cast my cares upon YHWH? to cast them again?
6. How have I experienced God's sustaining when I have cast my cares upon Him? How have I failed to experience that sustaining when I have taken the cares back again?
7. Why is it important to acknowledge the reality that we will fall? Why is it encouraging that YHWH will not let us suffer the shaking forever?

9

It's All Right to Be Afraid

When I am afraid, I put my trust in you.
In God, whose word I praise—
in God I trust and am not afraid.
What can mere mortals do to me?

PSALM 56:3-4

To be heroic doesn't mean you aren't afraid." Initially that comment surprises us, but then its truth sets us free. The person who is not afraid in a dangerous situation usually doesn't really know what is going on. The person who is aware of all the circumstances and proceeds anyway is the truly courageous one.

To be Christians does not necessarily mean that we are not afraid. In our desire for discipleship, we struggle to be more trusting and regret that we aren't more so. We're ashamed that we haven't reached the spiritual maturity that we think we ought to have attained. Then we feel lonely because we're not strong enough as Christians truly to belong to the community of God's people. Moreover, fear and loneliness are mutually reinforcing: the more lonely we feel, the more frightened we become in threatening situations, and greater fear makes us feel more alone because others don't seem to share our dread.

Into the midst of this escalation of both fear and loneliness, the words of Psalm 56 speak great comfort to us—especially because they follow Psalm 55, which so vividly displays the torment of having our trust betrayed. Now the great hero David admits honestly that at times even he is afraid. It is in those times that his trust in YHWH is particularly developed.

French lay theologian and sociologist Jacques Ellul insisted that Christianity is neither pessimistic nor optimistic, but rather realistic. To be true to our faith, we can't simply talk idealistically about God's action in our lives, nor concentrate gloomily on the discouragements or our human failings. Optimism expands the victories that God accomplishes in our lives beyond actuality, but pessimistic dejection ignores God's grace and mercy and leads us to despair. "Christian Realism," Ellul proposes, balances in a healthy sense the reality of sin and a trusting hope in the truth of God's ultimate victory over sin and evil in all their forms.[1]

In the Christian community both dimensions of our existence must be in equilibrium in our conversations together. That way we can identify with each other as human beings who have needs and failings and desires and motivations, but we can also see the training and healing effects of God's action in our lives. We can be encouraged both by what God is doing in others and by the progress we notice as we yield ourselves to His work in us. The poet achieves a good balance, with "when I am afraid" as a preface to the declaration "I put my trust in you."

More than our English translations, the original Hebrew construction emphasizes that trust can characterize those times when we are afraid. The sentence begins with the construct *the-day-of,* which signifies, when put together with a verb in the imperfect or incomplete-

---

[1]See Marva J. Dawn, trans. and ed., *Sources and Trajectories: Eight Early Articles by Jacques Ellul That Set the Stage* (Eugene, Ore.: Wipf & Stock, 2003), pp. 92-112.

action tense, "in the day when." In other words, at the very time when we are afraid, that is the time for trust.

Usually in times when we are frightened, we try hard not to feel fear. Attempting to push it under, however, can bring a volcanic explosion of panic or terror when we can no longer keep the lid on all that anxiety we've been struggling to keep corked. This psalm, by contrast, suggests a healthier managing of emotions—dealing with fear by accepting its reality and learning to trust in the midst of it.

In practical terms, this discipline of thought can free us from the frenzy of trying to stave off fear. At the time I was first writing this chapter, I experienced dizziness more severe than my typical problems with low blood pressure. Previously whenever I had tried to stop being afraid, fear had exploded instead into worry about how soon I would be incapacitated by my handicaps. Needing to understand why I had almost collapsed on the kitchen floor of the home where I was staying, I couldn't merely dispense with heightened feelings of fear.

However, because I had been meditating on this verse and was immersed in this psalm's handling of emotions, I tried to keep praying like this: "LORD, I am afraid of what is going on in my body right now. I don't know why it is malfunctioning like this, and I'm scared about it. But I do know that you are a God who takes care of your people, and I know that you are here to help me with this. Teach me to trust you even though what I feel right now is fear."

Though this example might sound silly, that freedom to be afraid released me from the panic that usually compounds my problems. It enabled me to think more rationally about the symptoms, take bouillon to raise my blood pressure and something sweet to raise my blood sugar. Within an hour I was functioning normally and able to lead the Bible study that was scheduled for the congregation I was visiting.

The whole process illustrated for me the validity of the psalmist's approach to fear. When we are scared, we are invited to concentrate on who *YHWH* is and that He is trustable, rather than on the cause of our anxiety. We do not have to squelch the emotions that are an uncontrollable reality; let us undergird them instead with more truth so that they can be channeled constructively. Then we can actually delight in the presence of the LORD with us in the midst of whatever is so alarming.

We can react to fear in this way because we have complete assurance that *YHWH* will take care of us. His covenant relationship with us has provided us with promises that are foundations for our trust. That is why the psalmist continues by proclaiming, "In God, whose word I praise." His word is to be praised because it reveals to us the character of our faithful God. Scriptural accounts give us more than enough evidence that the LORD is eminently worthy of our trust.

The term *word* in Hebrew signifies not only one's speech itself, but also the content or fulfillment of one's words. Thus, the biblical narratives give us not only the record of God's promises in the Scriptures, but also the substance of those commitments, most specifically in Jesus, who is the Word of both promise and fulfillment in the New Testament (see John 1:1-14). That is why we recognize the Bible profoundly as The Revelation of God.[2]

For the people of the First Testament, the "word" was the instruction that they received through the speaking of Moses and the prophets, who proclaimed the speech of *YHWH* concerning God's covenant relationship with them. Now, having the Scriptures recorded for us, we can continually turn to them to learn the magnitude of God's declarations to us so that we can rely on them in times of fear.

Furthermore, the discipline of memorizing the Scriptures can put the Word in our thoughts, readily available for us to be reminded of the character of our God. Then we have something tangible to lean

---

[2]See chapter eight of *Sources and Trajectories*.

on—specific promises addressed to us to cling to when we are afraid.

After the emphasis on trusting God in our fears, the Hebrew text continues with an important progression that is not so noticeable in the English renditions. In verse 3, which begins with being afraid, the phrase "I put my trust in you" uses an imperfect verb, which designates incomplete action. When we are afraid, we need to keep working on the trust. However, in the fourth verse, after the psalmist has emphasized that in God we have received the revelation of His Word (for which we praise Him), the verb *trust* is in the perfect tense, which designates completed action. Once we have learned that the God who is revealed to us in the Word is trustable, then we can respond decisively with trust.

For this reason the poet can continue, "[I] am not afraid." Once our minds have moved through the progression of managing our fears by means of trust in YHWH, we will come to the point at which we are not afraid anymore.

In the final phrase of verse 4, the poet adds this extra reason why we no longer have to be afraid: "What can mere mortals do to me?" The Hebrew text uses the word we often translate "flesh" to indicate frail or erring human beings as compared with God, who is sovereignly wise. What can mere human assailants do to us when God is on our side?

We are impressed by the courage of Christian heroes such as Oscar Romero and other priests and sisters in Central America or Desmond Tutu and other anti-apartheid activists in South Africa, who, though in danger of death, went boldly on with their ministries. Such saints serving in strife-ridden places have not been oblivious to the dangers inherent in their roles and geographical locations. Rather, they have worked through their fears and have come to the insights of this psalm. What can a mere human do to us, after all?

Jesus refers to this freedom from fear of physical harm when He urges, "I tell you, my friends, do not be afraid of those who kill the body and after that can do no more" (Luke 12:4). Shortly thereafter He comforts us with this truth: "Are not five sparrows sold for two pennies? Yet not one of them is forgotten by God. Indeed, the very hairs of your head are all numbered. Don't be afraid; you are worth more than many sparrows" (Luke 12:6-7).

We frequently hear sayings such as "The only thing we have to fear is fear itself" or "You are your own worst enemy." We fail, however, to identify the genuine biblical roots of these expressions and thus don't recognize the larger truth of all that we have on our side. God said long ago that we do not need to be afraid of others. Disciplined study of the question "What can flesh do?" enables us to move more boldly and constructively into whatever produces fear in our own lives.

Are we afraid to tell others about our faith because of what they might think or how they might mock us for our "ignorance"? Are we afraid of economic consequences because of our Christian principles? Perhaps we might be fired if we refuse to cheat or if we won't automatically flunk a student who has problems that cause us concern. What can mere human beings do to us?

Are we afraid of going to jail because of our protest for godly principles in the government? In many countries Christians are being persecuted and tortured, but they persist in their witness and their work for justice. Think also of the model of the apostle Paul, who wrote from prison with a convincing boldness and Joy. What can mere human beings do to us?

They might mock us or reject us, but what does that matter anyway, when we are so profoundly undergirded by the promises and future of YHWH? They might imprison us, but often that increases the power of our witness to the love of God. We might be harassed in academic programs because we don' t accept the vain philosophies of contemporary culture, but this can become a great vehicle for manifesting the integrity and truth of the gospel and for helping us learn what we really want to do with our lives. (My own life was redirected toward theology partly because of harassment in my graduate program in English.)

Many people have been attracted to Christianity when human endeavors failed, drawn by the witness of those who know that mortals can't do anything to us that God doesn't allow and ultimately bring to our benefit. This is but one of the many words of assurance in the Scriptures to which we can turn when we are afraid, so that we might learn to trust.

Psalm 56:3-4 shows us what to do with our fears. If we begin by looking at the character of the God on whom we rely, and if we concentrate on trusting Him even though we fear, then we will be able to move to thanksgiving for the truth of His Word, which will set us free to trust without being afraid. Realizing that mere mortals cannot hurt us helps us in that discipline of mind. What can flesh do when we have a God whose Word can be trusted and whose promises are sure?

For Further Meditation

1. When and why am I afraid?

2. What happens when I try simply to squelch that fear?

3. How can I learn to manage that fear instead?

4. How does the Word of God give me hope as I trust in Him?

5. In what situations have I experienced the successful mastery of fear? What did I learn about my fear in the process?

6. Why do I not need to be afraid of what people can do? In what circumstances am I afraid anyway? How could I deal with those fears?

7. Why is the progression of verses 3 and 4 in Psalm 56 so important?

10

Our God Records Our Tears

Record my misery;
>*list my tears on your scroll—*
>*are they not in your record?*
Then my enemies will turn back
>*when I call for help.*
>*By this I will know that God is for me.*
In God, whose word I praise,
>*in the LORD, whose word I praise—*
in God I trust and am not afraid.
>*What can mere human beings do to me?*

PSALM 56:8-11

You have kept count of my tossings;
>*put my tears in your bottle.*
>*Are they not in your record?*
Then my enemies will retreat
>*in the day when I call.*
>*This I know, that God is for me.*

PSALM 56:8-9 NRSV

Why is it that a child might cry wildly when her father is in the room, but, if he ignores her and walks away, the sobbing ceases? The weeping might be a plea for empathy. If it doesn't work, the tot will soon try some other means to get attention. On the other hand, if someone who is concerned actively listens to the child, the crying ceases because it isn't necessary. The youngster feels understood.

The verses to be studied in this chapter from Psalm 56 enable us to cease crying, not because it isn't working, but because we know that God is listening and cares and comprehends. God does indeed pay thorough attention to our tears and confusions; YHWH can't get us out of His mind.

The Hebrew text begins with a word that means "wanderings" and has the pronoun *my* attached. Since this is the only place that this noun occurs in the First Testament, we see the poet's precision in choosing it to describe his situation. The word displays the aimless wanderings of a fugitive and portrays graphically the life of someone nobody knows.

The picture reminds me of a woman who lived for a while in our EPHESUS community when it was still a home for crisis ministry. She came with hardly any money, stayed a few months, and suddenly left. After several months she came back, left her car with us, and went to Alaska to work for the canneries. We couldn't reach her when she was there, but suddenly, long before the fishing season was over, she returned to get her car and was gone again. Her wanderings usually had no set destination, and we couldn't know her because our care couldn't follow her. Though some of her possessions stayed for more than a year in our home, we had no idea where she was and if or when she would ever come back. We cared very much about her, but we had no way to keep track of her.

This image in the psalm was made poignant for me by my concern for her: "You, YHWH, have taken account of my wanderings." Even though sometimes we might feel that no one really keeps track of us, though we might wander as far out of sight and mind as that houseguest, still YHWH closely observes us. He really cares about every little thing that concerns us.

Differences in translations reveal the Hebrew text's ambiguity—almost as if in keeping with the poet's wanderings. The New Revised Standard Version reports that *YHWH* has "kept count of my tossings." The NIV renders the Hebrew noun as a "lament" to be recorded. The Jerusalem Bible uses the word *agitation,* whereas the New American Standard employs the idea of "wanderings." The TNIV, which we are primarily using in this book, registers our "misery." The point in all these versions is that God cares about us. In the midst of our confusions, aimless wanderings, agitations, tossings, lamentings, and miseries, the LORD is taking record.

The poet goes on to note how carefully *YHWH* observes our pain. An imperative verb calls for the LORD Himself to put our tears in His bottle. We know that He will do so, for the poet continues with the question, "Are they not in your record?" (NRSV). That last noun, rendered "record," is related to the verb *count,* which was used in the first line of this verse. Since it is also a rare noun, used only here in the First Testament to signify a document or book of record, it seems the poet is implying that God has indeed kept accurate count. These root relations link the sentence together poetically to underscore the truth that God heeds intimately every little detail of our lives.

The command to God to "put my tears in your bottle" (NRSV) is an arresting image. The child who cries in our presence wants us to share in her sadness. Similarly, our tears are usually easier to bear if only someone knows about them. If there could only be somebody significant to consider that we have cried ourselves to sleep! The poet asks God to keep all those tears in His wineskin, lest they will have been cried in vain.

That picture amuses even as it comforts. Imagine God's huge wine cellar, filled with rows and rows upon rows of wineskins. Each one is labeled with the name of an individual, and, when that person cries, *YHWH* catches all the tears and stores them in the right flask. I sometimes think He has had to use at least seventy flasks for me. Indeed, that is the point of the verse. No matter how extensive our bewilderments or wanderings or weepings, God has cared intensely about them all.

When I was first alone after more than seven years of marriage, I was trapped in a deep depression that lasted for months. Caught up in my work of teaching the Scriptures at retreats on weekends, I found great Joy. But during the week at home alone, I often cried myself to sleep with wrenching sobs that lasted far into the night. It was especially comforting to me that God would really want to store up every tear in His bottle.

Because the LORD keeps our tears in His wineskin, we can know that we will not drown in them. Though it seems sometimes that we will be swallowed up by the billowing black clouds of despair, in the midst of them God is always present to protect us. Ultimately, tears cannot overwhelm us because God has recorded them.

With confidence, therefore, the poet can continue, "Then my enemies will turn back when I call for help." The original Hebrew phrase for verse 9 includes the "in the day" construction and thereby parallels the phrase "in the day when I am afraid" that we considered in the previous chapter. When we call upon God, He will not let adversaries triumph.

The stronger Hebrew phrase insists, "Then shall the ones hating me turn back [in fear and shame] in the day when I cry out for help." Because God is on our side to record our tears and fears, the foes will be either ashamed or terrified of the power He uses on our behalf.

The concluding phrase of verse 9 proclaims even more assurance. "This I know, that God is for me" (NRSV). We might not know any other comfort in the troubles of our lives, but this is not an empty promise: our God is for us.

The night I first wrote this chapter, three people called me for counseling. As the last caller was concluding, she apologized for dumping so much bad news on me so late at night. I tried to assure her that, even though I had no specific answers for her struggles, I was glad she talked through her griefs with me to sort them out. Though I was an inadequate helper, at least now I knew more accurately how to pray for her, and I wanted to be as supportive as possible. We each, much more effectively, receive perfect care and support and a thoroughly attentive listening ear from God.

The tragedy of our loneliness is that we have to bear its pain alone. That is not a redundant sentence; instead it acknowledges that our sense of despair is multiplied by the fact that we bear it unaccompanied, which in turn increases the emptiness of our solitariness. Therefore, we intensely need assurance, such as these words on a plaque given to me by Marguerite, who faithfully stood beside me through all my tough times of aloneness: "Don't forget—I'm your friend, no matter what."

The Covenant *YHWH* is offering that comfort to us through the words of the poet David. Therefore with confidence we can respond with the psalmist, "This I know, that God is for me."

As the apostle Paul says, "If God is for us, who can be against us? He who did not spare his own Son, but gave him up for us all—how will he not also, along with him, graciously give us all things?" (Romans 8:31b-32). If God is with us, will we lack anything else that is essential? (This question will be addressed more thoroughly in chapter fifteen.)

Do our Christian communities offer this kind of assurance and comfort? Most people need God's presence to be incarnated in human skin, so these verses are a call to our churches to make sure someone is there for those who are lonely or grieving—someone who can embody God's promises to be present and graciously to spare nothing.

Verses 10 and 11 of Psalm 56 return to the refrain lines from verse 4 that we studied in the previous chapter, with one notable addition. Besides saying, "In God, whose word I praise" (the phrase in verse 4), this time the poet adds a parallel line: "In the LORD, whose word I praise." The doubling of the idea not only reinforces it, but also significantly adds the declaration that the one who is my God is YHWH, the Covenant Keeper. Upon His promise we can rely.

The refrain reminds us that we can trust in God without fear, that mortal flesh cannot do anything to us that matters in light of our relationship with God. To read those phrases again after the assurance that God has recorded our tears and cares, our fears and prayers, is a double accentuation, since we now appreciate how much more is involved in His concern for us.

We can trust YHWH's word to us because He has listened and recorded our tears. His word contains the comforting hope that not only dries those tears, but also promises someday to take them away forever.

Therefore, we respond with thank offerings. The poet promises to fulfill his vows, and we turn with praise to use our lives in gratitude and Joy-full acclamation. After all, this is what we know: our God is for us!

For Further Meditation

1. When in my spiritual life have I felt like a wanderer?

2. How can I be sure that God knows and observes my wanderings?

3. How does it affect me to know that God cares about all the littlest details of my life? Does that scare me or make me glad? Why?

4. Why is it comforting to think that God would keep all my tears in His bottle?

5. What if my enemies aren't turned back right away in the day when I call?

6. How do I know that God is for me?

7. What progression do I see in this psalm between the first use of the refrain (v. 4) and the second (vv. 10-11)? Why does that matter for faith?

11

The Right Kind of Fear

Know that the LORD has set apart the godly for himself;
    the LORD will hear when I call to him.
In your anger do not sin;
    when you are on your beds,
    search your hearts and be silent.   *Selah*
Offer right sacrifices
    and trust in the LORD.

PSALM 4:3-5 NIV

Tremble, and do not sin;
    Meditate in your heart upon your bed,
    and be still.   *Selah*
Offer the sacrifices of righteousness,
    And trust in the LORD.

PSALM 4:4-5 NASB

I had promised Tim that I would pray for him all the while that he and the doctor discussed a new treatment for the failure of his kidneys. For several years Tim had had to insert two huge dialysis needles into his arm three days a week so that his blood could be circulated through an artificial kidney for more than eight hours per run.

To change to a constant dialysis across the peritoneum would free him from the lengthy routine of setting up and coming off the run, the time-consuming care of his dialysis machine, and the great chemical swings that left his body debilitated; but the new treatment held the risk of other complications. I promised to pray as Tim weighed the advantages and disadvantages, but I didn't know how.

My usual meditation on the Psalms in the swimming pool became an excellent vehicle for prayer. Though I had never prayed for someone for two hours before, the experience grew exciting when I thought about the phrase, "Know that the LORD has set apart the godly for himself" (NIV). From Psalm 4 I learned many important lessons about my friendship with Tim, about how I could trust God to take care of him, and about the proper place of fear in loneliness.

First of all, the psalm assured me that Tim had been set apart by God. The Covenant YHWH had chosen him particularly and continued to use him for a special youth ministry. At that realization a huge wave of confidence swept over me. I looked forward to all that I would learn about prayer and that Tim would learn in his decision process.

We are commanded to know this truth: "The LORD has set apart the godly for himself." The imperative implies that such knowledge will have important consequences in the way we live with it. One is in the next line: we can trust the LORD to hear when we call to Him. Other consequences will be considered later in this chapter and in the next.

If YHWH has set apart the godly for Himself, we must ask if the godliness comes first and causes Him to set apart those who exhibit it—or does God's setting them apart create the godliness? In the context of the rest of the Scriptures, we interpret this text to mean that God is the actor in the setting apart. The passage emphasizes this; it insists specifically, with emphatic pronouns, "for himself." Godliness is a gift first and then a response, not a characteristic that itself causes YHWH's choice.

To be set apart means to be made distinct, to be separated out for special aims. Sacred vessels were thus consecrated for use in the temple sacrifices. Different from other vessels because of their designation and service as sacred, they were used only for the purposes of worship.

The name that the NIV translates "godly" comes from the Hebrew word *chesedh*, which we encountered in chapter one. (The TNIV renders it instead "his faithful servant," and the NRSV simply says, "the faithful.") God alone is characterized by perfect *chesedh*, the active, steadfast, faithful loving-kindness of grace. Persons named godly or faithful are those who are pursuing and developing such a disposition by diligently practicing God's tender compassion. They are able to do so only because they have first passively received God's *chesedh* as it has been directed toward them. Thus, this psalm phrase emphasizes the paradoxical active passivity that characterizes the believer's life.

Tim illustrated this formation well. He had a very deep sense of the forgiveness of God. As a result, he actively sought to incorporate that sort of love into his own life as he reached out to minister to those around him. He would have been the first to admit his failures, but he was always growing in godliness. God knows how far he had come since he had first been His.

Some of us might be saying, "But I don't want to be separated. I'm already lonely; I don't want to be cut off any more." Blessedly, we are not separated to be alone, but to be part of a community, the people of God. Furthermore, we are separated not only *from* the world (in the sense of cultural practices inimical to the gospel), but also *to* the LORD and therefore *to* the world in His service. *YHWH* has called us apart for Himself to make available to us all the gifts of His work in our lives. Our loneliness is eased by the care of the community into which He places us and by His caring gifts to us.

The first of those gifts, the assurance in this verse that He hears us when we call to Him, is much like the choosing of a beloved. One whose attention is fixed upon someone special will more eagerly listen to that person's requests than those of others.

It is our delight that God chooses each one of us that way. When a person selects a beloved, everyone else is eliminated. But the special position and relationship with Himself that the LORD creates guarantees that He will hear each one of us when we call to Him.

This assurance comforts us profoundly as we pray for each other. During the entire time I prayed for Tim, I rejoiced that the benefits of those prayers might be very apparent. Indeed, later Tim said that he had felt thoroughly enfolded in God's wisdom as he deliberated with the doctor.

The next phrase is translated from the Hebrew in several ways in various English versions. The NIV urges, "In your anger do not sin." The Jerusalem Bible commands, "Tremble; give up sinning." The King James Version charges, "Stand in awe, and sin not." The TNIV and the New American Standard Bible render the phrase, "Tremble, and do not sin." Many of these translations convey the idea of trembling because the first Hebrew verb carries the connotation of "come quivering," in the sense of fear.

Because the next command is to keep from sinning and the preceding concept is that of being set apart, I think we wisely heed that "quivering" as a call for awe, as well as agitation and perhaps perturbation. The verb for sinning is here the one that signifies missing a goal or going wrong. Thus, the whole phrase introduces this very important but usually overlooked issue in the Scriptures: the proper place for fear in the believer's life.

In his writings Martin Luther ties the subject together closely with his perception of the right use of the Law. The reformer kept stressing that the Law cannot make us good, but it is a mirror to show us what sinners we are and how much we are in need of a Savior. By its standard we can see that we utterly fail to act like the saints that we are by virtue of God's gracious declaration and atoning work. Though the LORD has set us apart as godly, our human nature keeps us from ever living like that.

That is why we must properly fear. When we realize with awe and trembling that we have no right to stand before a holy God (compare, for example, the experience of the prophet in Isaiah 6), then we will rejoice more profoundly in the magnificent love that the Trinity demonstrates in the death of Christ for us, His enemies (see Romans 5:8).

The hymn, "What Wondrous Love Is This," proclaims the mind-boggling fact that Christ should lay aside His crown in order to become human and die for us. That seems almost too good to be true. With a proper sense of our unworthiness and inadequacy and failures, we sing in wonder at the immensity of God's love and respond to it with an eager desire not to sin.

We must be warned against the wrong interpretation of fear. God does not hold a threat over us all so that we are too terrified to misbehave or to omit a kindness. Rather, when we behold the consequences of evil that we deserve and notice alongside those the immensity of grace that rescues us from sin and death, in fear and awe we intensely desire to follow God's desires. This is the "fear of the LORD" that is "the beginning of wisdom" (Psalm 111:10; Proverbs 9:10). The more we rightly fear God in His holiness, the more profoundly and richly we will respond with warm love to the immensity of God's gracious and tenderhearted love.

To stress this dialectical balance, Martin Luther begins all of his explanations to the Ten Commandments with the phrase "We should so fear and love God that we . . ." When we hold fear and love in a proper tension, our recognition of God's wrath, which we rightly fear because we deserve it, is overpowered by gratitude and wonder at the mercy that has borne that wrath for us. Thus we can never take God's grace for granted, and reverent thanksgiving rather than stark terror becomes the motivation for our good behavior. Furthermore, Christ's atoning work involves many more aspects than most Christians usually realize. We properly fear God because we are delivered from fears of our enemies—all the principalities and powers of evil—for Christ has conquered them to rescue us from their power.

The NIV and TNIV lessen the emphasis of the next clause in Psalm 4 when they both begin with the idea "when you are on your beds." The Hebrew phrase begins dramatically instead with the imperative *search*. The godly person is instructed to consider within and to be silent. That command is also reinforced by the liturgical addition of the word *selah*, which most likely instructed worshipers to pause for a while to consider what has just been said.

If the verse tells us what to do in our anger (as in the NIV and TNIV), then in our hearts we are to search out the truth of what has made us angry so that we respond without sin (see the context of the quotation of this verse in Ephesians 4:26). If the commands are to "tremble" with fear (instead of anger as suggested by the NASB footnote) and to "meditate" (as in the NASB), then what must be considered in silence upon one's bed is a right relationship with God—the facts of one's sinfulness and the LORD's grace, and the response to that combination in a desire not to sin. Silence is the fitting response as we pause in wonder over those freeing truths. Just as the snowy splendor of magnificent mountains sometimes overwhelms us into silence, so the immensity of God's towering grace calls us to be still in awe before Him.

Silence also expresses our shame and humility and acceptance. I almost wrote the word *resignation,* but I don't think such a negative passivity characterizes our silence. Rather, we wait hopefully, eager to learn more of who the LORD is, very much in the manner of this command from Psalm 46: "Be still, and know that I am God" (v. 10).

The interpretation "fear and do not sin" is reinforced further by the next phrase of the psalm. The poet continues with the invitations to "Offer the sacrifices of righteousness, And trust in the LORD" (NASB). In the last chapter we learned about trusting as our reaction to being

afraid. Here trust is the corollary to our presenting offerings of godliness.

We cannot be righteous by ourselves. To be so before God, as with
holiness, is granted to us when the LORD sets us apart for Himself.
The First Testament people of Israel who heard these words obedi-
ently offered the specific sacrifices of righteousness commanded by
the law, but those offerings were not sufficient to make them righteous. They were instead a reminder of God's covenant with them,
confirmed by sacrifice (see Exodus 24). Through our New Testament
prism, we see them as a foretaste of that One who was coming to be
the perfect sacrifice to make righteousness available to us all as a gift.

For us in the New Testament era, the requirements of specific sacrifices no longer apply, since Jesus has fulfilled them for us. But the
exhortation to present offerings of righteousness is for us a constant
invitation to respond to Christ's sacrifice of Himself with lives that
seek what is right and just. Paul's prodding to "offer your bodies as a
living sacrifice, holy and pleasing to God—this is true worship" (Romans 12:1) remembers and expands this verse from the Psalms.[1]

The best part of our offering is to trust YHWH. What God desires
from us most of all is that we believe that His love is given to us freely,
without our thinking we can earn it in any way.

Because YHWH has set us apart for Himself, we want to respond
by choosing righteous ways to fulfill God's will. For those of us who
are lonely, this is a call to morality, an invitation to servanthood, an
exhortation to give ourselves fully into whatever God might call us to
do as we care for those around us.

In our trusting we realize that our sacrifices are perfectly accept-
able to God. That sets us free to respond even more thoroughly.
Moreover, in offering ourselves first to God and then to others, we are

---

[1]For deeper explication of this verse, see chapters one through three of my book
Truly the Community.

often to our delight set free from loneliness to find new purpose and fulfillment and wholeness. (This will be considered further in later chapters, but it is introduced here by the implications of our text.)

The final command to "trust in the LORD" actually completes our study of Psalm 56 and the progression that we have considered there from being afraid and still trusting to being not afraid (see chapters nine and ten). The absence of the wrong kind of fear is now matched with our understanding of the proper kind of fear, the kind that enables us to choose not to sin. We are set free from fears that would inhibit us and given right fears that keep us in check. We are thus liberated to offer ourselves as living sacrifices—holy and pleasing to God—because the LORD has set apart the godly for Himself.

For Further Meditation

1. What does it mean that *YHWH* has set me apart for Himself?

2. What does it mean that I am godly? How does that affect how I live? (Be careful not to turn this into legalism, but let your answer be Good News.)

3. How does God's setting me apart give me assurance that He will hear me when I call?

4. How does the proper kind of fear keep me from sin?

5. How can I find the appropriate balance of fear and love in relation to God? What will sustain it?

6. What will be the result if I consider these things and am silent upon my bed?

7. What does the idea of "offering sacrifices of righteousness" mean to me?

12

Joy When Nothing Seems
to Be Good

Many are asking, "Who can show us any good?"
Let the light of your face shine upon us, O LORD.
You have filled my heart with greater joy
than when their grain and new wine abound.
I will lie down and sleep in peace,
for you alone, O LORD,
make me dwell in safety.

PSALM 4:6-8 NIV

Even the comic strips aren't funny these days. Several find dark humor in the downsizing of the job market, in the ridiculous decisions of corporate management, or in the immorality of our times; some jab at such governmental actions as cutting support for people on welfare. Instead of bringing laughter, the "funnies" show us that the world isn't very funny. Underneath all the sad humor seems to lurk the question, "Is there anything good anywhere?"

David's world in Psalm 4 is a similar culture of despair. When the godly are suffering distress, when the world is filled with delusions and idolatry (see vv. 1b-2), the poet hears the people around him asking, "Who can show us any good?" (NIV) or "Who will bring us prosperity?" (TNIV).

We see a search for good in the large shopping malls that glut the U.S. landscape. Stores filled with trinkets and toys, the latest styles and gadgets, offer us "just the thing" to lift our spirits forever. Even some of the names of the stores suggest that we might be able to buy happiness there.

I listened to some Christmas advertisements on the radio before getting up one morning, and their pressures filled me with a brooding sadness. "See your little girl's eyes light up when she receives this doll for Christmas." "What fashions have you selected for the Christmas parties this year?" "Let me tell you what to serve at the party everyone will be talking about till next Christmas." When all the right kinds of clothes and entertainments are failing to produce lasting happiness, many are asking, "Can anyone show us any good?"

The verb translated "are asking" in verse 6 is in Hebrew a participle indicating a state of being or continuous action. People keep on searching for good somewhere, somehow, because they are constantly finding themselves dissatisfied with what they acquire.

The psalmist offers a solution tied to the principle that YHWH has set apart the godly for Himself (as discussed in the previous chapter). In the Hebrew, the first sentence that follows the agonizing question of this psalm pleads fervently, "Lift up upon us the light of your face, YHWH." The Hebrew imperative entreating God to lift up His countenance upon us comes from an attitude of humility. The poet, appealing for this sign of God's grace and mercy, is fully aware that only by God's loving action and lifting up is the gift of His light bestowed.

"The light of your face," probably an allusion to what is called the Aaronic benediction of Numbers 6:24-26, is a graphic image to describe God's shining concern for His people. We experience that image vividly in human terms when someone who really cares about us looks at us. A few days before working on the original version of this chapter, I returned from a four-day trip to California that had turned into three weeks of recuperating from emergency surgery for an intussusception (when the small intestine strangles itself and turns gangrenous). The shining radiance on the faces of my friends who met me at the airport showed me the fullness of their love for me.

The poet's request for *YHWH* to lift up the light of His face upon us uses human terms we can imagine to describe a divine radiance that is inexpressible. When the LORD's face shines upon us, we know that we will receive all the fullness of His gifts. Inevitably there will come a genuine Joy that is available only to God's people.

This Joy that *YHWH* gave in "my heart," the poet declares, is greater than all the happiness others experience when their grain and new wine abound, because it is based on facts that will not change, not merely emotions or unstable circumstances. *Heart* in the Hebrew designates what is grasped by the will. We might not feel happiness, but we can know and claim the divine Joy that is ours by grace. The universal search for happiness has no satisfaction apart from a genuine personal relationship with the LORD who made us and chose us for Himself.

I have been capitalizing the word *Joy* when writing about that notion ever since I first wrestled through to an understanding of the biblical idea over thirty years ago. At that time I was leading a Bible study on Paul's letter to the Philippians at the University of Idaho, where I worked in campus ministry. One of the participants in that group couldn't understand how the passage "Rejoice in the Lord always. I will say it again: Rejoice" (v. 4:4) could be possible. The following "three-level theory" illustrates Paul's frequent exhortations to Joy.

First of all, we have to remember that the Greek verb is plural, which means that we don't do this rejoicing alone. Moreover, the verb is a continuing imperative; the Christian community can rejoice at all times because of our mutual remembrance and incarnation of the reasons for Joy. We could better translate Philippians 4:4, "Keep on rejoicing, all y'all, in the Lord always, and again I say, keep on rejoicing, all y'all."

Compare our Joy in Christ, furthermore, to the life of the normal person without a relationship with God and thereby involving basically only two levels of existence: the experiences of happiness and those of sorrow. Placing our two hands on top of each other can illustrate these two aspects of reality. The top hand is the happiness level of life, which we experience when all goes well—when a person has plenty of money, a loving spouse and/or deep friends, good relations with parents or boss, straight A's in school, a smoothly running household, and so forth. The other hand, the lower level, is the sorrow side of life, when things aren't going so well—when a person fights with his or her spouse or has been abandoned, has lost a dearly loved friend or relative, is getting lousy grades, is drowning in a shambles of a household, does not get along well with others, or is running out of money. Everyone has experienced both of these levels of existence at various times and to a greater or lesser degree.

The Christian, however, has a third level of existence. Now place both of your hands on the floor—the happiness one on top of the other. Imagine that the floor is infinite, stretching on beyond the ends of the room forever. Assume that the floor is powerfully hard, like stone that cannot be broken through. This floor is the bedrock for the Christian's other two hands of existence. It stands for one simple, foundational fact: the truth that Jesus Christ rose from the dead and thereby demonstrated for all time our reconciliation to God. Nothing can crack that fact; nothing can destroy the eternal victory over death and evil that it entails. The Scriptures call this Joy: a confident reliance upon the infinite, uncrackable resurrection fact.

The truth of Easter brings Joy for at least five major reasons. First of all, Christ's resurrection is proof of His victory over all the principalities and powers of evil—the last enemy of which was death.

Therefore, none of those forces can have dominion over us any longer. Second, because God loved us even as we killed Him when we were His enemies, we know that our sins are forever forgiven, that we have been completely reconciled to God. Though scholars argue over the "how's" of the atonement and why Christ's death could take our place, we are assured by the Scriptures that the life and suffering, death and resurrection of Jesus do atone for our sins.[1] Third, because Christ rose from the dead, we know that we, too, shall rise and live eternally with Him. Fourth, the resurrection is the next-to-the-grand-finale of the story of the promising God and proof that He always keeps His promises; thus, we look forward to the day when He will dispense with evil forever and wipe away every tear from our eyes. Finally, the victory of the resurrection assures us that we, too, can find strength for our everyday struggles in the constant presence of the living Christ with us and in the power of the Holy Spirit.

Lift both your hands into the air, and you see existence without the resurrection. Tossed about by circumstances, the two levels float around with nothing substantial as their base. Take away the happiness hand (when earthly pleasures fail and problems multiply), and all that remains is the hand of sorrow, being battered by the storms and tempests of change and disappointment.

Next, place your two hands again on the floor and turn to look at the Christian life, in which the levels of happiness and sadness are permeated with the Joy of that infinite, never-to-be-cracked resurrection base. Pretend that everything has gone wrong in the believer's

---

[1]For an excellent discussion of and examples of wider images and interpretations for the atonement, see Joel B. Green and Mark D. Baker, *Recovering the Scandal of the Cross: Atonement in New Testament and Contemporary Contexts* (Downers Grove, Ill.: InterVarsity Press, 2000), and Mark D. Baker, ed., *Proclaiming the Scandal of the Cross: Contemporary Images of the Atonement* (Grand Rapids, Mich.: Baker Academic, 2006).

life. Take away the top level of happiness so that all that remains of the original two levels is the hand of sorrow. Yet look! Underneath is that level of Joy that no one can take away.

How large is that hand of sorrow compared to our infinite floor? The apostle Paul writes, "For I reckon that the sufferings of this present time are not worthy to be compared to the glory which shall be revealed in us" (Romans 8:18 KJV). The fact of the resurrection, proving the truth of God's promises for us, remains unshaken. Though I have gathered together an inordinate amount of handicaps, though you might be afflicted by intense sorrows, even though the world is being crushed by violence and injustice, how large are those sufferings compared to an eternity of perfection in God's presence?

Besides, continuing with our illustration, we need only spread the fingers of the hand of sorrow to see the greatness of the Joy underneath. As Paul proclaims, "We know that in all things God works for the good of those who love him, who have been called according to his purpose" (Romans 8:28). Even the fingers of sorrow in our lives draw Joy from the spaces between them as God weaves their elements together into a harmonious whole, working together for good. In the midst of struggles with handicaps, I see God's faithfulness in doctors, friends who give me rides or support, miracles of healing, God's provision for all my needs.

Joy is not merely an abstract concept; the poet praises God for filling his heart/will with a genuine actuality. Even so, Joy undergirded my life even in the saddest days when I was first alone. For months I was sustained by the hope that someday all my sorrow will be swallowed up in the Joy of my own resurrection into an eternal life free from pain and heartbreak. The hand of sorrow is so small compared to that infinite floor. And meanwhile I saw throughout the first four years alone as I began writing this book that God took my sorrow and turned it into benefits for others through the teaching I was doing. Underneath the hand of sorrow is a Joy that permeates grief and changes it into good, not only for ourselves, but also for others.

We do not have to slap a top hand of superficial happiness onto our existence and pretend that all is well when it is not. Happiness is temporal, dependent upon the circumstances that create it. Joy is eternal, dependent upon the accomplished fact that Christ has risen from the dead and demonstrated that reconciliation with God is an established, eternal truth.

Human "grain and wine"—or any other devices for that matter—might make us happy for a while, but that soon passes away.[2] In bright contrast, the true Joy created by our relationship with the LORD can never fade or fail.[3]

I don't think that to be a Christian necessarily means that we will be happy. For those of us struggling with loneliness, there are many times when we cannot be happy. But we *can* "rejoice in the LORD always," because He does indeed lift up the light of His face upon us—and because the command to rejoice is plural and reminds us that we are glad in the midst of the Christian community, which carries the Joy for us even when we can't find it or feel it.

We can also know the LORD's peace, Psalm 4 declares. In verse 8 the poet asserts that he will lie down and sleep in *shalom*. In chapter twenty-six we will consider *shalom* more thoroughly, but here we note that biblical peace goes hand in hand with Joy. As our relationship with God keeps enabling us to deal with the sorrows of our lives, we will have enough tranquillity, the poet anticipates, both to lie down and to sleep. We will not be kept awake by the agitations of the world (v. 4). In our silence we will have come to trust the LORD (see the previous chapter).

YHWH alone can enable us to dwell in safety. The Hebrew noun

---

[2]See chapters six through eight of my book *To Walk and Not Faint: A Month of Meditations on Isaiah 40*, 2nd ed. (Grand Rapids, Mich.: Eerdmans, 1997).
[3]See my book *Joy in Our Weakness*.

for "safety" is related to the verb *trust*, which we have encountered already in many psalms. There is no security in the things of the world, just as there is no lasting happiness. Therefore, by means of a noun that signifies "isolation" or "separation," this final verse of this chapter's study emphasizes that no one else but YHWH alone is able to create for us that kind of safety. Not only can we be awake with Him in Joy unspeakable, but we can also sleep in Him with peace illimitable.

For Further Meditation

1. In what ways do I get caught up in the futile quest for happiness that drives the society around me?

2. What enables me to be bold enough to ask God to lift up the light of His face upon me?

3. What does the image of the light of God's face convey to me?

4. What is the Joy of the LORD? What is the difference between happiness and Joy?

5. How is it possible always to rejoice, as Paul exhorts?

6. How does my relationship with YHWH enable me to lie down and sleep in peace?

7. Why is it that only YHWH can make me dwell in safety?

13

The Right Kind of Boasting

I will extol the LORD at all times;
his praise will always be on my lips.
I will glory in the LORD;
let the afflicted hear and rejoice.
Glorify the LORD with me;
let us exalt his name together.

PSALM 34:1-3

My soul will boast in the LORD.

PSALM 34:2a NIV

I didn't feel like writing this chapter. Though I am always eager to talk about texts with others and discuss their ideas, the disciplines of study and organizing and writing all have to be done alone. When I began work on this chapter, the solitude of my labors made me feel particularly lonely.

Hoping to find some motivation to get to work, I called my good friend Tim for some conversation, but he was feeling ill earlier than usual on his dialysis run and didn't want to talk. So I sat at my desk and cried and watched the pity party develop. My fingers were sore. My feet were cold. My head was swimming. I would have given anything to have someone to hug me and to encourage me to begin writing.

My attitude changed when I called up my prayer partner, Elaine, and told her I was in trouble emotionally. We talked together about extolling the LORD at all times. Discussing the themes of this chapter with her, I experienced the great benefit of the disciplines of prayer and fellowship that Psalm 34 espouses. The two support each other.

According to the canonical title of Psalm 34, David wrote it when he had to feign insanity to escape from Abimelech. (The account is given in 1 Samuel 21:10—22:2. Differing records cause some confusion over his enemy's name. Probably the title of this psalm uses the dynastic family name of the king, whose personal name was Achish, king of Gath.) After David fled from Saul, he began to gather around him others who were oppressed. Most likely this psalm was written much later, after enough time had passed for reflection on David's experience, his reaction to it, and its value for his life. The poem is obviously a studied one because it is cast as an acrostic, which means that each verse begins with the next letter of the Hebrew alphabet.

As David looks back, he recognizes that YHWH was in ultimate control of his life, and therefore he responds to God's love with these words of praise. His words urge us to choose the discipline of remembering the character of the God who cares about us. Even when we don't feel like praising, there is comfort in the very habit.

David begins with a verb that has its root in the word meaning "to kneel" or "to adore with bended knee." In the intensive (Piel) form, this verb means "to bless, to extol." Its roots suggest that extolling the LORD at all times is based on humility, our own kneeling recognition that in spite of surface evidences to the contrary YHWH is always worthy of our praise. We have considered in previous chapters this act of conscious intentionality. Though the normal nastinesses of everyday life will tempt us away from extolling the LORD "at all times,"

the choice to praise is made easier not only by YHWH's supreme wor-
thiness, but also by our surprise at the benefits of praising, which we
will discuss later in this chapter.

"Continually his praise in my mouth" is the ordering of the line
that parallels the opening sentence of the poem. The noun for "continuity" is used here as an adverb, and there is no verb to accentuate
this state of being: that adoration and thanksgiving will surely be in
our mouths.

Because I get discouraged about the periodontal problems that
have caused my jaws to deteriorate, I kid my Christian dentist that I
have named my partials "His Praise," since they are continually in my
mouth. That joke has turned out to be a good reminder when, after
hours and days of teaching, they cause painful irritation. At those
times their very presence, accentuated by the discomfort, nudges me
to keep my words constant in reflecting worship.

In the second verse the psalmist declares that he will glory in
YHWH. The Hebrew emphasizes "in YHWH" by placing it first in the
line. The statement reminds me of Paul's comments about glorying
only in the cross of Christ; nothing else is worth our boasting (see
Philippians 3:7-11 and Romans 5:1-11).

Because it teaches us some important truths about our faith life, let
us look at the rest of the first line of verse 2 in the New International
Version. The statement that "my soul" shall boast in the LORD is much
larger than we might think at first. As we saw in chapter four, the Hebrew word nephesh, or "soul," means the whole being, the true essence of a person. In other words, with his deepest self the poet
David recognizes that his boasting should be about YHWH's character
rather than his own.

The concept of boasting is easily distorted by Christians. We are
so afraid of prideful boasting that we don't know how to do it right,
and we resort to a false humility. To boast properly is to recognize
humbly where credit is due. Thus, to boast in YHWH means to point

out to others what He has done and how we have seen Him at work in our lives and, more important, in the world.

Too often the "testimony" given in worship services or public conversations elevates improperly the person doing the speaking. We are not left thinking, *What a wonderful God that person has!* Good testimony leaves everyone knowing *God* better.

The purpose of our boasting is made clear by David's next line, which promises that the afflicted ones will hear and be joyful. We need more genuine witness in the Church so that those who are weak or humbled or oppressed can be glad with the one testifying. The two Hebrew verbs, *shamah* and *samach,* make a word play in this phrase to reinforce dramatically their message. Hearing (*shamah*) is closely related in both sound and experience to being joyful (*samach*).

David's words urgently call us to apply them actively in our Christian circles. If we more thoroughly appreciated the immense value for others that comes from speaking about what the LORD is doing in our lives, we would do it more often and thus would be further strengthened. What is the topic of conversation in our congregation's narthex after worship? Is there space in our worship services for giving testimony and rejoicing together in what God is doing? Do we read several lessons from the Scriptures to remind us of our great story, the account of God's work on behalf of the world through the people Israel and the early Church?

The prevalence of support groups in our society indicates the need for finding strength in the positive experiences of others who have gone through what we are encountering. The Church could more thoroughly be a safe haven where the afflicted can be nurtured in hope.

The next set of poetic parallels (two lines that offer corresponding perspectives on the same subject with synonymous words and phrasing) underscores the importance of the fellowship of those

who boast in the LORD (v. 3). The poet calls his listeners first to
magnify the LORD with him. The Hebrew verb in this first line implies causing something to become great. We can't make YHWH
greater than He is, but we can delight in making His greatness obvious to those around us.

We find it easy to praise our friends who are talented. I like to
show the art of my former housemate Julie to others or invite them
to listen to her magnificent singing. Those who see or hear will undoubtedly benefit from her gifts.

In the same way, we gladly magnify YHWH because we know that
those who are introduced to His presence and purposes and compassions will greatly profit. We have no doubts that God will faithfully
prove Himself worthy of praise to anyone who accepts the challenge
to get to know Him. Evangelism becomes a delightful privilege and a
natural reaction. We don't raise YHWH up; we simply enable others
to see His prior elevation.

The poetic parallel "let us exalt his name together" makes the invitation more intimate. Since the term name designates a person's
character, to exalt YHWH's name emphasizes recognizing His chesedh
and all the other attributes we have been discovering in these chapters. The invitation is for us to do that together as a community in
action. Since we each have our own unique perspective on God's
character, we need each other to see more of what God is like.

The best part is that such glorifying together in a bond of praise
eases our loneliness. When I called my prayer partner that night
when I first began working on this chapter, our "boasting" together
about the faithfulness of YHWH motivated me to begin writing. Soon
the subject itself became so exciting to me that my fingers began to
fly on the keys. Praise God!

Later I called Elaine back to tell her the good news that our prior
conversation had been exactly what I needed, and then we could
again "glorify the LORD" together. Such a profound experience of the

truth of this passage from Psalm 34 filled me with rejoicing—that Joy in the LORD that is our strength (Nehemiah 8:10b) and that is always the undergirding of our lives (see the previous chapter of this book).

Later still that evening I paused for a moment to check my wood-stove and saw there a reinforcing image. Since I had added another log a short while before, the fire was burning much better. One log can't burn very well alone, but when two were propped against each other, the fire added a lot of warmth to my cold basement study. The togetherness of God's people similarly causes our praises to burn more brightly.

If you were here with me right now, I'd pick you up from your chair and dance around the room with you to the accompaniment of the exuberant piano concerto that is playing on the radio. Exhilarating moments of remembrance like these as I finish revising this chapter deepen my desire to keep the praise of God always in my mouth.

In the rough moments when we can't crank ourselves up to get going, we don't have to manufacture our own Joy or pretend our energy. Renewal is readily available to us in the habit of praise and in fellowship with other Christians. As we bless *YHWH*, we are blessed. As we boast in His love, the recounting fills us with His presence. And when we do that together, we are doubly encouraged.

For Further Meditation

1. Can we really praise *YHWH* at all times?

2. When we lose the praise from our mouths, how can we recover it?

3. How can we keep our boasting godly?

4. Do the afflicted really hear and respond with rejoicing when I boast? What might be unhelpful about my witness? In what ways is it effective?

5. Which friends do I especially like to invite to magnify the LORD with me? Why?

6. If I don't have many such friends, how might I find a Christian community in which I could be strengthened by supportive sisters and brothers?

7. How could my congregation become a genuine community that helps people to exalt the LORD's name together?

14

Radiance and Angels

Those who look to him are radiant;
  their faces are never covered with shame.
This poor man called, and the LORD *heard him;*
  he saved him out of all his troubles.
The angel of the LORD *encamps around those who fear him,*
  and he delivers them.

PSALM 34:5-7

I knew that my face was beaming. Perhaps that should have been embarrassing, but I couldn't help being pleased at the performance of the young pianist. I had sometimes followed the score as my spiritual student had prepared for this concert. Consequently, I knew the tricky spots as they were successfully performed, and I felt a radiant delight in the pianist's mastery of the keyboard.

David uses a similar picture to describe the people of God. The original text says that "they looked unto him and beamed." The first verb form stresses that they paid close attention. Focusing on *YHWH* with intensity caused them to shine. A figure for Joy, this second verb implies that such radiance is a natural response to what is observed. When the people of God look to Him, they are made radiant by the wonder of His embracing holiness and love.

Immediately we think of Moses, who had to wear a veil over his face after he came down from being with *YHWH* on Mount Sinai for forty days and forty nights. The people could not look upon him because he was so luminous, according to Exodus 34:29-35 and 2 Corinthians 3:7-13. In the latter passage, Moses' secret is let out of the bag. After he had been down awhile, his face began to lose its luminescence because he was no longer in the presence of God Himself.

Moses' need to wear the veil to hide his fading radiance urges us to stay continually in the presence of *YHWH*. The brightness of which David speaks is not a once-given gift that lasts for all time, but a reflection of what we are observing. The more we look to *YHWH*, the more we will continue to be changed into His likeness, from one degree of glory to another, as Paul stresses in 2 Corinthians 3:18.

At times I was not radiant about the young man's piano performances. A high school student, he lacked self-discipline in practicing and sometimes suffered severe memory slips. Then my trust was put to shame (although I didn't love him in Christ any less for that). In relationship with the LORD, however, we can trust that our faces will never be shamed. God will always be true to His character.

Pause with me to consider if we have ever been humiliated as we have looked to *YHWH*. If in our grief we answer yes, we must inquire more deeply. Usually we feel mortified because of our failure to keep searching, or we feel embarrassed because things don't turn out as we wish. Then we think that God has let us down.

A young Christian woman once insisted to me that God, who promises to give us the desires of our hearts, must answer her prayer for a certain man to marry her. Her shame at the failure of her prayer was certainly of her own making, for surely she had not been regarding seriously the whole context of the LORD's promise. Her misunderstanding points out once again the need for consistent study of the Scriptures in their entirety.

Careful reading is also necessary for the next verse of the psalm, lest we misinterpret and think again that God has failed us. The Hebrew poetry says, "This poor one called, and *YHWH* heard, and from all his distresses He delivered him." The word for "poor one" is the same noun that we encountered in the previous chapter and signifies whoever is oppressed. In the canonical framing of this psalm, David would be most likely describing his own experience and using the demonstrative *this* to point to his own crying out for the help of the LORD when his life was threatened by Abimelech.

The faithfulness of *YHWH* (as we have seen it so often already in our study of the Psalms) is underscored by the fact that here again He has heard and delivered the afflicted one from all distresses. The final verb in the sentence is the one that we studied in chapter eight, which means "to give width or breadth to, to liberate." The word for "distresses" is the noun that we found (in chapter six) to mean adversities that come from being bound or straitened. *YHWH* has set this poor one free from those things that have put him in a tight place.

We must read that carefully lest we complain that God hasn't extricated us from all our struggles. The verb suggests that in those challenges *YHWH* creates for us range and scope so that we have enough space to stand firm. The particular adversities in which we find ourselves might not be taken away, but God gives us a way to escape so that we can endure (as Paul says in 1 Corinthians 10:13).

These sentences are especially liberating for those of us who are single and lonely. If we say, "God has failed me. He has not given me someone to take away the agony of my loneliness," we would not be accurately grasping God's provision for us. He saves us out of all our troubles by giving us strength to hold on and friends to stand with us and by creating enough space and peace so that we can more sanely handle our difficulties.

At the time when I first wrote this book, it seemed that I would probably engage in the complications of being alone for the rest of my life. Yet God never failed in all my single years to give me some means of encouragement, such as my prayer partner, Elaine, whose assistance in motivating me to write was previously described.

Sometimes it is music that invites us into God's presence. A call or a card from a friend may be what uplifts us. Sometimes merely the memory of something that a friend has said is sufficient. In our roughest moments we might have to reach out and ask someone in the Christian community for the comfort we need, but God does not fail to provide. I pray as we work through this book together that the faithfulness of God for your loneliness is becoming more and more real. Sometimes the LORD provides ways we would least expect, but if our eyes and heart are open, He has all sorts of surprises up His sleeve (as if He had a sleeve!)—and His Word is always there for us, with surprises of its own.

My favorite surprise is the angels. I first wrote this chapter the day after the first Sunday of Advent, the beginning of the new liturgical year. Since this is the season of repentance in preparation for Christmas, I always celebrate it by putting up an Advent calendar and wreath, a manger scene, and an angel choir.

We don't really understand angels and can't picture them. That is why I especially enjoy the wide variety of paper, yarn, ceramic, wood, and straw angels who join my Advent celebration each year. The promise of *YHWH* in Psalm 34 is that His encamping angel encircles the ones fearing Him, to be an agent for the LORD's deliverance. My friends tease me that either God has given me extra angels or the ones assigned to me do double duty. With my physical handicaps and extensive traveling, divine protection by angels is not just a childhood fantasy for me.

The Hebrew phrase begins with the verb participle *encamping*. This word stresses that in all the angel's excellence, wisdom, and powerfulness, this messenger of *YHWH* continually remains with the ones fearing (in the sense of honoring in awe and humility) *YHWH*.

Then the prepositions for "around about" lead into the fact of deliverance. The angels' encamping around us makes it possible for them to draw us out of difficulties.

Sometimes the phrase *angel of the* LORD in the Scriptures seems to suggest *YHWH* Himself. At other times the word *angel* appears to signify a human being who functions as the messenger of God. We each know "encamping" persons who have been ministering angels to protect us and speak God's words to us. My former part-time secretary Sandy sometimes even cleaned my bathroom or did the dishes for me to protect my hands from cracking so that I could type and lead music with my guitar, and to give me extra time for study and writing.

The Scriptures also speak specifically of literal angelic beings, invisible warriors who guard us and fight for us. The Enlightenment idolatry that truth can be measured only in terms of scientific rationalism robbed us of a sense of mystery, of an appreciation for the supernatural, and, above all, of the recognition that the things of God are infinitely beyond our human ability to comprehend. On the other hand, angels have become too much of a New Age fad these days— and the tendency is to believe in them only for our personal benefit.

In contrast, the Bible does name angels, archangels, seraphim and cherubim as part of the heavenly hosts and invites us to be grateful for their ministering work, including their constant war with the "spiritual forces of evil in the heavenly realms" (Ephesians 6:12). We have scattered glimpses of them in such diverse places and roles as the call scene of Isaiah 6, the interpretations of Gabriel and the warfare of Michael in Daniel 8—12, the appearances to Zechariah and Mary in Luke 1, or the work of the angels in The Revelation, especially chapters 14—16, but we never discover much about them.

One favorite Bible story summarizes all we need to know about angels anyway. When Elisha is in danger for his life, his awed servant panics because he can see only the horses and chariots of the Aramaean army surrounding the city of Dothan (2 Kings 6:8-23). When he cries to Elisha, the prophet calmly answers, "Those who are with us are more than those who are with them" (v. 16); then he prays for YHWH to open the servant's eyes. Immediately the latter is amazed to see "the hills full of horses and chariots of fire all around Elisha" (v. 17). The protection of YHWH was very real, even though not particularly described. Because the name *seraphim* (as in the call scene of Isaiah 6) comes from the root meaning "fire" and, therefore, seems to mean "fiery beings," they might have been part of that hillside host.

Our problem is that we don't usually see them either. We need the LORD to open our eyes to recognize His messengers for combating the travails of our loneliness. They encamp around us to bring us the truth of God's presence. When we are afraid because we are alone, we need to take angels seriously as the forces that God constantly provides to protect us and take care of us.

I think specifically again of my friend Sandy. When I came home from a speaking engagement in Minneapolis many years ago with a severely painful ear infection, she met me as soon as she could at the hospital emergency room, helped me get medicine and handle details, took me to her home, made supper for me, took care of me all evening, put drops in my ears, took me back to my own home (where I was alone for the week), and tucked me into bed. The next morning I awoke to her ministering care.

Thinking about her as I write this chapter has brought me tears of gratitude for all the angels that God has placed around me. Perhaps the study questions below can help you think further about, and thank God for, the angels in your own life.

For Further Meditation

1. What experiences have I had of being supernaturally cared for? What accounts have I heard from other Christians of more-than-human safekeeping?

2. Who are the human ministering angels in my life?

3. How have I discovered that looking to *YHWH* produces radiance?

4. Have I ever been ashamed of God in my relationship with Him? Why?

5. How have I observed that *YHWH* has delivered me *from* my distresses, though not necessarily *out of* them?

6. How should I understand notions such as this one of angels that seem exceedingly "outdated" and yet are specifically recorded in the Scriptures?

7. How have I had opportunities to be God's angel for others?

15

Tasting the LORD's Goodness

Taste and see that the LORD is good;
*   blessed are those who take refuge in him.*
Fear the LORD, you his holy people,
*   for those who fear him lack nothing.*
The lions may grow weak and hungry,
*   but those who seek the LORD lack no good thing.*

PSALM 34:8-10

Blessed is the [strong] man who takes refuge in him.
Fear the LORD, you his saints.

PSALM 34:8b-9a NIV

W idely varying resources available these days offer exercises for discovering one's primary learning channel or principal intelligence. The tests have numerous questions grouped under a number of categories to determine whether a person learns best visually, through hearing, by touch/movement, intuitively, or however.

For all the time I spend reading and studying, I would seem to be primarily a visual learner. However, about twenty years ago I was surprised when on one such test I checked as applicable only three items in the visual and auditory columns, whereas nine statements under the touch/movement category described my way of life at that time. Evidently I learned best in tangible ways in those days. That discovery freed me from worrying about what had seemed an inordinate need to be hugged.

Finding our best learning modes can help us deal more effectively with our loneliness. Depending upon the kind of person we are, we will be comforted most by listening to a CD, reading a book, or being with somebody who touches us with the love of God.

The eighth verse of Psalm 34 seems to be meant just for sensate learners. The poet doesn't merely say, "Check out the goodness of YHWH." He encourages us to "taste and see that the LORD is good." The verb translated "to taste" urges us to examine by experience, by jumping right into God's goodness. How can we know YHWH is trustworthy unless we give Him a try?

That statement is a strong motivation for our witness to others. Many people have not entered into a relationship with God because they have never tasted His mercy, His truth, His generosity, His excellence. They might have heard or read all kinds of complaints about God or they might have been deeply offended by the failure of Christians to live in ways that demonstrate the gospel, but they have never really had the opportunity to examine the biblical claims in tangible ways.

Several years ago a Christian journal carried the story of a young woman who had become a believer because someone had challenged her to test whether the Scriptures "worked." In practicing a principle that she had read concerning not retaliating against enemies, she discovered the truth of the Christian life.

When we are lonely, we wallow too easily in our pity parties. Knowing for sure that we will not be disappointed, David urges us instead to go tasting. Having experienced God's goodness fully, he can be confident that it will never fail.

The Lord's Supper provides Christians with an opportunity to taste God's goodness in three tenses—past, present, and future. In that tangible partaking, believers look back to what Christ actually did for us in the breaking of His body and the pouring out of His blood in death. While sharing the bread and wine, we also experience Christ's presence in our eating and in the present community of those gathered around the table. Finally, we look forward at that table to the fulfillment of Jesus' promises that someday we will feast with Him and all the saints at the great banquet of heaven.

Throughout my adulthood, one of my best ways to ease loneliness has been to invite others to share the LORD's presence with me in a meal. Conversation, the delight of being together, the aromas and textures of foods from God's creativity, and holding hands in prayer enable us to taste and feel the goodness of *YHWH*.

In the poetic parallel of the eighth verse, David adds that the person who goes to *YHWH* as a haven, in the sense of protection or shelter, will be blessed. In fact, the Hebrew phrase is more of an exclamation. I have included the NIV translation here because the Hebrew word that the NIV translates "man" signifies a male of strength, in contrast to women or children, and the word *blessedness* is in a construct form as if to say, "Oh, the blessedness of the warrior who seeks refuge in" *YHWH* instead of himself. This is a statement of tangibility also, for such a sheltering implies warmth and physical harboring. This is an extremely important insight: even the one who might trust in himself because of his strength is far more blessed by seeking protection from the LORD instead.

Next, David urges us to fear *YHWH*. The verb that occurred in chapter eleven, in our discussion of the biblical balance of love and fear (in the sense of an honest assessment of how one deserves but does not receive God's righteous wrath), is not the verb David chooses in this psalm. In verse 7 and twice in verse 9, he selects instead the verb that means "to reverence or to honor" Him. Because of the context—the previous words about the blessedness of those who take refuge and the next statement that those who fear lack no good thing—we can hear in this word *fear* an invitation to thankfulness and praise. When we honor God, we learn to recognize His goodness in all that is around us, and in that reverent awareness we are more likely to respond with gratitude.

The ones who are to fear the LORD are His saints. That name reminds us that God has chosen us to be set apart as His people. In doing so, He has given us that very quality of sanctity that is His.

The scriptural pictures of God's holiness, such as the scene in Isaiah 6, are breathtaking visions. The prophet was filled with fear and horror and shame at his own sinfulness when he observed the holiness of God in His majestic enthronement and heard about it in the calling of the angels. You might want to read that chapter at this point and meditate upon it to try to imagine the magnificence of God's holiness. Whenever we confront the perfection of God, we, too, are forced to fall on our knees and cry out, "Woe is me! I am annihilated." Like the prophet, we also are persons of unclean lips, and we dwell among people who are the same.

Yet the Joy of our faith is that God has made us holy through being covered over with His righteousness, through our incorporation into the body of the perfect Christ. Like the prophet in Isaiah 6, we have been cleansed with the burning coal of grace. That is why Paul addresses his letters to the "saints" of the various New Testament churches.

I have often asked participants at retreats or conferences to raise their hands if they are saints, but I have yet to find a group in which everyone does. For some reason we Christians have not yet learned that our sainthood is something that we already possess by the Trinity's declaration, action, and gift. Its truth does not depend upon whether or not we act like the saints that we are.

The Joy of our relationship with God, furthermore, is that the Trinity continues to enable us to act more like the saints we are by means of forgiveness and affirmation and gracious empowerment. Nevertheless, the fact of our sainthood remains, whether or not we are living it out.

Therefore, we who are rejoicing in that sainthood want, of course, to fear the LORD. We want to give God the proper honor and to receive the holiness He is creating in our lives.

David continues by recording the promise that those who are saints honoring YHWH will lack nothing. That we will have no need of anything is hard to believe when we are lonely. We say, "But I lack a friend" or "I long for someone to care for me intimately." Is David lying to us?

Why does God sometimes seem to deny us what we need most deeply? Is David just speaking about food-and-shelter kinds of things? We might think that because of the way he continues with the subject of lions.

It seems to me, however, that the poet is not speaking only of suffering from lack of food. Rather, it appears that David chose lions for his illustration because they symbolize bloodthirstiness and power. Even in their forcefulness, David asserts, they might be in want and go hungry. We observe by means of them that power is not the instrument through which our needs are going to be met. We will not find a person to satisfy our longings by any manipulation, exploitation, vindication, or bloodthirsty revenge.

Instead, David continues, the ones seeking YHWH will not lack any good thing. The verb for "seeking" in this tenth verse is the same one that David used in verse 5. There the word emphasizes investigating the deity through prayer and worship, coming into the presence of YHWH in order to know Him.

David's assertion is very carefully constructed to remind us that only by honoring YHWH do we not lack any good thing. We might miss certain elements that we think are good, but if we are seeking YHWH's purposes, we will not fall short of anything that *is* good for us.

The Tower of Geburah, an older fantasy by John White, illustrated this point well. A child named Wesley is adventuring in another world and encounters Gaal, the Shepherd, who images Jesus. In a time of great danger they converse earnestly as follows about whether fighting evil is worth the effort when the venture might not be successful:

> [Wesley:] "I suppose you want me to say that it's always worthwhile to fight evil even if you know you're going to lose. But that doesn't make sense. Yet you want me to say it does."
>
> [Gaal:] "You seem to know a lot about what I am thinking. What I really wonder is whether you trust me or not."
>
> "Trust you?"
>
> "Yes, you seem to suspect that I do wrong to send you on a dangerous mission like this."
>
> "It sounds awful when you put it that way."
>
> "And I think for the moment that you're going to have to trust me even though I don't tell you all that's going to happen."
>
> "But Gaal, of course we trust you."
>
> "You mean you believe I know what I'm doing?"
>
> It would have been insulting to say no, so Wesley uncomfortably said, "Yes, I suppose so—I mean—*yes.*"
>
> "Do you think I don't care about you? Am I, perhaps, not a shepherd after all?"
>
> As Wesley looked into Gaal's eyes he knew deep down inside himself that Gaal *did* care. What's more, he suddenly knew that Gaal knew what he was doing. He also knew that his questions had been pretty insulting to Gaal. He felt small and cheap.
>
> "Then do as I bid you. The dangers are real, so beware of all I told you. It is not for you to see into the future, only to live in the present moment. And that involves being able to trust me."[1]

---

[1]John White, *The Tower of Geburah* (Downers Grove, Ill.: InterVarsity Press, 1978), p. 315.

If the LORD were here and we looked into His eyes, we, too, would see that He cares for us after all. Even though He seems to have neglected something that would be good for us, He does know ultimately what is best—and He grieves with us in our heartbrokenness in the meanwhile.

Once again, we are thrown back upon the character of God. Is He good or isn't He? Sometimes we don't see that goodness, but we are invited to try it out—to search for it, in fact—because it is there.

It is true that human evil often gets in the way of God's perfect will. For example, YHWH certainly intends for all the people of the world to have adequate food (seen in His original creation design in Genesis 1:26-31), but human greed and the materialistic consumption of the First World violates God's intentions. We in the Christian community must become more deliberate about participating in God's purposes for all to be fed.

Too often we are so intent on receiving whatever we lack that we think is good for us that we miss God's best. Perhaps if we are alone, we might be angry at God because we do not have a person to comfort and accompany us.

Then it sounds like a cruel thing to say that "the good can be the enemy of the best," but in my years alone I learned that that aphorism is true. For all the times in those seemingly endless years that I longed for someone to help and hold me, God enabled me to realize in my wiser moments that He really was teaching me to trust Him, to turn to Him for eternal comfort that will not pass away. Whenever we continue to seek Him and to be open to what He wants to teach us, we learn why certain desires might not be what we really need.

Nevertheless, some things we will never understand. That is why Gaal's words above were so piercing to me when I first read them. Sometimes it is imperative simply to rest in what is happening today and not worry about the future—or about comprehending the reasons for the way things are. (I chuckled when I first revised this paragraph more than twenty years ago. God had led me to write many months before what I needed to read later as I lay on a hospital bed seven hundred miles from home. While I was out in the mountains of California to lead a retreat, I suffered an intussuscepted intestine, and after an excruciating two-hour drive down to the hospital and a day of traumatic waiting as the doctors tried to discover what was wrong, midnight emergency surgery removed fifteen inches of it. Sometimes it is *necessary* simply to rest in what is happening today and not worry about the future—or about comprehending the reasons for the way things are!)

Blessedness is indeed promised to those who seek the LORD, but the key lies in the seeking. That means to study and pray, to search and wait, to worship and serve—even to be tested, to struggle and suffer. Such disciplines of mind and spirit are often hard to engage in when we are feeling lonely. In those times especially we are invited to cling to this promise: "those who seek the LORD lack no good thing." In believing that statement to be true, we find the contentment to accept whatever blessings are or are not in our lives.

You have probably heard this aphorism: "Contentment is not having all I want but wanting what I have." Unless our wants are refined by seeking the LORD as David urges, our wants are probably larger than our needs. On the other hand, when the LORD meets our needs, then we can learn to say with Paul, "I have learned, in whatever state I am, to be content" (Philippians 4:11b RSV). Then we will know the Joy we discussed in chapter twelve.

This chapter has moved through a surprising progression. We began with the acknowledgment that *YHWH* enables us to know His goodness in tangible ways. Here at the end, however, we have learned not to depend on what we can sense. Sometimes we will be able to taste and see how good God is, but true maturity of faith will recognize His love even though from a human perspective we might lack good things. That kind of maturity grows as we continue to seek

Him. Not in the power of a lion, but in the waiting of a saint we know the fullness of blessedness.

For Further Meditation

1. What are some of the ways in which I most deeply taste God's goodness?

2. Do I receive God's love best through hearing about it, reading about it, or tasting it?

3. What is blessedness?

4. What does it mean to me that I am a saint? How does it affect my daily life to know that I am one?

5. Have I ever thought that I lacked anything? What have I thought I lacked? How do I feel about that after studying this text? (Don't worry if this text still upsets you—it takes time for us to grow into the spiritual maturity of complete acceptance. We can be real with God when we are having trouble trusting Him.)

6. Have I observed others or myself trying to meet needs in "lion" ways? What are some of those ways, and why will they not ultimately succeed?

7. How does it affect my desires to know this promise from *YHWH* that if I continue seeking Him I will never lack any good thing for my life?

16

The LORD Is Near
When We've Lost All Hope

Come, my children, listen to me;
I will teach you the fear of the LORD. . . .
The righteous cry out, and the LORD hears them;
he delivers them from all their troubles.
The LORD is close to the brokenhearted
and saves those who are crushed in spirit.
The righteous may have many troubles,
but the LORD delivers them from them all.

PSALM 34:11, 17-19

Surely it was the saddest day of my life. Marguerite had listened to me many times through the agony of my husband's abandonment. She had given me a plaque that promised, "I'm your friend, no matter what"; so I went to her home to sit in her rocker and cry. I didn't expect to be able to find any comfort.

When I arrived, she got out several Bibles and read to me her own mixed-translation rendering of the eighteenth verse of Psalm 34. "This verse is just for you," she said:

The LORD is near to the brokenhearted
and saves those who have lost all hope.

I had lost all hope of ever being able to face life again—even to smile again, much less to deal with this fierce anguish. All I knew was the despair of rejection, desertion, poor health, and betrayal. Why go on?

Marguerite helped me to find the courage for that day. It was here: "The LORD is near to . . . those who have lost all hope." I couldn't feel God's presence. I didn't know any of His answers. My marriage would not be restored, though I had tried for years. But I did believe (though faintly, through my friend's help) that the Comforter was near.

It is still hard for me, even twenty-five years later, to review what I once wrote about that hopeless pain, but I include it in this book because perhaps you are feeling such desolation or brokenheartedness right now. Or maybe you have felt that way in the past, or you will need to know where this chapter is for some day when you will comfort a friend or family member suffering acute grief or profound depression. We yearn to find in the depths of despair a basis for hope.

When I first drafted this chapter, it was also hard for me to write about despair because so many of my friends and family were going through great troubles at the time. Nancy was battling leukemia; Tim's kidney dialysis was being made more difficult by horrendous complications from the flu. Six of my close friends were unemployed, and several members of my family were going through traumatic times of decision and difficult circumstances. Where is there hope in the midst of all this anguish?

The New English Bible translates the first phrase of verse 18, "The LORD is close to those whose courage is broken." The verse could refer to brokenness of the will, but it might also designate a fracturing of one's moral character, in the sense that God searches and refines the "heart." In that case, the phrase would emphasize that *YHWH* is near to those who are crushed by their own sinfulness and guilt.

Another scene in John White's *Tower of Geburah* illustrates well this truth that the LORD remains close even when we are appalled by our failures. The girl Lisa has been deceived by the evil sorcerer and has feasted upon all sorts of delicacies that were not actual food. Then she tried to clean herself up in a shower of water that was not real. When she finally meets Gaal, the Shepherd, she is filthy and sticky and afraid that he won't want to touch her. Yet he gently takes her hand. Even when she wipes her dirty hand on his sleeve, he does not pull away. In fact, his robe remains white, and some of the stickiness is removed from her hand.

The nearness of the LORD to the brokenhearted implies the same tenderness. No matter how dirty our face, how dark our shame, how troubled our spirit because we have spoiled our relationship with the Shepherd or mistrusted His goodness because of the immensity of our sorrow, yet He still chooses to be beside us in our grief.

Much of the sorrow of the brokenhearted takes the form of those disabling questions, "Why?" or "What could I have done?" Our brokenheartedness is often multiplied by the intense guilt we feel (usually falsely). In the LORD's nearness we can learn more truly what is sin—for which we are freely forgiven—and what is false guilt—which *YHWH* will help us put away. Thus the apostle Paul begins and ends many of his letters with a reminder of that forgiveness and that release when he wishes his readers, "Grace to you and peace."

In the poetic parallel line to "The LORD is close to the brokenhearted," David declares that *YHWH* saves or delivers those who are crushed in spirit. The verb is from the root *Yashah,* from which we get *Yeshua,* the Hebrew word for our English name *Jesus*. This meaning of the name is noted when the angel Gabriel commands Joseph, "You are to give him the name Jesus, because he will save his people from their sins" (Matthew 1:21).

Looking back from our perspective in time, we New Testament people know *how* the LORD saves those who are crushed in spirit. No matter how shattered we are by our experiences, the Trinity has accomplished our deliverance through Yeshua, the Saving One.

"Crushed in spirit" may be interpreted in several ways. It is often understood as contriteness for flaws in moral character. In that case the salvation promised in this psalm is the gift of forgiveness and reconciliation for those who are repentant. In addition, we could construe the phrase more in the sense of being shattered or crushed emotionally—or as in the Good News Bible's version, to have lost all hope. In our most despairing times, we identify with this reading.

Whatever the nuances, this message is the same: YHWH is near and YHWH rescues. This is the hope to which I clung in the many months when all I could do was cling. When I felt so crushed that I didn't feel capable of holding on any longer, my pastor would reassure me, "Don't forget, Marva. God will never let you go." In the midst of the darkness of despair, we need to keep hearing the word of comfort that YHWH is near until we can believe it and see its true light.

The poet David is realistic. He continues by acknowledging, "The righteous may have many troubles." The alliteration of the Hebrew words raboth ("many") and ra'oth ("troubles") underscores our reaction of panic or grief to the multiplicity of our afflictions. Thus we add to our many problems one more—that sometimes we can't begin to deal with them because we are so overwhelmed by them. Many are the miseries or distresses of the righteous—the ones who desire to be just and good. We who choose God's ways set ourselves up for extra trials, not because we deserve them, but because the powers of evil are actively engaged in struggle against the good. That is why the Lord's Prayer includes the pair "Thy kingdom come" and "deliver us from evil," for the opposite side of the same coin of doing God's will and participating in God's kingdom purposes are the temptations to live that way for our own benefit and the possibility that we will idolatrously serve the purposes of evil instead of God.

The Bible tells us that we can rejoice when we encounter struggles in our spiritual lives (see James 1:2-8). They build our character and form us with godly virtues. However, the Bible also tells us that if we are leading godly lives, we will be persecuted (see 2 Timothy 3:10-12). That makes us wonder: *If I'm not being persecuted, am I really living the alternative life of the Christian community? Have I become so enculturated that my neighbors don't see in me the difference Christ makes?*

Furthermore, we have to realize that each of us is actively engaged in the cosmic battle between good and evil. If our desire is to fulfill the purposes of God, we will indeed encounter obstructions.

I don't mean this flippantly at all. We must realistically face the corollary between growth in faith and an increase in troubles. Several years ago the members of some discipleship groups that I was leading ran into all kinds of obstructions as they tried to establish habits of Bible study and prayer. One person kept oversleeping and losing the time she wanted for prayer and meditation. Another started running into irritations in her job that distracted her when she tried to study the Bible. A third complained that his mind always wandered when he tried to concentrate on prayer. Others noted family problems, mechanical breakdowns, crazy frustrations. As we talked about the various difficulties everyone was encountering, we realized that they were not merely human struggles. As Ephesians 6:12 reminds us, our battle is not against mere flesh and blood, but against the "powers of this dark world." We ought not to overspiritualize these powers; though Ephesians 6 does also mention "the spiritual forces of evil in the heavenly realms," the chapter primarily discusses "principalities and powers" that operate in this world through such modern manifestations as technology and politics and Mammon, the god of money. Many of the obstructions in our faith lives come from the ordinary things that surround us but get out of hand or overstep their roles and become gods dominating our lives.[1]

---

[1]For an elaboration of the biblical notion of the principalities and powers in the present world, see my book *Powers, Weakness and the Tabernacling of God* (Grand Rapids, Mich.: Eerdmans, 2001).

According to C. S. Lewis, there are two mistakes we can make about Satan and all these powers of evil (in whatever material or spiritual form they take). One error is not to take them seriously enough. We must pay attention to the realism of such phrases as "many are the afflictions of the righteous" (Psalm 34:19 KJV). The other mistake is to take them too seriously and fail to remember that in His death Christ defeated the principalities and powers by exposing them and disarming them (see Colossians 2:13-15). The Easter empty tomb is the seal of that victory.

Therefore, we can assert with the poet of Psalm 34 that though there are many troubles for the righteous, "The LORD delivers [us] from them all" (v. 19). This same verb for "delivers" has been employed earlier (v. 17), when David declares that when the righteous cry out, YHWH hears them and delivers them from all their hardships. In the Hebrew, repetition and parallel use proclaim these words doubly to enfold us more richly in their comfort.

The verb *to deliver* comes from a Hebrew root that emphasizes snatching away, so it produces an image of God rescuing us from the midst of those troubles. That verb choice is important because sometimes our circumstances—especially in aloneness—cannot be changed. If someone deserts us, God will not cram His will down that person's throat and force him or her to come back. Nevertheless, in the pain of that rejection YHWH comes near to those who are His and takes them away from that grief. We must be patient with the long process of healing, yet we can be confident that ultimately the LORD delivers us from our straits and distresses.

Because I wait for healing impatiently, I included verse 11 in this chapter's discussion. This invitation comforts us softly: "Come, my children, listen to me; I will teach you the fear of the LORD." Many times in my deepest woundedness, I longed for the security of being a child crawling into my daddy's lap and feeling his arms around me while he gives me the wisdom to solve all my problems. David certainly had plenty of experience in knowing the LORD's deliverance from his troubles; consequently, he can tenderly address his listeners as children to invite us to learn from him.

I think the text further invites us to learn from all those whose greater years with the LORD have given them deeper wisdom. We gain hope by listening to those who have suffered the same griefs we bear. We can glean from them how they survived their sorrows, how they have grown from them, and how YHWH was near in the midst of them. That is the great value of support groups and prayer partners, of biographies and testimonies of faith.

What distinguishes salutary biographies and testimonies from unhelpful ones, however, is the subject of the second line of verse 11. David says, "I will teach you the fear of the LORD." We are not aided by human words of comfort or pride in human achievements. We are given lasting comfort and eternal hope by whatever enables us to honor YHWH better and to turn to Him—expecting that God will deliver us and believing that He knows what He is doing.

As I look back upon the times of deepest heartbreak and sorrow, I realize that I was more helped by those who said, "Things are going to be tough for a while, but God is with you," than by those who patted me on the back with a glib "Everything will turn out fine." The first words might sound cruel, yet I remember rejoicing at their truth.

Just a few weeks before I first wrote this chapter, a very wise counselor admonished me to die to my own desires in order to pursue my ministry. He encouraged me to face realistically the fact that my work as a freelance Bible teacher might necessitate a solitary life so that I could be available to travel anywhere to teach. He analyzed my multiple handicaps and my commitment to serving God and concluded that it would be very difficult to find anyone to share them. My experiences over the years confirmed the accuracy of his insights. Even though those hard words meant disillusionment, they were the best words I had heard because they forced me to confront the truth and

to learn to find my need for companionship satisfied by God Himself.
(What an amazing surprise it was, then, when ten years later God
brought Myron into my life—just at a time when my handicaps became overwhelming—and he was remarkably willing to take on the
burden of caring for me even though we knew my physical problems
would only get worse.)

Psalm 34 here reminds us that we need to listen to instruction that
will help us learn to fear the LORD. That reality will truly help us deal
with our brokenheartedness, because in honoring YHWH we will discover that He is near. In fact, He is nearest in our humbled repentance and broken sorrow. When we are crushed—by our sin or by
our circumstances—then we know most deeply that the LORD comes
to love.

For Further Meditation

1. Why is it comforting to know that the LORD is near when I am
   brokenhearted?

2. How might my insights into these verses enable me to minister to
   a friend who is brokenhearted?

3. What does it mean that the LORD saves? (Don't limit this idea too
   much.)

4. Am I comforted by knowing that the troubles afflicting the righteous are many? Why or why not?

5. How can I cope when YHWH does not seem to be delivering me
   out of my troubles?

6. Who are my heroes of faith, those to whom I listen for words of
   wisdom and instruction?

7. Why is it important that they teach me how to fear the LORD?

17

I Thought I Would Die,
but the LORD Helped

Who will rise up for me against the wicked?
   Who will take a stand for me against evildoers?
Unless the LORD had given me help,
   I would soon have dwelt in the silence of death.
When I said, "My foot is slipping,"
   your unfailing love, LORD, supported me.
When anxiety was great within me,
   your consolation brought me joy.

PSALM 94:16-19

Your consolation brought joy to my soul.

PSALM 94:19b NIV

The whole day I had been anxious. Every dimension of my life seemed unsure and troubled. Several options had fallen through for how I could use my big, five-bedroom house for ministry. A nasty letter had come from someone I had been counseling, and I was angry (righteously, I thought) that after I had invested so much time my intentions had been so misunderstood. Also, disturbing news had come from my publisher about the manuscript of my second book. Finally I was overwhelmed by it all and called my friend Tim for help. Often when we lived in the same town and he was on kidney dialysis runs, we would converse on the telephone about matters of ministry and personal concerns. Tim was a church youth worker and musician and was several years older than I. As a skilled counselor, he really understood the struggles of my physical limitations as well as the hardships and delights of ministry, so we often worked together through our respective difficult times and questions.

But it wasn't a day for a dialysis run, and Tim wasn't home. I left a message for him to call, but he didn't for the rest of the late afternoon and evening—so it seemed to me (in my despairing and therefore irrational emotional state) that God had abandoned me, too, and didn't care. I went to bed uneasy and fitful.

A while later the phone rang. Tim had returned to his home, and since in those days I usually did my writing late at night, he had decided to call me in spite of the hour.

I hadn't been rejected after all! (Suffering desertion had made me extremely sensitive to anything that looked like rebuff.) As I poured out my hassles one by one, Tim kept rebuking me gently, helping to put things back into the perspective of God's love and care. I told him all the disappointments about my house, and he answered, "Is it God's house or isn't it?"

He was right. I had bought the large house in order to have enough room to welcome into my home those who needed asylum. Now the director of our crisis ministry had gone back to school, and I wasn't able to care for guests along with my traveling and writing. Surely God would help us find another way to use His house to minister to the needs of others. Tim's question made me feel ashamed that I doubted so much God's compassion for all my concerns.

I told him of my anxiety about my book, and he replied, "Did you put that book into God's hands or didn't you?" His words of admonition came out of such a loving spirit that no one could be offended. If my books were written to enfold people in the answers of the Scriptures, surely I should know that the God of those Scriptures would take care of those books. Tim's kind chiding turned me back to the comforting character of our God.

The surprise came when we had finished sorting through the struggles of the day and he didn't hang up. We talked into the wee hours of the morning—in uplifting ways and about pleasant things, so that I was not only comforted, but delighted. That conversation had changed an apprehensive and fearful loneliness into a deep security in receiving God's gifts of presence and love.

When I first studied them, the four verses from Psalm 94 at the head of this chapter struck me with the same wondrous progression that I have just described. First, however, this psalm calls upon God to avenge the poet on his enemies, who are jubilant and arrogant. The writer is distraught: troubles are crushing *YHWH's* people, yet God doesn't seem to be paying attention.

In the present time the United States is not oppressed by more powerful enemies in the same way as Israel was in the time of the Psalms—though many people in our world suffer such tyranny, and our life with God calls us to do what we can to end such brutality (especially if the oppression comes from us!). In our own personal situations, life is much more subtle. Adversaries aggrieve us through business manipulations, personal indifference, economic exploitation, and institutional injustice, so we might not readily envision them as foes. Therefore, when we look at this psalm through contemporary eyes, we must imagine the different sorts of enemies that our culture produces: stress, economic instability, insecurity, anxiety about our power or prestige or relationships, and so forth.

When these things attack us, we cry out with the poet, "Who will rise up for me against the wicked? Who will take a stand for me against evildoers?" Our frustration grows because no one seems to be on our side. On the day I described in the story above, nothing seemed to go my way—as if *my* way were best! At one point in my conversation with Tim I complained about the arduous struggle that life had been for me for so long, and Tim asked gently, "Is that really what this year has been like?"

His question shamed me, because that year I had experienced more hope than in the previous five. Yet at times when too many irritations pile up, it is easy for us to feel that no one is on our side.

Into our questions comes a resounding answer: "Unless the LORD had given me help." His assistance enabled the poet—and me—to find an escape and go on. The word *help* is the same Hebrew noun that is used in Psalm 46, where the poet declares, "God is our refuge and strength, an ever-present help in trouble" (v. 1). That night I discovered God to be such an aid through the person of my friend Tim. Those of us in the Christian community must always recognize how the care of God can be incarnated through us. How will our words of solace or support—or even of rebuke, as Tim found it necessary to speak to me—bring to others the help of *YHWH*?

The poet records in Psalm 94 how deep his fear and anxiety were. Unless the LORD had given him help, he "would soon have dwelt in the silence of death." The Hebrew word translated "soon" in the TNIV might also be interpreted as "nearly" or "almost." Without *YHWH,* he would almost have settled down in grave silence. Though the word *death* does not actually appear in the Hebrew text, it seems to be implied, and that matches our experience. In times of despair we think we are almost going to die—or wish we would.

This rising terror at whatever we might be confronting is perhaps one of the most critical causes and effects of loneliness; the terror both comes from our being alone and increases the sorrow of our solitude. When pain seems to overwhelm us with its crushing waves and no one takes a stand for us against the evil, then we panic. If God doesn't do something drastic, we will surely die.

The psalmist has recorded his anxiety to encourage us; someone else has felt so great a terror and has overcome it. We dare not treat lightly another person's panic or depression. The horror of evil rising up against us is very real, and a person being overwhelmed does indeed feel starkly alone and defenseless.

However, in the Hebrew text, the poet goes on to describe how mistaken he was. "If I said, 'My foot has slipped,' your *chesedh*, YHWH, will support me." In chapter one we learned that the LORD's *chesedh* connotes a depth of loving-kindness unmatched in the world's various kinds of love. When we feel we are slipping over the edge, YHWH's steadfast care will support our deepest being. On the day of my panic, the affirmation and love my friend Tim proclaimed to me were from the LORD.

I was still loved, even when I was fitful and complaining. This is what supports us best in our moments of pain and panic: the assurance that we are loved even though we are doubtful and disagreeable people. If we can know that we are cared about when we feel rotten about ourselves and our fears, then we can have the courage to change and not be afraid. The loving-kindness of YHWH is what we need to hold us when we feel we are slipping. Then we can discover that the sense of falling is a false one, for we are really being sustained tenderly by our LORD.

The last verse of our text contains the surprise. Not only does the *chesedh* of YHWH support us, but furthermore it actually brings us past the point of panic into a sense of well-being that can even issue in delight.

Even though our anxieties multiply, still the LORD's love can lead us beyond them. The original Hebrew text piles up phrases—"in the abundance of my disquieting thoughts in my inward parts." That thorough wording graphically illustrates the depth of distraction that afflicts us at times. Disquieting thoughts or uneasy doubts seem always to multiply, not just arithmetically but geometrically. Furthermore, they don't just aggrieve us on the surface, but they attack us in our deepest recesses, where they are harder to handle.

Our "inward parts" may literally be attacked; we might think, for example, of times when we have received bad news of one sort or another. We might think we are taking it all in stride and handling the anxiety reasonably well, until we begin to have serious digestive malfunctions. The tension is much deeper than we could be aware of on a conscious level.

We are troubled more and more deeply, and the vexing worries seem to snowball. However, into that reality thrusts this truth: the consolations of *YHWH*.

The word that the TNIV translates "consolation" is actually plural in the Hebrew. It comes from the verb root meaning "to comfort or to console, to have compassion upon someone." Used always in an intensifying plural, the noun depicts profound soothing.

The consolations of *YHWH,* the poet declares, take "the soul" to the point of delight. This verb *to delight* is in a continuing tense in the Hebrew and comes from a verb portraying "sporting." It is used in Psalm 119:70, where the poet delights in *YHWH's torah,* or instruction. It is also used in Isaiah 66:12 to depict a child being dandled upon the knees of a doting parent. The soul, signifying the seat of emotions or passions and, especially here, the place of Joy, is figuratively danced upon the lap of *YHWH* in His consolations.

Not only does God bring us comfort, but He brings us such an abundance of it that we are led out of the state of fear or anxiety that was plaguing us and beyond it into sheer ecstasy.

One of the best ways for me to sketch that movement from despair to euphoria is in terms of music. If I am discouraged, I play a favorite classical CD and, in listening, find myself transported beyond myself into a new realm of light and exhilaration. Much of this book was originally typed to the accompaniment of the stirring music of Rachmaninoff and revised to Bach.

What kinds of experiences uplift you like that? Do you ever pause to consider that those gifts to you are the consolations of YHWH, meant to bring you out of anxiety into a celebration of elation? What a loving LORD we have, furthermore, that He gives His bounty to us according to our individual personalities.

When I first moved into the big old house that we used for a crisis ministry, I became very discouraged at how much a stranger I seemed. I felt ripped away from all that had been my security, especially when a new wife took my place in my old home.

In that sense of being lost, I wondered who would "take a stand for me." Like the poet, I felt at times that if it were not for the LORD giving me help, I surely would have dwelt in the silence of death. But YHWH continued to give His largess of consolations.

I shall never forget the first night that I felt at home in the big house. Finally, my study/workplace was ready in the basement. My books had been unpacked at last and put in order in new bookcases. My typing desk filled the alcove, the woodstove had been checked, and the husband of one of my friends had connected my old stereo.

Late in the evening I lit the fire, made a pot of tea, turned on a favorite symphony, and sat in my rocker. At first I didn't even notice, but suddenly I became supremely aware that I'd come "home." I rocked and cried with bliss in the goodness of the LORD that at last I felt I belonged somewhere.

It wasn't the room. It was the place created by the LORD to bring me His consolations. They didn't merely comfort me; they reminded me of YHWH's surprising love, which lifts us beyond our troubles to heights of Joy.

For Further Meditation

1. At what times in my life have I felt that there was no one to stand up for me against evil?

2. When has the evil been so overwhelming that I wanted to die—
   or thought I would?

3. In those times, how have I known the help of my LORD? How have
   I seen His *chesedh* in action in my life?

4. How have I misperceived my circumstances and thought I was
   slipping when actually the LORD was supporting me?

5. How have I experienced the multiplication of anxieties deep
   within me?

6. How have the consolations of the LORD brought me not only out
   of anxiety, but also into delight?

7. How might I help someone suffering from anxiety to find the delight of *YHWH's* consolations?

18

The Wicked Aren't So Fat and Sleek

Surely God is good to Israel,
   to those who are pure in heart.
But as for me, my feet had almost slipped;
   I had nearly lost my foothold.
For I envied the arrogant
   when I saw the prosperity of the wicked.
They have no struggles;
   their bodies are healthy and strong.
They are free from common human burdens;
   they are not plagued by human ills. . . .
Surely in vain have I kept my heart pure
   and have washed my hands in innocence. . . .
When I tried to understand all this,
   it troubled me deeply
till I entered the sanctuary of God;
   then I understood their final destiny.

PSALM 73:1-5, 13, 16-17

The young man wept in my office. "It isn't fair," he cried. "Everything is going just fine for her. She's running around, having a lot of fun. And I'm in misery."

He had been on the verge of suicide because he doubted the justice of God. Psalm 73 surprised him with its intensely practical application to our everyday lives.

We have all felt at times like the psalmist Asaph did. He was a musician among those appointed by David to oversee music in worship (see 1 Chronicles 6:39) and sang at the dedication of Solomon's temple (see 2 Chronicles 5:12). Psalm 73 is the first of a set of eleven psalms (along with Psalm 50) attributed canonically to Asaph. In these poems he reveals keen insight into human experience. He understands with deep wisdom the tremendous resentment sustained by those who watch the ungodly have it all. This just doesn't seem fair: those who try to stay pure seem to suffer more than those who don't care.

Just like the psalmist, we rant and rail against the injustices of life. There had better be a good answer, or we won't be able to believe that God is really a good God.

Because we get ourselves into such a state of mind, the poet begins with a statement of faith: "Surely God is good to Israel, to those who are pure in heart." Later he will question whether or not it is worth the effort to keep one's heart pure, so he begins by asserting that it is; then he wrestles through to belief in the truth of that statement. The process is instructive for the times when the inequities of pain and suffering cause us to doubt.

The psalm itself begins with the word *surely.* The poet announces this thesis at the outset: God is indeed righteous and just to Israel, to those who are clean in their moral character and will. Purity is worthwhile after all, he proclaims, but then continues as if to say, "But let me tell you how I almost forgot."

In fact, he humbly admits, "As for me, my feet had almost slipped; I had nearly lost my foothold. For I envied the arrogant when I saw the prosperity of the wicked." That simple reality almost undid him and his faith. His spiritual feet tripped over the confusion in his mind.

This is a different reason for the slipping of the feet than we saw in the previous chapter. Here we envy the ease of the haughty, impervious to their sin. One day in a very lonely year a couple having an affair talked with me about how much they cared for each other and how important it was to express that love. Their evident happiness belied the belief that if we participate in sexual relationships outside of marriage, we will ultimately not be as fulfilled as if we continue to follow God's moral principles.[1] In my loneliness I envied their freedom to sin. Life would be much easier, I thought, if we could just have an affair and not feel so guilty about it.

If Christians who are single still choose God's design for genital faithfulness, we must battle not only our loneliness, but also the peer pressure of our sexually loose culture. We wonder why the others all have lovers, but we don't have anyone to hold us. Who will respect our efforts to stay pure?

"They have no struggles," Asaph declares. They don't seem to suffer spiritually or physically. "Their bodies are healthy and strong." In literal Hebrew, this description of the well-being of the wicked is cryptic: "For not the pangs. But fat their body." Not only do they not suffer from the bonds and fetters, but also their bodies are well provided for. In fact, they are fat. The word the TNIV translates "body" actually is the one for "belly," from a word meaning "in front of." Therefore, the expression implies that they are prominently fat—for most cultures a sign of prosperity, as is the conspicuous consumption of the rich in the United States. One can't help but notice how well off they are.

Why did and do so many of my friends suffer with such severe handicaps—Tim with kidney failure, Linden with paralysis, Nancy with leukemia—when the "wicked" seem to be "free from common human burdens"? "They are not plagued by human ills." Of the troubles or labors of ordinary people, there is nought for them. Contrary to what most people experience, they are not stricken. The last par-

---

[1] See my book *Sexual Character*.

ticiple in the Hebrew comes from a verb which emphasizes touching or assailing and is usually associated with diseases. They seem to escape contact even with illnesses. Why? The result is that "pride is their necklace" (v. 6).

No wonder that after several more verses describing their cockiness and scorn and mockery of God, the poet summarizes his immense frustration in these words: "This is what the wicked are like—always free of care, they go on amassing wealth" (v. 12). Some people have it all! Such disparity is more than we can take.

So the poet complains, "Surely in vain have I kept my heart pure and have washed my hands in innocence." The latter might imply ceremonial washings, and thus we might infer, "It really does no good to be faithful about matters of worship either."

The poet is exceptionally disgusted that he hasn't benefited from trying to be God's person. Eugene Peterson's *The Message* captures his jaded attitude well with this rendering: "I've been stupid to play by the rules; what has it gotten me?" (v. 13). To have expended such obedient effort has been a waste of time, he pouts. The "heart" of the first phrase and the "hands" of the second line remind us in poetic parallel that both the inside and the outside have been kept clean—but to no avail, it seems.

The poet doesn't want to speak about it publicly; that would upset the crowds. However, when he tries within himself to understand, everything is oppressive to him and troubles him deeply. The sorrow, the vexation, the pain of labor hadn't produced results. The more one tries to comprehend injustice, the more grievous it becomes. The Hebrew calls it "travail."

Repeatedly, what gets our faith into trouble is the attempt to analyze and figure things out. We keep asking, "Don't they know they have sinned? How can they not feel any sorrow that they have hurt me so badly? Don't they know how much harm their evil has caused?"

The more we try to decipher it and make things somehow fair, the more oppressive it becomes to us. Envy of another's well-being, even if it was not achieved by sin, can never be constructive. There must be a better way to deal with the vexation of it all.

The poet knows a superior way. After much discontent and irritation, he takes a wiser course. Verse 17 begins with a rare construction in the Hebrew to mark a decisive turning point—"until." Things were onerous as long as the poet was trying to interpret them with his own mind; the bitterness could be changed only by his going to the sanctuary of God.

Actually the Hebrew word is plural and says "sanctuaries," which might designate the temple and its many precincts about the Holy of Holies. Signifying many sacred places, the word is more easily transposed into our times. We need not necessarily go to a church building somewhere to get our minds straight about the inequities of suffering. We can enter any sanctuary. The word comes from the root *qadosh,* or "holy," and thus can refer to any place set apart, any space in which we encounter God.

When I first wrote this chapter, I paused at this point to put lotion on my fingers and to rest them because my skin was cracked. What an irony to have them bleed as I wrote these words about envy of those whose bodies are healthy and strong and who seem to have everything going for them in life! Yet when I entered the sanctuary of my writing alcove, I realized that I wouldn't trade places for anything. There in that silent holy place late at night, God was very present in the Scriptures. (Originally I wanted to title this book *God and I Are the Only Ones Up!*)

I'm sure you have some special sanctuaries too. When you go to those places (even if just in mind and not physically), there your searching intellect and troubled heart can find rest. In the sacred sites we meet with God to learn His answers to our probings. Indeed, only His answers will suffice. We will never be able to explain satisfactorily such problems as the prevalence of fatal diseases, the breaking of covenant marriage relationships, the limitations of physical handicaps, the quirks of history that keep us alone, or accidents of freakish nature or mechanical failure. We can't completely calm the agony in our minds by coming to grips with reality or gaining insights into it. Nevertheless, in the sanctuaries there are answers of another sort.

The poet says, "Then I understood their final destiny." The Hebrew verb in that clause emphasizes giving heed to or considering with great attention. When the poet enters the holy place, he puts all things into an eternal perspective, and that makes a huge difference in how we view life—and death—and life again.

We will look at the conclusions he comes to more closely in the next chapter, but here at least we note the different perspective. Always life seems unfair until it is put into the whole picture of forever. We who believe in Jesus Christ already possess eternal life. It is not just "pie in the sky in the bye and bye when we die." The verbs in John 3:36 ("Whoever believes in the Son has eternal life") are present tense verbs. If we already have that gift, then we must discern how it will affect our view of circumstances now.

The letter to the Ephesians proclaims that "God raised us up with Christ and seated us with him in the heavenly realms in Christ Jesus" (Ephesians 2:6). This insight means that we no longer view events only with human eyes, but we share Christ's mind and seek His perspective on the whole in the light of God's power active on our behalf.

Having an eternal outlook does not simply mean that we look forward to heaven, when all this pain will be over, or that we are glad because the wicked who seem to prosper now will really suffer in hell. In fact, the prospect of the latter increases our concern for everyone and motivates us to try to invite those who are evil out of their hellish lack of a relationship with God. Rather, having an eternal perspective means we learn to recognize that the reality of struggles in this life is not all that there is to truth.

I think, for example, of how much more I appreciate friends now than I did before I went through the agonies of lonely years. Our capacity for happiness seems to be greatly enlarged by the depths of sorrow through which we pass. Eternity enters into our appreciation of our relationships with friends now—and the fact that we already possess eternal life enables us to share it now in many ways with our beloved ones who have died.

When we consider the "end of the wicked," we recognize to what extent they experience agonies too. Though they appear to be fat and happy, deep inside a longing in them cannot be quenched. Sometimes they have to work dreadfully hard to hide that restlessness from themselves, and sometimes they seem to succeed. But where there is sin, there will also be guilt and sorrow and emptiness. Cruelty works its own rewards, and evil bears its own consequences. Therefore, seeking revenge does us no good. Rather, our frustrations can enable us to grow in compassion and in our eternal perspective. To that growth we will turn in the next chapter.

For Further Meditation

1. Can I assert with the psalmist that God is surely good to those who are pure in heart?

2. What experiences in my life have caused me to doubt that assertion?

3. Have I observed that the wicked seem to have no problems? How does that make me feel?

4. How do I deal with my own envy of their supposed well-being or with the pain that their hurting me has caused?

5. How does the Bible challenge our perspectives on the world's injustices?

6. What are some of the sanctuary places in my life?

7. How does an eternal perspective affect my view of the supposed "fatness" of the wicked?

19

In Our Brutishness, God Holds Our Hand

When my heart was grieved
and my spirit embittered,
I was senseless and ignorant;
I was a brute beast before you.
Yet I am always with you;
you hold me by my right hand.
You guide me with your counsel.

PSALM 73:21-24a

One day as I swam a long training workout, I experimented with counting laps by praying for ten different subjects on a repeated cycle. On the first lap I prayed for my housemate, who was still unemployed, and on others, for those who were ill and for my family. On the sixth lap I sprinted thanksgivings, and each tenth was filled with praise.

Repeating that sequence for three hundred lengths, I kept realizing the immaturity of my faith life. When I envy the wicked, I have forgotten how rich life with God is.

The poet's graphic picture of his previous ingratitude and poor attitude is something with which we can all identify. At times we have all reacted much as Asaph did to the prosperity of those who hurt us and of others we observe.

The first verb in the Hebrew text of Psalm 73:21 is a form of the root that means "to be sour or leavened." In the intensive reflexive form (Hithpael) this word emphasizes being embittered. (I would like to change around the final adjectives of the two lines in the TNIV rendition of v. 21 so it would say, "When my heart was embittered and my spirit grieved.") The poet says that his heart, signifying the seat of his will and intentions, was resentful when he saw the inequities we considered in the previous chapter.

Next, in the poetic parallel Asaph confesses that in his kidneys he was pierced. The noun *kidneys,* used as a particularization of the larger word *heart,* especially implies in the First Testament the involvement of one's emotions and often is added to phrases that place them as the object of God's examinations. Thus, when the poet acknowledges that in his kidneys he was pierced, he suggests not only the pangs of his emotions, but also perhaps that God, too, searches and knows the depths of his psychic pain.

His poignant envy had impaled him. We must admit that we, too, cause much of our own pain. Truly, much suffering comes to us from the outside, when calamities strike or when others hurt or reject us; however, we multiply it many times by our envy and our untrusting spirits. To accentuate the sharp stabbing that his own jealousy had caused him, the poet uses a form of the verb root that means "to whet or sharpen." The Jerusalem Bible illustrates the idea with this graphic translation: "When my heart had been growing sourer with pains shooting through my loins."

Beyond what was happening inside himself, the poet also realizes that his comparisons and attitudes affected his outward behavior. Verse 22 begins in the Hebrew with an emphatic pronoun, which exclaims, "But I *myself*—how terrible that this is how I was." There is no verb in the original text, which says literally, "I—brutish!" so the predicate adjective stands out more disparagingly. The word *brutish* (translated as "senseless" in the TNIV) is related to the noun for "beasts" and the verb "to be stupid or dull-hearted." In the Scriptures it describes the one whose spiritual sensitivities are too dull to perceive truth.

The TNIV translates with the adjective *ignorant* the Hebrew phrase "and I do not know." The Jerusalem Bible captures well the sense of this phrase with its rendition, "I had simply failed to understand." The result of such failure, the poet continues, is that he became a behemoth—that is, a brute beast or a hippopotamus—in his relationship with *YHWH*.

Like a hippo—not a very lovely picture for describing oneself, but perhaps we can identify with it very closely. Sometimes we are shocked at how beastly and blundering, ignorant and idiotic we have been, how we have not trusted when so much evidence points to the LORD's trustworthiness. *The Message* captures this whole sequence well in this paraphrase:

> When I was beleaguered and bitter,
>   totally consumed by envy,
> I was totally ignorant, a dumb ox
>   in your very presence.

I must seem like a beast to God because I seem so much like a monster to myself.

A necessary part of our spiritual growth is to see ourselves this way. We've got to face up to the senselessness of our lack of trust so that we can see, with Joy-full wonder, the infinite surprise that God would love us anyway, in spite of our ignorance and brutishness.

That surprise is captured well in *The Message*, which continues, "I'm still in your presence, but you've taken my hand."

After all our beastly attitudes and behavior, we are shocked that God should love us anyway. The original Hebrew again begins with an emphatic pronoun to say, "But I myself—greatly to the contrary of what I might have expected—continually with you." Again the absence of a verb accentuates with precise terseness, "I with you."

It is not an illusion. With you continually I myself *am.*
It is not an on-again, off-again deal. I am with you *continually.*
It is the relationship that matters above all.
Continually I am *with you.*

The word for "continually" (rendered "always" in the TNIV) is actually a noun meaning "continuity" that is used in significant places, especially in the Psalms and in the book of Isaiah, as an adverb. One of my favorite places is the eighth verse of Psalm 16: "I have set the LORD continually before me. Because He is at my right hand, I will not be shaken" (NASB). (Psalm 73 similarly emphasizes the right hand, which is held by *YHWH.*) We also saw this noun used as an adverb in Psalm 34:1, where David declares that the praise of *YHWH* will "always be on my lips" (see chapter thirteen).

The always-ness of our relationship with the LORD takes us away from our brutishness into the freedom of acceptance. Too easily we might take that continuity for granted or even think that we justly deserve God's love. A good, hard look at the beastliness of our ignorance is a necessary dose of strong medicine.

To say that we are with *YHWH* emphasizes that we are in His thought and care, as we have observed in other chapters of this book. But in verse 23 an unusual fact surfaces. The pronoun that is attached to the preposition *with* in the Hebrew is the feminine singular *you.* The feminine pronoun was also used in the previous verse in its connection to the Hebrew preposition *with* to declare that the poet became a behemoth "with you," the LORD. But in verses 24 and 25 the pronouns shift back to the masculine form.

These passages are made more poignant when we think of God with feminine images. To be brutish and ignorant like a hippopotamus before the feminine softness and gentleness of God sounds more ugly and crass. To be in wonder at the mother-love of a nurturing and tender God suggests a deeper enfolding. Since one of the strongest words for the compassions of YHWH in the First Testament comes from the root meaning "womb" (see chapter five), we are invited throughout the Scriptures to think of God's love and devotion in motherly terms. Thus, the wonder and surprise multiply, for when we have been beastly senseless, the LORD still directs maternal care toward us. God still holds us as special children in relationship with "Herself."

The contrast is also strong between the feminine relationship of our being continually with the LORD and the masculine grasping of our right hand that concludes verse 23. The verb I translated "grasping" emphasizes taking hold or taking possession, but it is used here in a gracious sense rather than in a manipulative or exploitative one. Yet it is a word of power. God does take us firmly by the hand in spite of our brutishness in order to pour out upon us His gifts.

The right hand among Semitic peoples functions prominently as a sign of goodwill. Thus, Jesus speaks about sitting at the Father's right hand (see Luke 22:69), and the apostle Paul exults because Peter and the other apostles extended to him the right hand of fellowship (see Galatians 2:9). That action connoted acceptance and empowerment.

To extend to a person one's left hand was an insult. By contrast, verse 23 underscores the gladness by ending with the adjective: "the hand, my right one." Because of the pun on "right" in English, we can see more deeply that God knows what He is doing in choosing to care for us even though we have been hippopotamuses: He holds our hands—the right ones. How can God love us in the state that we are?

That wonder fills us as we meditate upon these verses and relate them to our loneliness. Sometimes in the misery of being alone we are aghast at the horrendous hostility or maliciousness or blind ignorance of our lives. We didn't notice something, or we said the wrong things. We messed everything up or can't seem to get things right. Yet in the midst of feeling like a hippo in a china shop, we can share this glorious assertion: "Yet I am always with you; you hold me by my right hand." We remember that the "you" refers to YHWH with images of masculinity and femininity and realize that all of God's character (which far surpasses anything engendered) is fully available to us in our relationship with the Trinity. In our next chapter we will see further the results of this new awareness on the part of the poet—and of us.

First, however, we need the reminder that YHWH wants to guide us with His counsel (v. 24a). He is always with us and takes us by the hand so that we don't make such stupid mistakes so often.

In the context of the whole psalm, we remember that we need the guidance of the LORD to enable us to perceive truly the difference between the outcomes for the wicked and for ourselves. We require God's accompaniment to learn to be grateful for the ways circumstances develop and to look to Him for their development so that His purposes can be accomplished.

YHWH's instruction is our greatest need.[1] Many years ago my life was revolutionized by a professor who pointed out to me how God had answered my prayers for graduate school finances in ways I had not observed. Since then, I have been amazed by the frequency of my failure to perceive God's will. He wants to lead us in beneficial ways, but we often panic before we recognize His guidance, and then we try to discover our directions on our own.

---

[1]For a discussion of means through which God guides us, see my book *Joy in Divine Wisdom: Practices of Discernment from Other Cultures and Christian Traditions* (San Francisco: Jossey-Bass, 2006).

That is exactly what had happened to Asaph to make him embittered about the prosperity of the wicked. When he focused his attention upon them rather than upon *YHWH,* he was overwhelmed by the inequities of the world. However, if our focus is upon the LORD and His purposes, we are so busy being faithful to our calling that we don't have time to worry about the fortunes of others; nor do we have the space to be envious, because we are so filled with the enjoyment of our own ministries and God's gifts in our lives.

Many verses in the Psalms speak of God's faithfulness in guiding His people—such as Psalm 23:3; 31:3; 43:3; and 139:10. Our problem often lies in not realizing that *YHWH's* counsel comes to us in many different forms—through the Scriptures and books about them, through the wisdom of friends and advisers and the Christian community as a whole, through opportunities that develop and those that don't materialize, through our own insights gained in devotional meditation.

We need to believe that God wants us to know His will, so that we can be released from that terrible panic of trying to find it. That is why the psalmist makes this bold declaration: "You guide me with your counsel." Truly, when we pay attention to the LORD's instruction, we will not behave as hippopotamuses; we will not turn sour. Instead, we will recognize *YHWH's* guidance in our lives as part of the Joy of His continual presence.

For Further Meditation

1. How have I seen my own spirit turn sour in response to circumstances around me?

2. In what situations has envy pierced my kidneys?

3. In what manifestations have I seen and been ashamed of my own brutishness? In what ways do I spiritually resemble a hippo?

4. How do I know that I am continually with *YHWH?*

5. Why does *YHWH* want to stick with me when I am brutish?

6. How have I seen in my life that God has grasped me? How have I observed that the LORD has taken my right hand to accept me and to grant me His gifts of forgiveness and grace?

7. How have I experienced the counsel of the LORD? What means does He usually use to guide me?

20

To Desire Nothing on Earth

> *. . . and afterward you will take me into glory.*
> *Whom have I in heaven but you?*
> *And earth has nothing I desire besides you.*
> *My flesh and my heart may fail,*
>   *but God is the strength of my heart*
>   *and my portion forever.*

PSALM 73:24b-26

> *Whom have I in heaven but you?*
>   *And being with you, I desire nothing on earth.*

PSALM 73:25 NIV (1978)

On the far edge of the huge store were the grand pianos, and while my friends were pricing organs I was free to dabble. Giving up on the touch of one, I wandered over to a seven-foot-four-inch August Forster from Germany. The piano's touch was precisely balanced; its tone, lusciously rich; its workmanship, finely crafted. What delicate candlelight and raging fire the keys could pull from the heart of the strings! The salesman urged me to compare it with all the other pianos in the store.

There was no comparison. Nothing in that store could match the thrill of playing that August Forster.

Once we know the God of the heavens and gain a celestial perspective, how can we desire anything less on earth?

Two definite movements compose Asaph's final response to his former ignorance in questioning the prosperity of the wicked. First, as we saw in the previous chapter, he recognized his brutishness and knew that *YHWH* was yet with him to guide and gift him in this life. Furthermore, he perceived that there is a wholly (and holy) other dimension to our existence and to our relationship with the LORD.

Scholars debate whether or not the poet is thinking about eternal life in the second half of verse 24. The phrase "and afterward you will take me into glory" is an unusual statement for a Hebrew writer. Jews living at the time that most of the First Testament was written did not possess much of a concept of life after death. Only in rare places, such as Psalm 16:11 and Job 19:25-27, do we catch intimations of immortality. Subsequently, by the time of Jesus, controversy reigned between the Pharisees and the Sadducees—those who believed in life after death and those who didn't. The religious leaders tried to cast Jesus into the midst of that controversy on some occasions (see, for example, Luke 20:27-40), and the apostle Paul makes use of it in his self-defense (see Acts 23:6-11).

If Asaph is referring to eternal life here, he is certainly well ahead of his time. He could also be referring to the future in an earthly sense. In that case, he would mean that after his bitterness about the wicked had been erased and after God had guided him out of whatever had caused him so much grief, then he would assuredly experience *YHWH*'s glory. We could also interpret the Hebrew phrase to assert, "afterward you will bring me to honor." This rendering would suggest that the poet is speaking about securing justice in this life.

It seems to me more true to the earth as we experience it if Asaph is looking to life after justice has been fully inaugurated at the end of time, since it doesn't seem possible to bring it about entirely in our

world. However, as we are formed by this text, we recognize that the
eternal life to which we look forward will determine our attitudes toward this life now. A heavenly perspective must affect our desires, our
confidence, our ambitions, and where we put our trust.

The Hebrew word for "glory" stresses honor or dignity of position,
a life with the God of abundance. Thus, this text suggests numerous
eschatological ramifications. Eschatology is the study of the last
times, when we will experience the ultimate fulfillment of all God's
promises to us. In our walk of faith we know that the heaven to
which we look forward is also experienced to some extent, but not
fully, now. We call it *realized eschatology* when we partake of the Joy
of heaven in this time and space.

Because we look forward to the glory that someday will be our entire and permanent, unceasing possession, we discover that *now* we
are elevated to positions of dignity and abundance and honor in the
sight of God. If we believe, Jesus tells us in John 3:36, we receive the
gifts of eternal life now.

Texts such as Psalm 73:24 thus invite us into tasting the delight of
heaven, even though its best gifts are yet to come. How much better
it will be when we are fully taken into glory, without any vestiges of
pain or sorrow.

After all, the poet continues, whom do we have in heaven but
YHWH? He is the only LORD of all.

Elementary-school lessons about Greek and Roman mythology
made me think as a child about the difficulty of living under such a
system. Whenever troubles came, how could one figure out which
god was mad now and how to appease him or her without getting
any of the other gods upset?

Going to a Lutheran grade school, I thought already then how liberating it was to have only one God! As I grew older, that truth
brought even more comfort. As we have been observing throughout
our study of psalms together, whenever we learn to know better the

character of our God, then we grow in trusting *YHWH* and in receiving His *chesedh,* or steadfast love, for us. The fact that there is no competing deity enables us to rest thoroughly in the ultimate triumph of our God. We do not exist under a dualistic system, wherein the powers of evil have as much control as those of good. Because *YHWH* alone is God, nothing else can ultimately thwart His purposes. If we have Him alone in the heavens, we therefore know some particular truths about our struggles on earth.

The first issue that follows is this perspective: "And being with you, I desire nothing on earth" (NIV 1978). Having the LORD of all lords to be our ever-present God, would we ever again settle for anything less? Is anything on earth even remotely desirable in the place of being with the only true God? Even the magnificent August Forster or a Steinway or a Bösendorfer cannot begin to produce music such as His.

To choose discipleship necessitates some hard wrestling, however, because many times we do settle for less. The verses from Psalm 73 bring us back to a balanced (and godly) outlook on the things of this world. Sometimes we think we can't get along without a certain possession or a certain person or a certain kind of comfort. To insist on these is to make idols out of whatever we desire. I am horrified by the diversity, frequency, intensity, and stupidity of my idolatries.

My deepest spiritual longing is to be able to say with Asaph, "Earth has nothing I desire besides you." Necessarily, then, all divinized human cravings must be killed, but our rebellious nature oftentimes prevents that. Don't misunderstand this point: human desires themselves, such as the longing for someone's love, are not wrong. What makes them sin for each of us is when we elevate them to the place of God so that we want the satisfaction of our passions more than we want Him.

What ambitions become gods for us and distort our visions? Do we trust our job for our future security, rather than recognize that it is the God who created us with skills for our employment whom we can trust, even if the position ends? Do we believe that a marriage will satisfy our deepest yearnings, rather than remember that marriage itself is a symbol of the greater faithfulness of God, whose love is perfect and never wavers? Do we anticipate that more money will provide what we need, rather than perceive that our Creator's work lies behind both whatever we possess and the ingenuity of those who produced it? What do we substitute for total dependence on God?

What keeps us from trusting God—our need for love, our insecurities, our fears or sufferings or sorrows or doubts about God's character? What prevents us from following Jesus, from relinquishing our control to the Holy Spirit, from relying on the Father?

Do we know who we are primarily because we are the beloved of God? Are we willing to give up all the human possessions or relationships that become crutches to our self-identity? Our text from Psalm 73 reminds us that these secondary realities are not really worthwhile compared to our intimacy with God, whom alone we have in the heavens.

That point is underscored by the fact that, after all, our bodies are wasting away. Verse 26 concludes that even though our flesh and heart might be failing, yet our relationship with God will not. The verb for "wasting away" suggests being spent, used up or exhausted, and thus points us to the ephemerality of our days and vital strength. The word *flesh* signifies the physical power or the external expression of a person, as opposed to the heart, which denotes the inner self. Both inner and outer aspects of us will surely fade away. All flesh is grass, the voice cries in Isaiah 40:6, 8.[1] In fact, we experience this world's death every day.

In a clever play on words, the poet again uses the word *heart* to say that the gifts of the LORD will last forever if He is, to be precise, "the

---

[1]Compare chapters six through eight of my book *To Walk and Not Faint*.

rock of my heart." When our inner person, our true being, is focused on the LORD as its support and defense, then His might and grace keep us forever. The word for "rock," translated "strength" in the TNIV above, is used thirty-five times in the First Testament as a figure for God. Surely the people in Israel recognized the permanence of rocks, especially in contrast to the shifting sands, which are blown around by the desolate winds of the wilderness countryside. Rock stands silhouetted against the sky as a symbol of permanence.

Though my heart might fail, Asaph insists, the rock of my heart will endure. Moreover, the God who is my rock is also my "portion." This is the word that is used in Psalm 16:5 to emphasize that *YHWH* has given His people "a delightful inheritance" (v. 6). There the poet declares, "LORD, you have assigned me my portion and my cup; you have made my lot secure."

Here in Psalm 73 *YHWH* Himself is the portion. Even more than the gifts that God pours out upon His people, the LORD Himself is actually the best possession of His servants. How thoroughly we can know His intimate presence!

The phrase is a good summary of everything in this section of the psalm. The very God who alone resides in the heavens as LORD over the universe deigns to let His people possess Him. He gives Himself to those who believe in Him and desire Him above all else.

We can't possess God if we don't desire Him. If we make anything on earth a god in His place, then we neglect and deprive ourselves of His gifts (especially of Himself), available to us both now and in the future.

Such an eternal perspective is our hope against the inequities of time and sorrow. When the wicked seem to be prospering while we continue to suffer in serving the LORD, we are assured that our desire to remain pure is not a waste of time, but a movement toward, and to some extent a participation in, the genuine fulfillment of our deepest longings.

For Further Meditation

1. What are some images that help me envision the "glory afterward" to which Psalm 73 refers?

2. How does having an eschatological perspective increase my Joy now?

3. What passions, purposes, possessions, or people do I make into idols here on earth? Why?

4. How have I experienced the freedom of "desiring nothing on earth" because I have God in the heavens?

5. How does it affect my daily existence to know that there is only one God?

6. What does it mean to me that *YHWH* is the rock of my heart?

7. What does it mean to me that *YHWH* is my portion?

21

Even in Death, *YHWH* Protects Us

The cords of death entangled me,
>*the anguish of the grave came over me;*
>*I was overcome by distress and sorrow.*
*Then I called on the name of the L*ORD*:*
>*"L*ORD*, save me!"*
*The L*ORD *is gracious and righteous;*
>*our God is full of compassion.*
*The L*ORD *protects the unwary;*
>*when I was brought low, he saved me.*
Return to your rest, my soul,
>*for the L*ORD *has been good to you. . . .*
*Precious in the sight of the L*ORD
>*is the death of those faithful to him.*

PSALM 116:3-7, 15

*The L*ORD *preserves the simple;*
>*I was brought low, and He saved me.*

PSALM 116:6 NASB

My friend Nancy called one afternoon from a hospital in Seattle. Her cold had developed into pneumonia, and she was about to go into surgery for some cauterization to stop hemorrhaging. Her many-years' struggle against leukemia seemed to have reached its final weeks.

When Nancy first called to ask for prayers, a blood clot on the brain was causing severe seizures, but she had only a 30 percent chance of surviving any surgery to remove it. What is the place of God's comfort in the Psalms for the loneliness brought by severe illness or imminent death or the death of our beloved child or spouse?

The loneliness of the hospital seems to me the toughest thing about terminal illness. Friends can't be as supportive there, limited as they are by visiting hours, kept distant by sterile precautions. A few bright cards or drooping flowers cannot give a bare-walled room the warmth of home. Unfamiliar nurses and procedures, frightening machines and injections, and foreboding symptoms make the dying person feel alien to all that is living.

Perhaps that is your loneliness right now, or perhaps you know someone struggling with it. Perhaps you have just recently lost a loved one in death. Psalm 116 offers particular comfort for dying saints and for those who stand beside them or without them.

Actually, of course, we are all dying, but for some of us the process is going faster than for others. Actually, also, we believers are all saints already. We don't have to wait till our deaths to receive that title. By the Trinity's work to forgive and transform us, we were made saints when Christ reconciled us and the Spirit empowered us to know YHWH as the one true God. Since then, God has continued to refine us to make us into the saints that we presently are. These truths have deep effects upon our dying.

A friend once asked Nancy, "How can you counsel others about death when you yourself are dying?"

Nancy replied, "I'm not dying. I know where I'm going."

The friend protested, "Don't give me all that heaven stuff."

Nancy answered, "I'm not giving you 'all that heaven stuff.' I just know that I'm going home to be with my Father." Nancy's confidence made her battle against leukemia a remarkable testimony by which others were profoundly touched with the actuality and truth of God's love. That is the Joy.

However, let us also acknowledge the suffering and the loneliness of dying. The psalmist expresses well one element of its agony when he cries, "The cords of death entangled me." For someone battling terminal illness, the grip of death is an inescapable reality.

"The anguish of the grave came over me." This second line in the original Hebrew says more graphically, "The straits of Sheol befell me." "The straits" signifies the worst possible distresses, even that of the underworld Sheol, the dark abyss to which the First Testament people thought they would go after death and not be able to return. No wonder the poet was experiencing great "distress and sorrow." The first Hebrew noun pictures adversity and strain, whereas the second speaks of grief and mourning.

These two graphic word pictures motivate us in the Christian community to pay more attention to easing the afflictions of those in death's anguish and those left behind, for indeed the agony of suffering is terribly intensified by the aloneness of bearing it. No one else can do our dying for us or carry the ache of our cruel loss. No one can really comprehend the fears and doubts that go through our minds and spirits. But others can be with us, hold our hand, pray with and for us, sing to us, remind us that God is near.

Notice that the poet of Psalm 116 responds to his dying anguish of soul and body by calling on the name of the LORD. The second line of verse 4 uses in the Hebrew a strong particle of entreaty that introduces this phrase: "Ah, now, YHWH, let my soul slip away." The verb could also be rendered "be delivered." We don't have common English idiomatic expressions that give the thrust of the opening particle. The word means "please" but is very much intensified. More so than at any other point in our lives, the time of our death or the death of a loved one is a time for strong calling to the LORD out of all the questions of our mind and the anguish of our being. Now more than ever we will be helped by being honest with God about our feelings. Nancy was an example of being real with God in her prayers as she poured out to Him all the feelings of her suffering and discouragement. She knew she wasn't perfect; she knew her own stubbornness—so she was very real about being real.

But out of her wrestling, Nancy could genuinely assert with the poet, "The LORD is gracious and righteous; our God is full of compassion." The word *gracious* is used in the First Testament as a description for an attribute of God only. He is uniquely gracious in a way that no human could ever be, and that graciousness includes the fact that He declares us to be saints and creates us to be His faithful ones. Any virtue or benevolence in us comes in response to His.

Notice how this term is used in these two passages from the Psalms: "But you, Lord, are a compassionate and gracious God, slow to anger, abounding in love and faithfulness" (Psalm 86:15). "The LORD is compassionate and gracious, slow to anger, abounding in love" (Psalm 103:8). The context of each of these verses includes a description of how God's graciousness is evidenced in His care for the men and women who are His saints.

Furthermore, the poet in Psalm 116 adds that *YHWH* is righteous. What He does is eminently just. We might question how His justice can allow such evils as leukemia or heart disease, paralyzing or fatal accidents or kidney failure—but we must remember that human sin brought these things into the world contrary to God's creation designs, and God grieves even more intensely than do we. Furthermore, God has enlisted us in His purposes to fight the results of human evil, so ultimately His righteousness must be seen in light of His graciousness and His compassion, the third attribute of the trio in Psalm 116:5. The latter is again the word that comes from the Hebrew root for "womb," so it stresses the maternal love and tenderness of the LORD. Because of that intense love and the unique fullness of YHWH's graciousness, we can trust that what contradicts God's righteousness (the death of His saints) will be turned to ultimate good (their resurrection).

Because these three characteristics mark YHWH's relationship with us, the next verse is even more comforting. The poet declares that "the LORD protects the unwary," or "simple" (NASB). The Hebrew verb is one that emphasizes watching over in order to preserve or to keep safe, so it brings to mind an image of enfolding. The Hebrew text is especially soothing because the verb is used in the form of a participle, which stresses its continuing action. God doesn't just protect once in a while, but constantly, indefatigably, He guards His saints. If you are on a hospital bed, He is watching over your intravenous needles and blood transfusions, your respirators and heart pacers. He is more constant than the nurses to keep you in His care. When I have been deathly ill, that deep sense of His presence has been for me a strongly consoling assurance.

When human mistakes result in the death of one of His saints, we might think that God has failed to guard. It is exceedingly difficult for us to comprehend that God's love is so great He won't supersede human choices. In such cases we need the gift of His watching over us throughout time to sustain us as we learn what good (besides the resurrection into eternal life of our loved one) God will bring from the tragedy.

The New American Standard Bible's translation of the adjective in verse six as "simple" rather than "unwary" (TNIV) offers another faithful rendering of the original Hebrew, which seems to suggest innocence or naiveté. Perhaps it could refer to those who are simple-minded in the sense of being open to the instruction of wisdom. Perhaps "the simple" could denote those whose simplicity of faith keeps them trusting in any circumstances. Someone with that kind of faith can declare with the poet, "I was brought low, and He saved me" (NASB).

Surely to believe that *YHWH* still saves requires a simplicity of faith when one is suffering excruciating pain, battling against overwhelming odds, agonizing in suffocating loneliness, or mourning a tragic loss. Sometimes the LORD saves by delivering unto death, but then His salvation is experienced most fully. The important point is to recognize His saving action in whatever takes place in one's life— or death.

When a person who is dying can wrestle through to that kind of assurance, then that person can truthfully make the next statement with the poet: "Be at rest once more, O my soul, for the LORD has been good to you" (NIV).

When I was a senior in college, emotional trauma severely upset my insulin balance, and I wound up on the edge of coma. Long hours of spiritual struggle finally brought me to the point of knowing the LORD's protection and graciousness, and then at last I could be at rest. Believing in the LORD's goodness, I was ready to trust Him for whatever direction He might choose to take my life at that point. I was even a bit disappointed when I didn't die, for I really felt as Paul did when he wrote, "I desire to depart and be with Christ, which is better by far" (Philippians 1:23).

Remembering the LORD's character strengthens our faith to affirm that. Our lack of simpleness convinces us that we must understand everything before we can accept all the facets of our lives. The LORD's protection is more apparent to those who simply trust without all sorts of obstructing rebellion.

The Hebrew text of Psalm 116's seventh verse urges, "Turn back, my soul, to your rest, for *YHWH* has benefited you." The state of rest described implies a security that is vitally connected to the assurance that the LORD has benefited a person. If we know that *YHWH* has been, is now, and will continue to be good to us, we can rest securely in that gracious hand in spite of unanswered questions, gaping holes in our family life, or escalating symptoms of impending death.

More than anything, people in our confused and tumultuous society long for security. We who are Christians can look forward to our death, for when we leave this life of sorrow and pain and go home to our Father, as Nancy often said, then we will finally know a perfect security. Furthermore, in looking forward to that unmarred rest, we are able to rest securely now. "I know where I'm going, and I know who's going with me," a Christian song from the 1980s said. In the LORD's company we have assurance for the meantime.

Probably the most comforting message of all is the fifteenth verse of Psalm 116, wherein the poet declares, "Precious in the sight of the LORD is the death of his saints" (NIV), or "those faithful to him." The poet lived through whatever ordeal he was experiencing to write about YHWH's answer to his prayers and the deliverance he received. In his case this verse means that his death was so valuable to the LORD that He delivered him out of it. I must add that Nancy, too, at the time of the first writing of this book, was delivered from her fight with death, and, to the utter surprise of everyone, she experienced a complete remission of her leukemia. We who prayed fervently for God's healing in her life were filled with wonder at the miracle we observed. Several years later Nancy again surmounted a crisis when her kidneys failed and her heart stopped; God continued to do miracles. Finally Nancy died, more than fifteen years after this book was first dedicated to her.

As we reflect on it and immerse ourselves in its hope, this fifteenth verse has larger meanings. Our death is so precious to the Father that He gave up His Son to take away its sting for us. Through the death of Jesus, eternal life has been made available to the saints. Therefore, we know that our deaths are highly valued by the LORD; they mark our entrance into the fullness of His kingdom. He cares intensely about every death because His desire is for "all people to be saved and to come to a knowledge of the truth" (1 Timothy 2:4).

Furthermore, our deaths are precious to YHWH because of the very dying itself—even if that might be a terribly painful process. These days when U.S. society is clamoring for euthanasia, we who are God's people know that the LORD knows our sufferings and cares, and, though we can't understand His wisdom, He can bring good things even from the greatest afflictions (see Romans 8:28). When everything hurts, when we face the sorrow of leaving our loved ones, it is hard to remember that our God's character is marked by the infinite graciousness, righteousness, and compassion that we have discovered in this chapter. God wants us to know that these traits are His, even in the midst of our agony and affliction. Only then can we be comforted by such words as those of Paul to the Romans that the sufferings of this present time are not worth comparing to the glory that is to be revealed in us (see Romans 8:18). Or we can look to other promises and be assured that for those who endure, there is indeed a crown of life (see, for example, 2 Timothy 4:6-8 or Revelation 2:8-11).[1]

The preciousness is our comfort. We are helped by knowing that every concern in our dying matters infinitely to God—so much so that He will even use our dying as a means for drawing others to Himself. For example, more than five hundred teenagers were present at the funeral of my godson, Joshua, after his tragic death in a small aircraft accident several years ago, and they saw a video about his life that affirmed his trust and hope. The final interviews with him had been filmed just a week before, during a mission trip in which he had participated, and he had declared the praises of God and the goodness of life in relationship with Him. All those young people saw the words on the screen that believers in Christ shall always live, even if they die. The anguish of Joshua's death was eased for many by their knowing that even his funeral was a witness to the wonders of God's presence in his life—and his presence now with God.

Similarly, how gloriously God used Nancy's courage and love in the face of death to make others curious about her faith. Frequently Nancy

---

[1]Also see my book *Joy in Our Weakness*.

was able and ready to give an answer to those who asked her for an account of the hope that lay within her (see 1 Peter 3:15). Moreover, that hope was so evident in her near-dying that those of us around her were all greatly strengthened to see God's faithfulness at work. We also were encouraged by seeing how the LORD used us to minister to her in the tough times of her struggles. Truly we were all deepened by the manner of her last years. God's purposes are good beyond our comprehension. Certainly He won't let such a corrupted thing as death interrupt them. When Nancy's battle against leukemia and other illnesses was finally won (after all those years), when the LORD delivered her from those cords of death, then His earthly purposes for her became most fully complete. In that victory we all rejoiced at His compassion, even as we mourned the loss of her. Then she knew a perfect rest as the Father welcomed her home. God Himself then could tell her face-to-face how precious her death was to Him.

For Further Meditation

1. How can I bring comfort to those suffering the anguish of aloneness in dying?

2. How can I prepare for my own dying?

3. Am I really *with God* in my prayers? Do I make strong entreaties to Him? Am I real with God?

4. What is the force of the combination of the three attributes by which YHWH is described in verse 5?

5. Why is it that the simple are more able to receive the comfort and assurance of the LORD's protection?

6. Why am I able to turn back to rest when I know that YHWH has been good to me?

7. Why is it comforting to me to know that my death and the deaths of my loved ones are precious in the eyes of YHWH?

22

Lest We Forget That We Are Special

For you created my inmost being;
your knit me together in my mother's womb.
I praise you because I am fearfully and wonderfully made;
your works are wonderful,
I know that full well.
My frame was not hidden from you
when I was made in the secret place.
When I was woven together in the depths of the earth,
your eyes saw my unformed body.
All the days ordained for me
were written in your book
before one of them came to be.
How precious to me are your thoughts, God!
How vast is the sum of them!
Were I to count them,
they would outnumber the grains of sand—
when I awake, I am still with you.

PSALM 139:13-18

Despite all the emphasis these days on "self-esteem" (especially in public-school systems), most of the assertions of unique individuality sound hollow. Sometimes the voice proclaiming a person's significance (especially when students don't do their work) seems so strident that we think with Shakespeare, "He doth protest too much." Who is trying to convince whom?

Lack of personal confidence especially afflicts those who are lonely. If we have been rejected or we feel as though we have never been accepted or we have lost the beloved one who constantly affirmed us, we can't convince ourselves that we really are unique human beings with much to offer the world around us. We need texts like Psalm 139 to tell us objectively why we are so special.

Our importance is not determined by our own efforts; our Creator made us special because He is. Theoretically, we who know that should have no problem with our self-identity. Unfortunately, often our faith doesn't penetrate to our unfavorable feelings about ourselves. In the struggle to like ourselves, we need again and again to listen to the Scriptures, especially texts such as the promise in Romans 8 that nothing can separate us from God's love or these verses from Psalm 139, which show us how that love was at work in creating us exclusively.

Anyone who doesn't know the Creator cannot appreciate as well the intricacies of His creations. Unless we trust the Designer, we can't rejoice fully in the wonder of His designs.

The setting of the words of encouragement at the beginning of this chapter is a wisdom psalm that recounts the greatness of God in terms of His omnipresence, omniscience, omnipotence, and omnijudgment—the truths that He is everywhere present, all-knowing, all-powerful, and perfect in His evaluations. The mood of the psalm is one of wonder that the poet can be in a relationship with this God who is so "all" about everything. That relationship is the foundation for our worth and significance.

The very first line of this section of the psalm underscores our specialness. The Hebrew text says graphically, "For you created my kidneys." The word *kidneys* is used to signify the most sensitive and vital part of a person. Figuratively, then, it refers to the seat of the emotions and affections. Thus the Jerusalem Bible uses the phrase "inmost self," and the TNIV translates the word as "my inmost being." A contemporary paraphrase might be "the true me." Psalm 139:13, consequently, offers this great comfort: when our loneliness is intensified because no one seems to know our deepest emotions, God understands every facet of them. After all, He put us together.

Indeed, we are known by God intimately (see 1 Corinthians 8:3). When God originated our complex personhood, He designed us with special "kidneys"—the special affectional attributes that compose our sensitivities. His plan is good, for God is good. The truth of His declaration that the creation is good sets us free to accept our uniquenesses too.

The second picture of our text from Psalm 139 is equally compelling, for its verb, *wove,* implies great care and craftsmanship. The poetic parallel asserts, "You wove me together in the womb of my mother." God didn't just throw us together; He carefully chose all the threads and colors and then fashioned them together into the beautiful patterns that compose you and me. No two tapestries are ever alike, so we see personal tenderness and love in the crafting. The LORD uniquely chose for each of us the perfect combination of the color of hair and eyes and skin, the kinds of intelligence, the various aspects of personality and gifts, the abilities and strengths.

The poet responds to this splendid creation by vowing, "I praise you because I am fearfully and wonderfully made." The Hebrew verb *to praise* is often used ritually to signify formal worship, but it is also used throughout the Psalms to declare personal thanks or adoration. The two adverbs in this line are especially graphic. *Fearfully* comes from a verb that describes excellent and glorious things that are so awe-inspiring they cause astonishment. Truly we are amazed by the marvel of our creation—not with the fear of terror, but with the fear of reverence and honor.

The form of the second adverb, translated "wonderfully," stresses the accomplishment of something that surpasses everything or is extraordinary. In other places its verb root signifies that which is beyond a person's power to understand. The word comes from the root for "wonder." The extraordinariness of our fabrication is vastly beyond our comprehension.

We become more aware of the magnificence of human creation when we see how one organ's malfunctioning has so many adverse effects on other parts of the body. The failure of my pancreas in my teen years made it impossible for me to gain weight, to metabolize food effectively, to develop properly. Now the intricacies of balancing immunosuppressants and insulin with blood sugar and activity affect my gum tissues and jaw bones, my vision, my susceptibility to cancers and illnesses and the speed of healing, the sensitivity of the fine nervous system, the ability of my body to increase blood pressure to handle energy needs, and on and on. How could these interconnections have happened by accident?

The statistical probability of even one protein molecule being formed by random chance is too incredibly low to be possible. Even if we constructed a small protein molecule of twelve different amino acids, its chain could be fashioned in 1×10^{300} ways. If we had just one example of each of these possibilities, they would weigh 1×10^{270} grams—which is enough protein to fill the entire known universe (since the earth itself weighs only 1×10^{27} grams)! Such facts boggle the mind and make us wonder how anyone could doubt God's hand in forming the right molecules for our existence.

The poet seems to recognize the danger of skepticism, for he continues, "Your works are wonderful, I know that full well." As if he were reminding himself not to take the glory of it all for granted, he asserts, "Yes, LORD, I am amazed by your works. I really do recognize how magnificent they are."

The word *wonderful* echoes "wonderfully made" (v. 14a), so once again we are reminded that God's handiwork exceeds our ability to comprehend. Yet we can know exceedingly well that God is the performer of these works.

The verb *to know* is in a form that pictures a state of being, the constant action of knowing. We just can't forget how wondrous His works are once we get to know them (and Him).

The final word in the Hebrew text of this verse ("full well," TNIV) is one that is often translated "exceedingly." It comes from a root meaning "to surround" and implies a great abundance. This is the same word used in the last verse of Genesis 1, where God looks at all that He has made, including humankind, which was created on that final day; He declares not merely that it was good, as He had said on the previous five days, but that it was "good exceedingly." In response, then, the poet of this psalm knows "exceedingly" that the works of the LORD are superb.

Next, the poet rejoices that when he was created in the secret place (again referring most likely to his mother's womb), his frame of bones was not hidden from the LORD. *YHWH* saw, in fact, the embryo, the unformed substance. This statement is seen by the pro-life movement as a good argument from a Christian and Jewish perspective against abortion. If indeed God is part of the whole process of creating life and putting together the embryo, then it is murder to cut off that life before its process of formation can be completed.

Of course, the poet was not addressing the issue of abortion. Nevertheless, his rejoicing over God's knowledge and action in the process of human development must cause us to think more thoroughly about the subject; it urges us to be formed by this text to care about all life as God does. This will cause us to work to make sure that all children who are born have adequate food and provision, that the ghetto conditions which give rise to numerous abortions are ameliorated, that violence against life in all its forms is resisted and combated.

The verb *to be woven together* actually connotes great skill. It comes from a verb root that means "to variegate" and implies, therefore, the colorful cloth that workers in fabrics weave. Several years ago I was given a jacket made by craftspeople in Guatemala, and I am stunned by the immense variety of colors and patterns in the multiple squares. The verb recalls the image of being woven from verse 13 and brings to mind the same ideas of care and artisanship we encountered there.

The "depths of the earth" is figurative for the dark and hidden interior of the womb, where God skillfully develops the individual person. Certainly we must see how special we are that from the moment of our conception God was putting us together as lovingly as a many-colored, finely textured tapestry.

Next, the poet exults that in the LORD's book all of his days that were preordained were written down before any one of them yet existed. We must keep this critical concept clear of distortions. Our lives are not pre-fated so that we have no choice in them at all. That misconception is precluded by the tense of the verb *to write down,* which here signifies an uncompleted action. God is writing them, but we have a chance to choose what He writes. Nevertheless, they are "preordained." This verb is in the perfect (completed action) tense and in the intensive passive (Pual) form of a root that stresses forming or fashioning. This particular form of the verb stresses that God's purpose is to establish the days in a certain way.

When we put these two concepts together carefully, we can better understand their paradox. God's basic plan for our lives is set in the unique combination of our gifts and personalities, but we have enormous freedom in choosing how to live out that creation. If we choose to serve God according to His designs, we will experience His best. Yet we have the free will not to choose God's ways, and then, because He loves us so much, God will forgive our rebellions. He is even able to bring good out of our worst choices (see Romans 8:28). We won't have God's best if we follow our own will, but God can turn whatever we choose into good for us.

This dialectical tension between God's sovereignty and our free will sets us free from any fatalistic notions about our lives, yet it gives us the sweet comfort that God really does care and can do something about everything that concerns us. I ponder that frequently because I love my work so much. When I'm right in the middle of teaching about the Scriptures, I sometimes think, *This is what I was made for!* What joy we find when we live out the LORD's design for our lives, when we use our gifts and skills to serve God, especially because He doesn't force us to choose that. If we are obedient to His creation designs, we will find the deepest fulfillment.

That is why the poet continues by declaring how precious God's thoughts have become to him. He realizes how vast is the sum of them. The Hebrew word translated "sum" comes from the root for "head or chief" and might signify that which is the best or the choicest. Altogether God's thoughts are precious, and each is precious because it is best. God's designs and purposes become the deepest desires of our hearts. They are valuable to us because we want to be right in the middle of them.

The final picture in this section is one of my favorites in the Scriptures—especially because of its humor. The poet comments, "Were I to count them, they would outnumber the grains of sand," and then suddenly he adds, "When I awake, I am still with you." That is a terrific way to handle insomnia. The poet became so involved in counting all the thoughts of God that he fell asleep.

This final line also offers vast comfort: "When I awake, I am still with you." We can never fall out of God's thought and care. Even though we fall asleep, the LORD never will. We are again and again, repeatedly, furthermore, besides, yet, still, moreover, enfolded in His mind and heart. As Jesus promises, no one can snatch us out of the Father's hand (see John 10:29). We don't really know very many of the thoughts of *YHWH*, but this one we know for sure: He will always love and care for us. Nothing can separate us from His love—not even our falling asleep when we count His graciousnesses. Truly this picture of ourselves, marvelously designed, made with His tender care, should fill us with dignity and self-worth. We don't have to win God's approval; we had it even before we were born. We don't have to prove our worth; He wove it together. We don't have to impress Him with our goodness; He just wants to show us His.

For Further Meditation

1. How does it make me feel to know that God really knows my inmost being?

2. How does it make me feel to think about God weaving me together?

3. What parts of the human creation most fill me with wonder?

4. Do I know exceedingly well the wonderful works of *YHWH*? Why or why not?

5. How does it make me feel to think that God has ordained all my days? How can I reconcile the paradox of His preordination and my free will?

6. What perspectives do biblical passages give on various life issues debated by our society—abortion, euthanasia, capital punishment, disproportionate spending for war, the use of land mines, U.S. sales of military equipment to "Two-Thirds World" countries, and so forth?

7. Why does it comfort me to know that when I fall asleep over trying to count God's goodnesses, I am still with Him?

23

Help to Resist Temptation

I call to you, LORD, come quickly to me;
*   hear me when I call to you.*
May my prayer be set before you like incense;
*   may the lifting up of my hands be like the evening sacrifice.*
Set a guard over my mouth, LORD;
*   keep watch over the door of my lips.*
Do not let my heart be drawn to what is evil
*   so that I take part in wicked deeds*
along with those who are evildoers;
*   do not let me eat of their delicacies.*
Let a righteous man strike me—that is a kindness;
*   let him rebuke me—that is oil on my head.*
My head will not refuse it,
*   for my prayer will still be against the deeds of evildoers.*

PSALM 141:1-5

The struggle against being lonely is itself compounded by, and in its turn complicates, the problems of resisting temptations. Longing to be hugged and loved, we can more quickly meet our needs by immoral means. Or perhaps we are tempted to overeat and abuse our bodies. Unfortunately, we can too easily drown the sorrow of our loneliness and satisfy our cravings (but only temporarily) by giving in to our sensual appetites. We may be driven to alcohol or drugs in a hopeless attempt to drown out the pain.

Sometimes those temptations become overwhelming, and we feel, "What's the use?" Life is so miserable that we think we can vastly improve it if we give in to whatever temptation is oppressing us. Especially if we have been married, the desire is incredibly strong in us not only to satisfy our sexual needs, but also to prove to ourselves and to the world and perhaps to our former spouse or a prospective one that we are sexually attractive.

So how can we find the resources for fighting the seemingly insurmountable odds against us in the battles against temptations? I especially find helpful the words from Ephesians 6, which lists the armor that we are to put on to defend ourselves against all the powers of evil. Prayer is greatly emphasized as the most essential tool for the fight, as it is also here in Psalm 141. Both the beginning and the end of the psalm section that we will discuss in this chapter focus on prayer as our greatest weapon.

Another major emphasis in this psalm, which is only indirectly stressed in Ephesians though it appears often in the New Testament, especially in 1 Thessalonians 5, is the support and rebuke of fellow believers. In and through the Christian community we are strengthened to combat the temptations that besiege us. As a child participating in evening vespers, I always loved the liturgical sequence in which the pastor said, "Let my prayer be set before thee as incense," and the congregation responded with the chant, "And the lifting up of my hands as the evening sacrifice." At the time I didn't know what those lines from Psalm 141 meant, especially because in Lutheran churches we didn't usually lift up our hands in prayer, but I was stirred by the dramatic action in them and sensed that they involved a plea for relationship with God. Now I rejoice that in newer hymnals the entire congregation chants much more of this psalm.

We ask in this psalm that our prayers would be set before God as incense. The Hebrew word translated "set" comes from a root meaning "to fix or establish." The form used in verse 2 emphasizes arranging our prayers or laying them out in order as we present them before the LORD. Imagine with me the strong fragrance of sweet incense; see its smoke slowly curl upward as the priest raises the censer and swings it out over the people. The priest moves from side to side at the altar and gathers all the prayers of the people to present them to God as a pleasing aroma, a fragrance that is cherished. We ask in Psalm 141 with the poet David that our prayers, too, would be a sweet smoke of sacrifice before the LORD. We want the lifting of our hands in prayer and praise to come to God even as the grain offering was brought as a tribute at the evening time of worship.

The gesture of raising hands in prayer illustrates the nature of our relationship with God and puts us into proper humility before Him—stretching out our hands both to beseech Him and to reach for His hand of care. Dramatic fragrances and actions put our prayer life into perspective. Though we join the poet in asking YHWH to come quickly, we also know we must have proper respect and patience in our prayers lest we call in demanding ways or fail to acknowledge in propriety who we are before Him.

We always need the poet's caution, lest our speech be unbefitting before the LORD. Wanting all the words of his prayers to be righteous, he adds, "Set a guard over my mouth, LORD; keep watch over the door of my lips." Similarly, we don't want anything to violate our prayer life, to be irreverent or flippant, to come from wrong motives, to trivialize or blaspheme God.

Even the form in which the poet makes these requests underscores the reverence with which he speaks. "Set," "keep" and "let" in verses 3 and 4 are not simple imperatives, but add what is called a paragogic hē. This letter at the end of an imperative makes it softer, as if we were to add the word *please*. Thus, we are asking the LORD to station a guard for us and to watch over our speech, *please*. We don't want any dishonoring to disrupt the intimacy between our LORD and ourselves.

Nor do we want any evil to get in the way. The real problem in temptation is not only that it causes us to sin, but that it breaks down our relationship with God. Consequently, the poet asks that his heart not even be drawn in the direction of that which is evil, because to move in that course is to go away from the LORD. The word *heart* here, we remember, is understood more deeply than the way we use it in English. Rather than signaling emotions, the word in Hebrew (and in New Testament Greek) refers more specifically to inclinations, resolutions, and determinations of the will. We don't want our desires or intentions to be drawn to any wicked or immoral practices.

This thought prepares us for the words of Jesus that merely to look at a person with lust in one's heart is to commit adultery (see Matthew 5:28). Sin is rooted in the intentions, so the place where we want God's action to begin in helping us to fight temptation is at the very core of our being in our basic motives.

Especially in the battle against sexual temptations, our thought life must be purified. We want to not even want what is contrary to God's principles—so in our contemporary culture we must be careful about the clothes we wear, the films we view, the music to which we listen, the sites we visit on the Web.

When the poet asks that he not be drawn to what is evil, the expression used is unusually forceful in the original text because it first employs a rare Hebrew verb (translated "be drawn"); then the noun immediately following it comes from the same root in order to emphasize doubly how much the deeds are evil. That verb comes from a root that means "to practice or to busy oneself, to divert oneself in dealing wantonly." The noun that follows signifies "deeds," but it is almost always used to denote those that are intemperate or reckless.

We will see this noun used in a shocking way in Psalm 77 (chapter twenty-eight), where it describes the action of God, whose love is so generous that it seems almost wanton. Literally translated, then, the phrase asks the LORD to keep us from practicing evil practices or doing doings of wantonness.

That strong statement is amplified in the next phrase, which adds the poet's desire that he be kept from taking part in "wicked deeds." This word denotes even violence or crime—in other words, much more overt acts of evil. The poet wants to avoid getting involved in such wicked deeds with men who are habitual "evildoers" (women in that society had little opportunity for such deviousness). The Hebrew text calls them men who are "practicing falsehood," a word that stresses the nothingness or vanity of iniquity because it never truly is what it seems to be. Indeed, we will always discover that the evil to which we are allured turns out to be hollow, an illusion, a deception.

That last comment gives us more ammunition for our battles against evil. We are more thoroughly equipped to fight sin when we remember that it is never ultimately satisfying. Always its pleasure will turn to dust in our mouths. In C. S. Lewis' fantasy *The Lion, the Witch and the Wardrobe,* Edmund eats and eats of the White Witch's Turkish delight, a candy that he continues to long for, though soon after eating it he feels very ill.[1]

Even so, the poet David specifically says, "Do not let me eat of their delicacies." We might speculate about to what he is referring, but it is more important to recognize ways in which this text suggests the seductions of our own experience. For example, many of us wrestle against the enticement to overeat when we get depressed. The word *delicacies,* or *dainties,* comes from the Hebrew word for "pleasant" or "delightful." It implies something very genial on the surface

---

[1]See C. S. Lewis, *The Lion, the Witch and the Wardrobe* (1950; reprint, New York: Harper Trophy, 1994).

that is poisonous in truth. To eat of the delicacies of evildoers pulls us into their traps. In practical terms, falling to the snares of overeating precipitates further evils. Abuse causes people to gain weight, which robs them of their health and self-esteem, which usually causes them to do more binging. Temptations catch us in those kinds of cycles, which are always terribly ensnaring and destructive.

Consequently, David asks that he be kept from those temptations, and his plea makes the next verse all the more important. The poet continues by reminding us of our most precious aid for resisting seductions—the help of friends.

Verse 5 is much more cryptic in the Hebrew and thereby accentuates its point. Lacking verbs in key places, the original text reads as follows:

> Will smite me a righteous one—goodness.
> and he will rebuke me—oil of the head.
> Nor shall refuse my head,
> for still also my prayer against their evils.

Because our prayer is continually directed against the temptations of those who work wickedness, David urges us to be grateful when members of the community who are supportive help us to combat them. If someone smites me to correct me, he says, it is a goodness. Notice that the smiting comes from a *righteous* person. If that individual is a model to us of what we would like to be, then the discipline is a favor to us, and we appreciate the kindness.

If that same righteous one will rebuke us, chide us, correct us, it will be as oil to our heads. This verb *rebuke* comes from a root that signifies judging or deciding, proving in the sense of testing. The righteous one who observes us has weighed our behavior against the standard of God's principles and therefore admonishes. Oil in this case is a token of hospitality or a medicament. It brings us cleansing and promotes healing.

Notice that David's response to such correction is simply the phrase that his head will not refuse that kind of oil. He certainly will not hinder or restrain or frustrate the gracious training of the righteous. God's purposes are being worked out through the rebukes of godly friends, so we would obstruct God's discipline and purification in our lives if we refused it.

One day during my loneliest years I was criticized for always hugging my Christian friends. My critic thought that a person in my position as a teacher should be more reserved about giving affection. That criticism hurt because it seemed to me unjust, but it was necessary for me also to listen to it to make sure that my actions were genuine expressions of Christian love and not manipulations of people to meet my needs.

When godly friends criticize us, we do well to pay attention. They are frequently God's vessels for bringing correction and for rebuilding our lives. Perhaps you might pause awhile to thank God for those members of Christ's body who have been agents of God's admonition for you.

The rest of this psalm speaks about keeping our eyes fixed on the LORD when the wicked lay out snares for us. Significantly, this last section begins, "My prayer will still be against the deeds of evildoers." I think that means not only that we don't want those deeds to infect our lives, but also that we pray to counteract their power in the world. Perhaps some concern is also implied for those who are working evil. Maybe we can be helpful to them in drawing them away from their wickedness and back to the LORD.

How, then, can we face temptation when we are alone? Our prayer life is the most important key. Moreover, the rebukes of our godly friends dare not be ignored. Finally, as we grow in our relationship with the LORD, we will more thoroughly know the resources of His care, not only to counteract the evil that would draw us aside, but also to reach out to help others who face temptations too. More and more, we could become guardians of righteousness bringing goodness and healing oil to the heads of others.

For Further Meditation

1. How does the dramatic action of "the lifting up of my hands" help me to focus on the inner attitudes of my relationship with the LORD?

2. What is the reason that the state of the heart is so important?

3. To what kinds of practices by evil persons am I drawn? What sorts of temptations afflict me, especially in my loneliness?

4. How does my loneliness increase my susceptibility to temptation?

5. How does my local congregation provide support in fighting temptations? How do I wish it did?

6. Am I able to receive the rebuke of my Christian brothers and sisters? Why or why not? Am I able to admonish them lovingly?

7. What is the state of my own prayer life? In what ways might I deepen it in order to be able to fight temptation more effectively?

24

God Sets the Lonely in Families

Sing to God, sing in praise of his name,
extol him who rides on the clouds;
rejoice before him—his name is the LORD.
A father to the fatherless, a defender of widows,
is God in his holy dwelling.
God sets the lonely in families,
he leads out the prisoners with singing;
but the rebellious live in a sun-scorched land. . . .
You, God, are awesome in your sanctuary;
the God of Israel gives power and strength to his people.
Praise be to God!

PSALM 68:4-6, 35

I held my namesake, Joy Marva Fehring, on my lap while we listened to her brother and sister play their instruments in the high school Christmas concert. That afternoon the wonderful music was more than just a program because I was with my "family," who had made me part of them by asking me to be a godmother for baby Joy.

Earlier in the day in another city, I had listened with great delight to two friends who were guest singers for a worship service. After coming to the adult forum I then taught on "Keeping Christ in Christmas," those two spiritual brothers gave me warm goodbye hugs. Several such single friends, both male and female, were (and still remain) another kind of family for me.

After the class, congregation members came to thank me for the ten weeks I had been their guest teacher for a course on Isaiah. During those three months together, they had become a church family to me.

That same night also a fourth family was created. My housemate Julie and I became instant aunts to Jess and Hope, whose parents, Eugene and Toni Carson, were planning with us to become a Christian community together. At last God seemed to be providing the answer to my many prayers about His will for the big old house in which we had conducted a crisis ministry for a while. Of course, we six would all have to work through issues together to be a family in that place. But our love for the LORD was of the same mind, as was our desire to live in community in order to share our resources and be supportive of each other's ministries. I believed that God would knit us into more effective stewards and servants through our assistance and care for one another.

How fascinating is the timing of God that on the Sabbath before the day in which I had planned to work on this chapter about the solitary being set into families, He should set me into four different kinds so that I could encounter more thoroughly the grace of it! What love-surprises God has in store for us, if we can open our eyes to see them!

Psalm 68 does not fit into any of the typical psalm styles, such as laments or thanksgivings or hymns of faith. Though it might appear at first glance to be merely a collection of songs and poetic fragments, scholars tie it more formally to dramatic processions celebrating the Kingship of God. If the latter was the psalm's liturgical use (which is highly likely, since its canonical title dedicates it to the chief musician or temple choir director), then probably each part of the psalm was sung in connection with a specific element of the sacred ritual. (You might want to read through the whole psalm first to gain an overview of the entire context of the section we will be discussing.)

Perhaps you noticed that the psalm celebrates God's provision for His people as one manifestation of His Kingship. *YHWH's* dwelling on Mount Zion is also part of the reason for this celebrative procession, as are the deeds that He performed when He brought the Israelites out of Egypt and into the Promised Land. In the midst of all these descriptions is this verse, also quoted in the letter to the Ephesians in its section discussing the gifts God gives to His church to equip the saints for the work of their ministries: "When you ascended on high, you took many captives; you received gifts from people" (v. 18; quoted in Ephesians 4:8).

The psalm's descriptions of the procession itself (vv. 24-27) give us glimpses of the people's experiences as they worshiped together— with the singers and musicians, the maidens playing tambourines and the various tribes moving along in their proper order in the celebrative throng. This graphic section sets the tone for our discussion of the LORD setting the solitary in families. We feel "enfamilied" when in our minds we join the festal assembly.

Especially note the way the psalm ends, for the last verse is the grand culmination of the message of the entire festival. I love processions involving brass and banners and robed leaders in our worship services, for we can say in dramatic actions more than we can say in words—that our God is magnificent in His sanctuary. The Hebrew text praises God for causing astonishment out of His holy place. At the place out of which He speaks and exerts His power (the temple and its precincts), He continually fills those who observe with reverence and awe.

After all, the second to the last line of the psalm concludes, this is the God who "gives power and strength to his people." An emphatic pronoun is used here to underscore our knowledge that the God of Israel deals with His people in this manner. The verb is in a participial form, which emphasizes more strongly in Hebrew the continuous bestowing of resilience. *Power* refers not only to personal power, but in this context to the influence of the people as a whole, as a political and social entity. The word that is translated "strength" by the TNIV is a term used in a plural form in the First Testament only here, in order to intensify its point. We might translate that plurality with "abundant might." God bestows upon His people more than enough strength to triumph.

Because YHWH's gifts are more than enough, the psalm ends with an exultant refrain, translated by the TNIV as "Praise be to God!" This is not the same phrase that appears so often in Psalms 111—117 and 146—150, in which the Hebrew text concludes, "Praise the LORD." Here the verb signifies rather "Blessed be." Because the word is a participle again, it stresses that God is continuously to be blessed. The verb urges the humility of kneeling before God; the psalmist reminds us that God is supremely worthy of our constant adoration. Our fitting response to all that has been manifested about Him is to develop and practice the habit of honoring Him at all times.

Now, with this whole context of Psalm 68 in our minds, we can focus particularly on verses 4 to 6. First of all, several different verbs are used in this section to urge the people to praise God. The first invitation is to sing to God, and next we are called to play music to His name, which underscores the honoring of the LORD's character. The verb is related to the word for "pipe," so it suggests playing on a reed. Thereby we are urged to praise God not only vocally, but with the full range of instrumental music.[1] The next verb means actually to lift up,

---

[1] For discussions of criteria by which to choose the best elements and forms in worship leading, see my books *Reaching Out Without Dumbing Down: A Theology of Worship for This Urgent Time* (Grand Rapids, Mich.: Eerdmans, 1995); *A Royal "Waste" of Time: The Splendor of Worshiping God and Being Church for the World* (Grand Rapids, Mich.: Eerdmans, 1999); and *How Shall We Worship? Biblical Guidelines for the Worship Wars* (Wheaton, Ill.: Tyndale House, 2003).

posed to hunger and homelessness and hazards, and the widows subject to harsh treatment and oppression without a man to protect them
and secure justice in a patriarchal world—are victoriously cared for by
the One who is Father and Defender to them. Once again there is a ref-
erence to "God in his holy dwelling," the sacred place of apartness from
which He exerts His power on behalf of the helpless.

Next, His holiness is manifested on behalf of the solitary. As the
TNIV translates this passage, "God sets the lonely in families." Scholars disagree over the best rendering of the Hebrew phrase here. The
original text concludes with the expression "in the house." The New
American Standard Bible interprets this as "makes a home for the
lonely." For the people in the procession that this psalm celebrates,
the phrase might refer to the fact that the LORD had led them into a
homeland. They had been exiles and friendless, but now God had
given them the Promised Land.

The phrase is one of immense comfort, not only to the wandering
Israelites, but also to those of us who are alone and isolated. God enfolds those who are lonely and gives us a place of security. As the beginning of this chapter indicates, I experienced in the day before I
first wrote it a remarkable enfolding into four kinds of families.

The rest of the sixth verse speaks of God leading forth into prosperity those who are imprisoned, in contrast to those who are rebellious, who live in a sun-scorched or glaring and bare place. The
noun for "prosperity," translated "with singing" in the TNIV, is plural
for intensification in the Hebrew. In these final phrases of the verse,
then, we see the immense difference between the afflicted ones,
cared for by God's bountiful provision, and those who by rejecting
Him miss His gifts.

One of my biggest frustrations with contemporary churches is that
we don't live out very well the principles of this psalm's procession.
God has called His people to participate in His purposes of providing
for the afflicted ones, but we are not doing a very good job. Countless

women are reduced to poverty in our society, and, as sociologists document, most of our culture's social problems can be traced to fatherlessness in U.S. homes. Are we being agents in the mission of the God who is a Father to children in poverty and a Defender of minorities and the disabled and single mothers? These issues are massive and require the stewardship of the entire Church. We dare not neglect this challenge because its immensity immobilizes us; there are plenty of ways that we can participate in efforts to feed the hungry, create jobs for those on welfare, provide big brothers and sisters to lonely children.

In particular, what do our churches do for the lonely? How have God's people learned to love better so that we might be one of the primary families into which lonely persons are set? More and more as I travel throughout the country to teach, I grieve over the lack of concern, evidenced by the small number of single persons participating in congregations. Forty percent of the U.S. adult population is single, but very few churches include such a proportion in their membership. Consequently, I plead with you to be active, out of your own aloneness or out of your concern for a lonely person, to encourage deeper caring in your parish. Out of the healing that we experience can come a powerful ministry of sensitivity to the needs of others around us who also long to be "enfamilied."

All sorts of families might offer the lonely comfort and security or a place of ministry. Physical families can adopt single persons as extra aunts and uncles or grandparents. (Parents need the influence of other Christian adults upon their children as much as lonely people need their companionship.) Individuals can serve as godparents for children and help to raise them spiritually, to assist in introducing them to the LORD. We might consider more seriously the idea of Christians living together in communities. (As I work on the revisions of this book, I remember with great gratitude all the gifts bestowed in the years that the Carson family joined Julie and me in the EPHESUS community.) Also, marriage is not the only possibility for deep relationships; we can find many levels of nongenital intimacy with friends of both genders.[2] During my lonely single years, many of my closest friends were single men who were also church workers and whom I loved intensely and affectionately, though not in a romantic way at all. These are some of the kinds of families into which God might set you.

The LORD wants to place us all into a home, to enable us to experience security in our aloneness, to change our loneliness into being enfolded by His grace incarnated in the Christian community. As a tender Father and righteous Defender, He cares for us when we are orphaned or widowed. As Jesus promised, "I will not leave you as orphans; I will come to you" (John 14:18).

For Further Meditation

1. What is the value of dramatic action in worship services? What gestures or rituals best convey to me the nobility and sublimity of God?

2. In what ways does God give me strength and abundant might?

3. How can I sing or make music to extol *YHWH* in the worship life of my congregation? (This is important even if you do not consider yourself a musician, for worship implies the participation of everyone.)

4. What is the sense of victory that this psalm entails? How do I experience it?

5. Why is it important that "in *YH*" is constituted God's name?

6 Who are "the helpless" in our times? How am I participating in God's purposes to care for them?

7. Into what families has the LORD set me?

---

[2]See chapter eight, "Friendship," in my book *Sexual Character.*

25

Worship Really Matters

As the deer pants for streams of water,
so my soul pants for you, my God.
My soul thirsts for God, for the living God.
When can I go and meet with God? . . .
These things I remember
as I pour out my soul:
how I used to go to the house of God
under the protection of the Mighty One
with shouts of joy and praise
among the festive throng.
Why, my soul, are you downcast?
Why so disturbed within me?
Put your hope in God,
for I will yet praise him,
my Savior and my God. . . .
Send me your light and your faithful care,
let them lead me;
let them bring me to your holy mountain,
to the place where you dwell.
Then I will go to the altar of God,
to God, my joy and my delight.
I will praise you with the lyre,
O God, my God.

Why, my soul, are you downcast?
    Why so disturbed within me?
Put your hope in God,
    for I will yet praise him,
        my Savior and my God.

PSALM 42:1-2, 4-5; 43:3-5

These things I remember
    as I pour out my soul:
how I used to go with the multitude,
    leading the procession to the house of God,
with shouts of joy and thanksgiving
    among the festive throng.

PSALM 42:4 NIV

The times were filled with anxiety and grief. My home had fallen apart through my husband's involvement with a girl in our youth group; my life's ministry was beginning to move in new directions; I was unsure of everything. One bright spot in my week was the opportunity to go to chapel on the day I commuted to the seminary for work on my master of divinity degree. I had deeply loved the chapel services when I was an undergraduate in a Lutheran teachers college, so it was not only the soreness of my circumstances that made me so hungry for worship during my lonely years. To this day I have a deep craving for more frequent and more profound corporate worship.

The Scriptures are a treasure chest from which we can continually take insights both old and new (see Matthew 13:52). We can study a text for one theme and then come back to it another time for an entirely different perspective. Because of the emphasis in Psalms 42 and 43 on the soul's longing for God (which is often obstructed by formalized religion that involves us in all sorts of superficial activities that prevent us from spending time deepening our relationship with God), we might easily overlook the other major theme of these psalms—the poet's delight in corporate worship. That theme is stressed especially in the repeated refrain which occurs in 42:5, 11 and 43:5 and which seems to indicate that the two psalms were originally one poem.

You might wonder what all this has to do with loneliness. Unfortunately, our materialistic and alienated culture hides from us the truth that God created us in His image and designed us to have fellowship with Him. The great tearing of sin into the world disrupted our relationship with God and, consequently, with each other. Human beings started blaming one another instead of communing with each other and with God.

God's image in us, however, is not lost completely by our fall into sin. These two psalms describe in a profound way the huge longing we all have deep inside of us, not only for God Himself, but also for intimacy with others who are His people. Notice how often statements in the poem imply corporate worship.

At the outset, the poet compares his desire to that of a hart that longs for streams of water. We must remember that he is writing in the land of Palestine, which is mostly terribly dry and sun-scorched. It's hard for me to identify with that craving for the brooks because I live in western Washington, where it rains much of the time. We must envision ourselves in the fiery and blinding desert wilderness of the Middle East in order to imagine the intense longing that the poet describes.

The poetic repetition underscores that intensity. The third line of the psalm announces again that the poet's soul, the core of who he truly is, thirsts not for just anybody, but for the living God, the One who alone is the vigorous fountain of life.

That longing leads naturally in the poem to the following question: "When can I go and meet with God?" We always wonder when we are going to be able to satisfy our appetites and meet our needs. Children ask, "When are we going to have dinner?" or "When can we have some ice cream?" This poet begs, "When can I have some worship?"

Today such an unusual question must stop us short. How many people that you know are begging for worship? Most children resist, screaming, "I don't wanna go to church!" Much of the weakness that we see in churches results from their failure to offer a vibrant fellowship of genuine community practicing rich traditions of worship that both stir up and satisfy our deepest longings for God. Perhaps we should each pause at this point to assess the worship of our congregation. Do we offer a holy place and splendorous time in which people can come to meet with the living God?[1]

Next, the poet remembers the times that worship has been refreshing and meaningful to him. As he pours out his soul in this time of grief and searching, the memory of worship brings him in touch with his deepest need. Observe carefully his description. (The meaning of the Hebrew original in verse 4 is uncertain; the following comments refer to the NIV translation cited above and the NRSV.)

First of all, the poet notes that he went to worship with the multitudes. He might be recalling specific times of pilgrimage when bands of believers traveled together to the temple in Jerusalem to celebrate

---

[1]Many churches confuse the need for true worship with a craving for excitement and think that the solution to participants' apathy is to offer hyped-up worship services; but these do not satisfy the longings expressed in these psalms for an encounter with the true God. Some churches discard the traditions of the Church in order to make worship more "appealing," but this flimsy strategy also misses what this poet yearns for in his request for the ritual worship of the people of God. What is needed is worship that is deep enough to give its participants more of God. See my three books on worship listed in the footnote on page 193.

Jewish festivals. The point is that part of the Joy of worship was being together with many others who were believers too.

Second, the poet was one of the leaders. He was an active participant in the celebrations and headed up the procession to the house of God.

Third, the multitudes traveled with shouts of Joy and thanksgiving. The times of pilgrimage and worship were times of celebration in awareness that God had poured out many gifts upon His people. These times were uplifting as the people gratefully recalled together the character of their God.

Fourth, the poet says once again, "among the festive throng." The idea of the group both begins and ends his description of his memory. His emphasis upon that fact indicates that one of the most important aspects of those times of worship was that he was among the others in the Jewish rituals (which connected him to God's people Israel over the entire period of their history), celebrating together the magnificent love of God.

Quiet devotional time alone is vitally important; however, it is also necessary at times not to be alone in worship. Our spirits crave corporate worship, a throng of people celebrating together, a sense of the entire cloud of witnesses of God's people throughout all time and space.

The refrain of these two psalms moves dramatically from despair and discouragement to the great *yet* of "Put your hope in God, for I will yet praise him, my Savior and my God." The poet realizes that one of the solutions for his being downcast and disturbed is to gather together with God's people. Praising God with others will usher in again a time of hope. The rejoicing of God's people carries us—even when we are too discouraged to feel much of anything.

Surely that matches our experience. When we are deeply depressed over failure or rejection or loneliness in our lives, times of worship with an assembly or times of prayer with a small group are some of the greatest means for uplifting us. When the soul is thronged with doubts and despair, comfort is found in the fellowship of the throngs of the saints.

The poet tries to calm his soul by reminding himself that soon he will be able to worship. The verb root *to wait* is put in a form that extends it to mean "to hope." The word that we translate "yet" expresses addition or repetition, the fact of more. *Yet* the poet will be able to praise God, who is his personal Savior and God. He is indeed *my* God, the psalmist insists, and the Deliverer of my self (literally, "my face"), so he eagerly anticipates praising Him. The poet knows that such an action will help to ease his discouragement and free his disturbed spirit.

In order to focus specifically upon the theme of worship as it bridges the two psalms of the poem, we are necessarily skipping over many other themes in Psalm 42. You might want to observe carefully some of these other main themes, such as prayer, deliverance from enemies, and so forth in your own daily devotions.

In Psalm 43 the third verse brings us back again to the theme of corporate worship. The poet asks God to send out His light and faithful care. The verb *to send* implies a commissioning, a dispatching for a specific purpose—which is, in this case, to guide the poet.

Light is a common image in the Psalms (and, of course, in the teachings of Jesus). Figuratively, light is needed for guidance. When coupled with the notion of faithful care, which also implies God's undergirding steadfastness, the pair of words suggests God's assistance for the poet to be able to discern what is best for his life. He begs God (the Hebrew is strong with "let them" and an emphatic pronoun) to allow His light and faithful care to lead him in the path of true bliss. Particularly, he seeks the leading that will bring him for worship to the mountain of holiness (i.e., Zion, the Temple Mount).

The psalmist wants intensely to be able to go to the place where God dwells so that he can meet with Him. Specifically he longs for the special feast times at the temple in Jerusalem, but his calling for

light and faithful care to guide him lets us immerse ourselves in the
same longings for a worshipful place. Where can we find an assembly
that will enfold us in the steadfast care of God and bring light to direct our own pilgrimages?

Furthermore, the poet asks particularly for the opportunity to go
to the altar. According to the canonical title at the head of Psalm 42,
this double poem came from the "Sons of Korah," who were a part of
the descendants of Levi in charge of the music when David was king
(see 1 Chronicles 6). Thus, the psalmist was probably one of the tribe
of officials for the temple services. At this point he particularly asks
to be able to praise God with his harp. Most likely, as one of the temple musicians he longs for the day when he can play for the celebrations again.

That longing is part of my experience too. Playing the organ for a
festival service on Christmas Eve was my happy privilege one De-
cember when I was alone. Now, since I'm often gone on Sundays for
speaking engagements, I rarely get the opportunity to play instruments, direct a choir, or sing in one for worship—and that leaves a
large hole in my life. There is in each of us a deep desire (often un-
recognized) to use our gifts in the praise and worship of our God.

That is why we can see an important connection between our
loneliness and our need for worship when the poet again speaks the
refrain of his discouragement and then the word of hope. We join
him in looking to worship for the "praise way" out of loneliness and
despair.

Worship is not simply a panacea of happy songs to cure forever
our being downcast. It will not bring an end to our loneliness unless
it truly offers us the way to meet a triple need—our longings for
closer communion with God, for deeper fellowship with His people,
and for the opportunity to use our gifts to express praise. This is why
we can continue to hope in disturbing times: for surely *we will yet
praise Him*. We will know Him as our personal Savior and God as we

join together with other believers in the assembly of light and faithful care.

For Further Meditation

1. What other themes do I see in these psalms for further personal study?

2. How have I experienced the longing about which the poet speaks?

3. How is corporate worship a healing agent for loneliness?

4. Why does the poet need God's light and faithful care to guide him to the holy mountain? Why can't he find it himself?

5. Why do I need God's light and faithful care to guide me into genuine worship?

6. In what ways would I like to deepen my participation in corporate worship? Why are public rituals necessary?

7. How have I experienced the thrill of leading in worship—through singing, playing a musical instrument, reading, directing children's worship, making a banner, preparing the altar, bringing flowers, or any other means? How did those experiences affect my spiritual and personal life?

in the sense of casting up a highway, though it is used here to urge
Israel to lift up a song of praise to the one riding through the desert
places. The TNIV translates the final word in that sentence as "clouds,"
but includes in a footnote the possibility that it means "desert." The
word evokes images of the Exodus because it is often used in the First
Testament to describe the wilderness or the steppes through which
the Israelites traveled to come to the Promised Land after their deliverance from bondage in Egypt.

The TNIV rendition of the end of the next phrase, "His name is the
LORD," only hints at the fullness of this point. The original Hebrew
says without a verb, "In *YH* his name." The nickname *YH,* only two
letters of *YHWH* and the end of the word *Hallel-u-jah* (which literally
says, "Praise, y'all, Yah!"), is used only in psalms of praise from later
in Jewish history. The sentence underscores that "His name consists in
YH." The Hebrew preposition *in* is most significant in this instance because it emphasizes that God's "name," which is His character, consists
in all the attributes of *YHWH,* who has revealed Himself through history with an infinite love and grace. He is indeed *YH,* the Covenant
Keeper, who is faithful to His promises to provide for His people.

That is why we are invited to rejoice before Him. The Hebrew text
does not use either of the two most common words to express rejoicing, but instead uses a rare word that highlights more exulting in triumph. The word is akin to the one used by Hannah in her song of
ecstasy because of the long-awaited gift of her son, Samuel (see
1 Samuel 2:1). (The same exuberant Joy is expressed similarly in
1 Peter 1:8.) Such a word is more in keeping with the exhilaration of
the context. This festival is a triumphant procession reveling in the
victory of our God, the King.

This is a significant introduction, then, to the next section, which is
the focus of our interest in this chapter. In such a mood of elation, we
remember that our God is "a father to the fatherless" and "a defender
of widows." Those who were typically the helpless—the orphans ex-

26

Finding the Strength to Go On

Ascribe to the LORD, you heavenly beings,
ascribe to the LORD glory and strength.
Ascribe to the LORD the glory due his name;
worship the LORD in the splendor of his holiness.
The voice of the LORD is over the waters;
the God of glory thunders,
the LORD thunders over the mighty waters.
The voice of the LORD is powerful;
the voice of the LORD is majestic.
The voice of the LORD breaks the cedars. . . .
The voice of the LORD shakes the desert. . . .
And in his temple all cry, "Glory!"
The LORD sits enthroned over the flood;
the LORD is enthroned as King forever.
The LORD gives strength to his people;
the LORD blesses his people with peace.

PSALM 29:1-5a, 8a, 9c-11

When the strength isn't there, it isn't there.

One of the greatest frustrations in my life is that when my blood pressure is too low and my metabolism too slow, I simply can't get up—up hills, up stairs, up from a chair. I have enough strength; it just isn't available to me fast enough. That gets very discouraging, especially when the people around me don't understand and complain that I am too pokey. Too many nightmarish experiences of getting left behind during my years of betrayal and abandonment furthermore led to an inability to accept my own physical limitations. The lack of wholeness, therefore, was not so much in my body as in my spirit.

Psalm 29 offers immense comfort for all of us, no matter what kinds of deficiencies we might suffer. Perhaps you don't lack for strength, but you feel inferior to others in certain kinds of intelligence or in appearance or social finesse. Whatever our weaknesses, they cause a lack of wholeness, and certainly the latter is the greater problem. Into the insecurity of all that, this psalm brings a tremendous word of hope.

Before considering its particular verses, however, we will be helped this time if we look first at some aspects of Hebrew poetry. Psalm 29 is one that is best read aloud to catch the impact of its parallel lines. Notice, for example, the parallelism of the first two verses. The phrase, "ascribe to YHWH" occurs in the first three lines and is matched in the fourth by the phrase "worship YHWH." Then the second half of each of the lines contains a phrase about might and glory.

Next, the poetic structure revolves around seven uses of the words "the voice of YHWH," but notice in the psalm all the other poetic repetitions of key words. Finally, the last two verses use parallel expressions depicting the LORD sitting enthroned and announcing the gifts that YHWH gives to His people.

The final word, *shalom*, or "peace," is accentuated by making it the final word—inverting the word order of the line it parallels just above. By moving "his people" into the middle of the line and "peace" to the end, the poet gives more force than ever to that last word. All the impact of the literary buildup throughout the poem comes to a grand finale in that great word *shalom*.

Stop for a minute and read the whole psalm aloud from some version of the Bible that has set it up in poetic lines, and accentuate as you read all the uses of *YHWH's* name and His voice. Notice the tremendous crescendo of power as the poem progresses. Altogether it creates a vivid picture of the immense strength of *YHWH* as He handles all of creation and all of history with His majestic voice.

One great affliction in our loneliness and grief is the lack of strength, which often is the physical symptom of our emotional brokenness. "How can I find the strength to go on?" is a common question among those who suffer. Thus, we are powerfully encouraged by seeing all the elements in this psalm assuring us that the LORD will indeed provide us with all the strength that we need.

First of all, the angels or some other supernatural beings are called to give God praise, for which He is eminently worthy. The phrases "you heavenly beings" and "O mighty ones" are the TNIV and NIV interpretations, respectively, of the Hebrew, "sons of the strong ones." The root for the latter phrase is *el,* which means "god."

We can only speculate why the poet initially calls upon spiritual agents to worship the LORD properly. The poetic device of calling both the heavens and the earth to praise is typical in Jewish literature, perhaps to remind us that our praise is inadequate; God is so worthy as to require cosmic praise. Moreover, God's heavenly messengers certainly know so much better than we all that *YHWH's* strength entails. They have been observing it and praising it from eternity, and, of course, they do so from perfection, whereas we struggle with our finite humanity. The point for us is to pay attention to them in order to learn more fully what the strength of *YHWH* involves—and what true praise must be.[1]

Next, we must note that the "heavenly beings" are called to ascribe

---

[1]See also the praise of heavenly beings in Revelation 4–5 and 7, and in chapters fifteen, sixteen and nineteen of my book *Joy in Our Weakness.*

to the LORD both glory and strength. The word *glory,* as we have seen in chapter twenty, suggests the honor or reverence that should be attributed to *YHWH,* recognizing *YHWH* in His rightful position.

In the third line, the word *glory* is expanded to remind us that it is due His name. *YHWH* is supremely worthy of this ascription of praise because His character is glorious and mighty, as has been revealed not only in the heavens, but also to us through history and in the Scriptures. Consequently, His character has become the object of our knowledge and love and praise.

The fourth poetic line stresses in its parallelism that the mighty beings are to bow down in worship, to prostrate themselves before *YHWH,* "in the splendor of his holiness." This ambiguous phrase reminds us that an element of mystery infuses the majesty of worshiping an ineffable God.

The word *splendor* is always used in First Testament texts in a Hebrew construct form that links the word more tightly together with the following word for "holiness." Thus, the phrase highlights the adornment of God's apartness and stresses in connection with public worship that, when the praise of God is made known, the place where the praise is offered is made holy. Some biblical translations use the image of worshiping God in "holy array" to capture the sense that the act of adoration sanctifies the space and/or participants. We can widen our appreciation for this image by looking at some similar uses of these words in their contexts, such as in 1 Chronicles 16:29, 2 Chronicles 20:21, and Psalm 96:9.

In all of these verses of adoration, notice in their context the deep Joy and reverence of the worship. To praise the LORD in the splendor of His holiness brings that profound sense of His sanctity into the very place where we are worshiping and fills us with reverence and wonder at His majesty.

Next, we are reminded, together with the mighty heavenly beings, of the magnificence of the voice of the LORD and what it has accomplished in the history of the world. The number seven in Jewish thought stands for perfection, so the seven pictures are vivid images of *YHWH* in all the creative acts and historical deeds, represented symbolically, by which He has dealt powerfully with and for the sake of Israel. In the first use of the phrase "the voice of the LORD," the repetition of the terms *waters* and *thunders* sets up a graphic sound picture of God's creative word bringing the world into being from chaos. The noun *glory*, moreover, links this section with the psalm's opening call to praise.

Next are images of storms, and probably and specifically the tremendous tempest upon Sinai when *YHWH* appeared there to make clear His covenant relationship with Israel. His shaking of the desert of Kadesh reminds us that His people were brought out of the Egyptian bondage, kept by Him through all their wanderings in that wilderness, and made a special people by His words to them at the great mountain.

No wonder all the beings in the temple (earthly or heavenly) respond, "Glory!" All the hosts of heaven and all the people in the temple at Jerusalem recall that *YHWH* has used His voice in these powerful ways. Therefore, all the dwellers in God's temple must shout out "the glory due his name."

When we worship in our earthly temples, we respond to the recountings of God's actions in creation and history also with "Glory!" Certainly we are astounded with the extent of the LORD's might when we observe the reverberations of His voice. All that which He has accomplished by a simple word must fill us with amazement at the immensity of His total strength.

This final picture is added to the montage: the LORD sat enthroned over the flood. The word for "flood" that appears in this tenth verse occurs nowhere else in the Scriptures except in the Genesis account of Noah and the ark. At the time of Noah, God was completely in control; therefore He could promise that such a flood would never take place again. He was, after all, sovereignly its ruler. For that reason we can join the poet in discerning the greatness of *YHWH* for His enthronement over it.

That is proof, David seems to say by the addition of the poetic parallel, that *YHWH* also sits enthroned over all events. He sits enthroned as King of the universe forever. Not only does He rule over all space and nature, but also He reigns over all time and history.

Now what are the consequences of this tremendous strength? We have seen by a colossal crescendo of magnificent images just how strong the great LORD and King of the cosmos is. Now we are specifically reminded personally that this same *YHWH* chooses graciously to give that strength to His people. This is another sentence that we must frequently hear to realize the impact of its meaning: *YHWH does give strength* to His people.

The verb *gives* is in the imperfect tense in the Hebrew, which means that the action is incomplete. That could signify either that *YHWH* will give power in the future, or more likely that He is constantly giving it, as in the TNIV rendition with a present continuing verb, "The LORD gives strength to his people." We can count on it now. The simple answer to that terrible question, "How can I find the strength to go on?" is this strong assurance: "*YHWH* provides power to His people."

Finally, the culmination of this overwhelmingly encouraging psalm is the poetic parallel to the promise of strength. Not only does *YHWH* give us the might that we need, but moreover He blesses us with *shalom.*

When I struggle against slow metabolism and low blood pressure, not only do I need the energy to keep going, but more than that, I need the wholeness that will allow me to accept myself in my limitations. That is the promise of this final line of the poem—so mightily emphasized by the placement of the word *shalom* at the very end of the psalm. The greatest blessing of *YHWH* to His people is the gift of wholeness.

The noun *shalom* carries with it immense connotations in the First Testament. We do the word an injustice if we limit it to the idea of peace, although that is where it begins. First of all, *shalom* commences with reconciliation with God. Then, because of that peace, God's people can have peace with themselves—and because they are at ease with themselves, they can work for peace with their neighbors in the sense not only of absence of war, but more broadly in regard to positive relationships. Such peace issues further in both health and wealth—health because the body is spared from the psychosomatic effects of anxiety and discord, and wealth because the self is free to enjoy the richness of blessings received.

These truths lead in turn to benefits of tranquillity, satisfaction, contentment, and fulfillment. All the preceding is summarized in the word *wholeness*, which is what we long for most deeply as we search for healing and freedom from loneliness.

Finally, the word *shalom* contains within it the promise of commitment. If we say *shalom* to someone and mean it sincerely, we are binding ourselves to that person so that whatever we might have that he or she needs to be whole we will gladly give. James seems to allude to this covenantal aspect of peace when he writes as follows:

> What good is it, my brothers and sisters, if you say you have faith but do not have works? Can faith save you? If a brother or sister is naked and lacks daily food, and one of you says to [him or her], "Go in peace; keep warm and eat your fill," and yet you do not supply their bodily needs, what is the good of that? (James 2:14-16 NRSV)

Shalom includes making the effort necessary to provide what is lacking for such wholeness to be secured for the other person.

As we conclude our study of Psalm 29, we draw the mountain of images to a snowy peak in the largeness of the *shalom* with which God blesses His people. *YHWH* creates for us reconciliation with

Himself and, consequently, the peace with our neighbors and with ourselves that leads to healing, abundance, serenity, enjoyment, fulfillment, and completeness. God is committed to all of that in us so that, when He gives us the strength to go on, He also gives us the courage to overcome whatever hinders our strength.

God gives us not only the physical power, but also the spiritual and emotional ability to continue. The fullness of His *shalom* frees us to accept our limitations and rest in His sufficiency. After all, His voice can make the whole forest of Lebanon dance. Certainly that strength will enable us to dance again too.

For Further Meditation

1. What is the literary and theological purpose of such a poetic crescendo in this psalm?

2. Why should the "mighty heavenly beings" be called upon to sing YHWH's praise?

3. Why is glory due God's name?

4. What does it mean to worship the LORD in the splendor of His holiness?

5. What specific instances in First Testament history are called to mind by the "voice of YHWH" passages?

6. How does the fact that YHWH was enthroned over the flood enable me to trust His enthronement over all inundating situations in my life?

7. How does the fact that YHWH adds *shalom* to the strength that He supplies us make its potential larger for me? Why is the gift of *shalom* such a strengthening gift?

27

Comfort Even When
There Is No Assurance

So I remained utterly silent,
   not even saying anything good,
But my anguish increased;
   my heart grew hot within me.
While I meditated, the fire burned;
   then I spoke with my tongue:
"Show me, LORD, my life's end
   and the number of my days;
   let me know how fleeting my life is.
You have made my days a mere handbreadth;
   the span of my years is as nothing before you.   *[Selah]*
Everyone is but a breath,
   even those who seem secure.
Surely everyone goes around like a mere phantom;
   in vain they rush about, heaping up wealth,
   without knowing whose it will finally be.
But now, Lord, what do I look for?
   My hope is in you.
Save me from all my transgressions; . . .
Remove your scourge from me;
   I am overcome by the blow of your hand.

> *When you rebuke and discipline people for their sins,*
>   *you consume their wealth like a moth—*
>   *surely everyone is but a breath.*   *[Selah]*
> *"Hear my prayer, LORD,*
>   *listen to my cry for help;*
>   *do not be deaf to my weeping.*
> *I dwell with you as a foreigner,*
>   *a stranger, as all my ancestors were.*
> *Look away from me, that I may enjoy life again*
>   *before I depart and am no more."*

PSALM 39:2-8a, 10-13

We were hiking in the woods. My two older brothers had run on ahead to jump out and scare my parents and me when we caught up. But we had gone to the end of the trail and still had not met them, in spite of all our calling. Were my brothers lost forever?

"No," my dad assured me calmly, "they will be all right." Nothing in the circumstances could convince me of that. But my father had said that my brothers would be safe, so I believed it with all the energy of my five years. He had never been wrong before in my experience, so somehow in my fright I was convinced that he could make everything right.

Part of our loneliness can come from seeing absolutely no basis for assurance. But the poet here in Psalm 39 continues to hope, even though everything seems to be against him. In contrast, only Psalm 88 ends with utter anguish. Describing the bleakest of bleaknesses that psalm ends as follows:

From my youth I have been afflicted and close to death;
   I have suffered your terrors and am in despair.
Your wrath has swept over me;
   your terrors have destroyed me.
All day long they surround me like a flood;
   they have completely engulfed me.
You have taken my companions and loved ones from me;
   the darkness is my closest friend. (Psalm 88:15-18 NIV)

Why should we consider such gloomy psalms in a book that is intended to give comfort and hope and encouragement to those struggling against the ravages of loneliness and depression and grief?

These psalms of despair are encouraging, first of all, because they remind us that we are not alone. Other believers have struggled against seemingly insurmountable odds and yet were able to continue to believe.

However, that would not be sufficient comfort without another truth and another gloomy psalm. Psalm 22 begins with these words:

My God, my God, why have you forsaken me?
   Why are you so far from saving me,
   so far from the words of my groaning?
My God, I cry out by day, but you do not answer,
   by night, but I find no rest.
Yet . . . (Psalm 22:1-3a)

Because this psalm was cried out by the One who changed our lives and destinies for us, we can find comfort in the despairing psalms. Though God seems to have forsaken us or we have no basis for assurance, yet we can trust, knowing the character of the One who speaks to us and knowing how He has cried out for us and what He has done to deliver us from this earth's sufferings.

The morning of the day I first wrote this chapter I was profoundly consoled in my devotional time by the assigned reading from the letter to the Hebrews. Let these words sink deeply into your sorrowing heart or troubled mind:

> Therefore, since we have a great high priest who has ascended into heaven, Jesus the Son of God, let us hold firmly to the faith we profess. For we do not have a high priest who is unable to empathize with our weaknesses, but we have one who has been tempted in every way, just as we are—yet he did not sin. Let us then approach God's throne of grace with confidence, so that we may receive mercy and find grace to help us in our time of need. (Hebrews 4:14-16)

Sometimes we wake up sad. When we try to understand ourselves and get past the grief, we are overwhelmed by our list of sadnesses. Nothing gets sorted, and having no one with whom to share the pain makes us feel all the more lonely. What can the Psalms say to us in the midst of such anguish?

As He carried all our sin and the brokenness of the entire cosmos on Himself, Jesus in His extreme pain of body and soul called out to the God whom He couldn't find. And because He bore that total forsakenness for us, we know that we will never have to experience it. Like the poet in Psalm 39, we may speak out of despair, but we never have to speak out of abandonment. The psalmist recognizes God's chastising, but he also realizes that his sin and human brokenness have caused his state of woe.

You might be saying at this point, "But I haven't sinned. I am the victim"—who has been rejected or deserted or treated cruelly, who has been underprivileged throughout life or has suffered a tragic loss or who has simply wound up alone because of callings and commitments. Yet in the recognition that we are victims in a sinful world and that God is God, we can finally come to peace. It might

not be our particular fault that we are undergoing our present suffering, but human sinfulness brought all this evil into the world—
and we bear undeserved consequences because we can't escape our
basic humanity.

Stay with me while we hammer out this tough theology. I constantly wrestle with it because I always want to understand everything before I can accept circumstances in my life. Why does God let
us go through such horrible tribulation?

Often when piles of things are making me sad, most of the items
on the list are things I can't comprehend. Why didn't my housemate
Julie find a job—didn't God realize how discouraged she was getting?
Why was singing for a wedding bringing back so many distressing
memories? Why couldn't I get past all this grief stuff? Why is there so
much evil and pain in the world?

I was asking these questions even as I typed the first version of this
book because my persistent cough, caused by medicine to prevent
total kidney failure, had become asthmatic and, as a result, had led
to severe inflammation of the cartilage in my rib cage. I was in excruciating pain and couldn't take anti-inflammatory medications or
painkillers because they are hard on the kidneys. Overwhelmed by
the misery, I wondered how I could finish the work.

Into the midst of such wrestling, my friend Linden inserted this
perspective: "I just believe that God is still in control and that He will
bring good out of all things." Toward that simple faith I still grope. I
long for the maturity—and simplicity—of faith that Linden possesses.

Linden's trust that God is in control is all the more profound because he is a quadriplegic, paralyzed by an automobile accident. A
few years younger than I, he has always put me to shame by the
strength of his confidence in God—no matter what happens.

Many phrases in Psalm 39 show evidence of a similar faith, even
in the midst of the poet's grief. The fact of sin, the obstruction of human understanding, and the sureness of God's presence even in the

greatest darkness are truths reinforced by this psalm's progression of thought.

Just after expressing the anguish and the emotional burning that continued even when he was silent, in verse 4 the poet David addresses his God as *YHWH*. He has courage because he knows that his God is the Covenant Keeper. Specifically he asks the LORD to show him his end and the measurement of his days. This is the only place in the First Testament where the idea of measurement is used in terms of time. The psalmist is asking God to put him in touch with how ephemeral life is.

When he looks at the brevity of his life, he requests further instruction. He humbly says to *YHWH*, "Let me know how lacking I (am)." The notion of "lacking" comes from a root meaning "to cease"; it is rarely used as an adjective in the First Testament, as it is here. Such a unique word choice stresses how much we need *YHWH* to show us the inability of our transient existence to perpetuate itself and, consequently, our utter dependence upon Him. When we come to such a point of absolute weakness and submission, then we will reorder our attitudes and be able to look up to the LORD for the gifts that He is able to bring out of even our deepest griefs.

This progression is accentuated in the Hebrew by the emphatic pronoun *I* at the end of the sentence: "The one who lacks is *I*."

Immediately our human pride gets defensive. We object, "But I've been driven low enough. Why does God continue to allow me to be scourged? How does it help me to know my life is finite?" Sometimes we sink to the depths of darkest despair recorded in Psalm 88.

Surely we dare not be superficial in addressing this intense pain and violent anguish through which we pass (as almost everyone does at some point in life). From experience I know that the words, "Well, we must get the right perspective," aren't very comforting. Nevertheless, because we fight so hard against being reduced to the point of total weakness, we don't really believe God for the good purposes He can bring out of the terrible things in our lives.

I learned that lesson a few weeks before writing this chapter, when I taught a class on coping with divorce at a singles conference in Minneapolis. My best qualification for teaching that session was that I hadn't coped very well. The class and I considered the various dimensions of our existence—physical, emotional, social, financial, intellectual, spiritual—and out of our brokenness began to minister to each other. God used the most horrible periods of our lives to equip us to be sensitive to the struggles of others and able to enfold them in grace.

Though I hated the months of dark despair that kept me so deeply depressed for so long (and still those moments struck me occasionally when I first wrote this book), yet I began to realize that God was using even those times to draw me closer to Himself, to teach me invaluable lessons about His love that I never could have learned otherwise, to create in me new discernment and compassion for the many people in the world who suffer in dreadful ways, to increase in me the desire to do something about that pain, and to give me new purpose in my existence and new goals for my life once my old basis of understanding had been destroyed.

Not everything felt good yet as I first typed these pages—my body certainly didn't. But as we learn to believe God for what He is able to do with even the darkest times, we become more able, in turn, to help others through their times of bleakness.

Nevertheless, we need first the humbling, the recognition of the ephemerality of our lives so that they can be placed back into God's hands for His inexplicable and inscrutably wise purposes to bring good out of evil. This is the poet's emphasis: "You have made my days a mere handbreadth; the span of my years is as nothing before you. Everyone is but a breath, even those who seem secure." He is not saying that we aren't worth much. We are incredibly valuable to the God who made us, but we are, after all, mere human beings and not God. As I like to say frequently, God is God, and we are wee. Our minds are too small to grasp the infinite mystery of God's ultimate and infallibly perfect purposes. When we get that straight, we are more able to trust Him in the darkness.

That is why the poet continues, "[A] man is a mere phantom as he goes to and fro: He bustles about, but only in vain; he heaps up wealth, not knowing who will get it" (NIV). Here the Hebrew noun is not the generic word for "person," but the poet holds up a specific man and his ambitions for us to observe. The point is that our frantic human efforts to find worth and meaning through wealth or whatever are empty. The process itself is changed when we begin with the right perspective and priorities. Therefore, the poet next makes this plea: "But now, Lord, what do I look for? My hope is in you. Save me from all my transgressions."

The phrase "surely in vain" or "surely a vapor" occurs in this psalm three times—in verses 5, 6 and 11. Because of that, verse 7 states the alternative simply with the Hebrew introduction "but now." Thereby the poet seems to say, "Therefore, drawing a conclusion from what has just been stated." Since we now have a proper awareness of our transience, what are we looking for?

It seems significant that at this point the poet does not call God by His covenant name. Instead, he uses the word *adonai,* which means "Lord" in the sense of a master or ruler. (The French translate this "Lord" as "le Seigneur" rather than as "l'Éternal.") Even outside of the covenant relationship, the poet recognizes that, after all, God is the Lord or Sovereign One. There is no one else to whom we can look. "My hope," he declares, "to you it." The word *hope* here is derived from the verb *to wait* (which is the root used in the refrain in verses 5 and 11 of Psalm 42 and verse 5 of Psalm 43; see chapter twenty-five). No one else is worth waiting for. Nothing else can give us a hope that does not disappoint (see the context of Romans 5:5).

Nothing else deserves our eager searching.

From our sin we must be freed. Therefore the poet continues, "Save me from all my transgressions." The final word comes from the verb *to rebel*. The poet recognizes that our defiant nature refuses to wait for God to bring good out of our hurts and struggles. We want to work things out by our own methods (sometimes manipulative ones; other times, stubborn resistances), and we thereby block the LORD's guidance and transforming love.

Consequently, the poet concludes with a plea for the LORD to finish His disciplining and then, using the name of the covenant YHWH again, to hear his prayer, to listen to his cry for help, to be not deaf to his weeping. There has been an important progression just before this plea; the poet has moved from saying that each person's *life* is but a breath (v. 5; see the NIV rendition) to admitting that each *person* is but a breath (v. 11). In that recognition we are amazed that YHWH is not deaf to our weeping; our covenant God listens, though we are nothing. Though the poet feels like an alien and a stranger, yet he knows that he dwells with YHWH.

My Hebrew lexicon defines the phrase "with you" from this passage in terms of being "in the service of" or "of the house or family of." Notice that this interpretation implies a close connection, even though David feels like an outsider. This is a key for us in our bleakest times: though we feel like strangers with God, yet He has deigned to make us part of His family. Still He is our covenant God. When we can put our ephemerality and His grace and wisdom into proper perspective, we have made a giant step toward healing.

We can't expect to be out of depression immediately or think that there should be no more suffering or sadness. Wounds are deep, and despair can be profound. Yet our hope is in the LORD, even though with the poet we wish God would look away from us for a moment to give us relief from the truth.

For Further Meditation

1. How do I answer the unanswerable question of why there is suffering in the world?

2. How does it help me to know the transience of my life?

3. How can it be helpful in despair to acknowledge that transience?

4. In what other things do I sometimes place my hope?

5. How do I try to solve my own problems in ways that are not the best? What is the result of trusting my own devices?

6. How can I learn to turn to the LORD when it feels like I am an alien or stranger with Him?

7. How do I know that YHWH will hear my prayer and not be deaf to my weeping?

28

Putting Our Grief into Historical Perspective

I thought about the former days,
  the years of long ago;
I remembered my songs in the night.
  My heart meditated and my spirit asked:
"Will the Lord reject forever?
  Will he never show his favor again?
Has his unfailing love vanished forever?
  Has his promise failed for all time?
Has God forgotten to be merciful?
  Has he in anger withheld his compassion?"   *[Selah]*
Then I thought, "To this I will appeal:
  the years when the Most High stretched out his
    right hand.
I will remember the deeds of the LORD;
  yes, I will remember your miracles of long ago.
I will consider all your works
  and meditate on all your mighty deeds."
Your ways, God, are holy.
  What god is as great as our God?

You are the God who performs miracles;
    you display your power among the peoples.
With your mighty arm you redeemed your people,
    the descendants of Jacob and Joseph.   *[Selah]*

PSALM 77:5-15

I just can't take it any more," I whimpered.

My friend Marguerite gently chided, "I wish I had a tape recording of all the times you have said that and then gone on." She then proceeded to remind me of many of the times in the long trek toward healing when I had become so discouraged that I felt I couldn't handle life anymore. "But each time God gave you the strength to keep going."

Marguerite is one of the friends who helped me most to bear the pain of an unwanted divorce. We met in the congregation for which I worked before I became a freelance teacher. We became good friends because of common interests in Bible study and classical music, but I grew to love her deeply with gratitude for her insightful mind and gentle support. When things had first begun to fall apart in my personal life, she noticed that something was wrong and invited me to talk. Sitting in a rocking chair in her family room, I poured out all the grief that had been bottled up in my heart for so long. Soon her rocking chair became a frequent haven for me, and often as I sat there I cried that I could not go on. Each time her comforting words, empathetic presence, or timely admonishment sustained me and gave me courage. Now as I look back and remember her enormous care, her love stirs me to be sure that the Christian community of which I am now a part works diligently to enfold those in anguish with the consolations and support of God through His people.

It helps us immensely if we can learn to put our grief and loneliness into a historical perspective. In remembering ways that God has helped us in the past, we can find solace for the present and hope for the future.

That is what the poet does in Psalm 77. As the psalmist mourns some unknown distress, he pauses to put his trouble into a larger historical framework so that he can trust God to rescue him from the trial he is presently undergoing.

The poet deals with his gloom and anxious spirit with a firm discipline of mind. The verb *to think* is used in the first verse of this section in an intensified form that suggests deeper consideration or mindfulness. The psalmist focused his thoughts on the past, the previous ages in which God's love had been clearly seen. God's dramatic deeds on behalf of His people were the subject of many songs of faith, to which the poet might be referring when he asserts that he remembered his songs in the night.

His self-discipline is further reflected in the fourth line: "My heart meditated and my spirit asked." The "heart" is used here to mean the inner person, the comprehending mind and will. Though we use it in English simply to signify emotions, the word *heart* in Hebrew, as we have seen, instead emphasizes thinking and reflection, the objective basis for our subjective affections. Thus, to meditate with one's heart suggests contemplation and deeper study.

The word translated "asked" (or "inquired" in the NIV) is an intensification of the Hebrew word *to search*. The noun *spirit* is used in some of the later poems of the First Testament to denote the organ for mental acts, but in the context of this psalm there are also connotations of a troubled disposition. When the poet struggles against his doubts and fears and wonderings, he responds to that disquiet in his spirit with disciplined searching for the truth.

This offers us a wonderful model, very much in keeping with all that we have been learning in these meditations on the Psalms. By the grace of God we can prevent ourselves from becoming so overwhelmed by our emotions that our faith is incapacitated. With the support and encouragement of others in the Christian community, we can deal with ourselves in our grief by putting things into God's perspective and thereby finding comfort and hope.

Next, the poet asks six profound rhetorical questions. Each one is so worded that we want to shout negations of utter disbelief: *"No! Of course not! Who could imagine such a thing? We know better."* Carefully listen to these questions in an awkward but more literal translation that more clearly and starkly emphasizes their point:

Will the Lord reject us to everlastingnesses?
Will He not ever again be pleased with us any more?
Has His *chesedh* [loving-kindness and steadfast faithfulness]
    ceased to perpetuity?
Has the word come to an end for age upon age?
Has He forgotten to show favor [or bestow His loving
    redemption]—God?
Or has He shut up in anger His compassions? *Selah*

The word *Selah* at the end of the strophe causes us to pause, too, and consider these questions. They stir us almost to an angry response. Our God isn't like that. Could God forget to show favor—God? That would be a contradiction in terms. No! He hasn't forgotten. No! this can't last forever. No! He hasn't closed up His compassions toward us.

The poet discloses how ridiculously obvious the answers to those rhetorical questions are when he continues with an appeal to the many "years when the Most High stretched out his right hand." This name is often used for God in the Psalms, and the entire phrase refers to all the time that all Israel, including the poet, has spent in the place of intimacy and fellowship with this highest and only God.

We worry about loneliness or grief in terms of months or even years; in contrast, we need to learn the habit of remembering the LORD's love in terms of scores of years and centuries and eons. Think for a while of your own history. How has God led your family through crisis and through difficult circumstances in order to preserve them? How have you personally seen His faithful love over the long haul?

For example, I think of how my grandmother as a young girl escaped with her family from Russia, wandered all over Europe, went to South America, and finally wound up in Canada, where she married her eighth-grade teacher. Consequently, my father and many relatives have all been dedicated Lutheran educators, so that the love of the Scriptures has been in my bones since childhood. God led me from teaching literature of the Bible at a university, through the back door into campus ministry, then into a parish, and finally into freelancing, through many years of loneliness and several graduate degrees in various theological fields and then—surprise of all surprises—into the bliss of marriage to a faithful man who loves me profoundly and cares for me even as my handicaps escalate.

What gratitude is stirred when we look back over the years that the Most High has stretched out His right hand on our behalf! Even if members of your family are not people of faith, I am sure that you can see God's protecting and guiding hand in some of the events that have brought you to your present position in life.

In the next four lines, the poet uses four different Hebrew words (in the TNIV rendition, "deeds," "miracles," "works," and "mighty deeds") to name the actions of the LORD. The Hebrew writers often group things in fours to stress universality—as if to name the four corners of the earth and thereby to include everything else in between. One sees this arranging of fours especially in the book of Revelation, where the writer John declares that God saves a great multitude from every "nation, tribe, people and language" (Revelation 7:9

and elsewhere). The set of four terms here in Psalm 77 underscores the awareness that God does everything that is necessary for the sake of His people.

Notice that only in the first line of these four is the name *YHWH* used in this psalm. Significantly, here the psalmist recounts deeds as the works of a Covenant God, who faithfully provides the "deeds" required to care for the people He chose for Himself.

The first and the last words for His works ("deeds" and "mighty deeds") are unusual because they both come from a Hebrew root that is usually associated with bad practices. The word for "mighty deeds" actually means "wantonnesses." Just as a prostitute is too generous with herself, so God's goodness is so outrageously profligate that He seems sinfully wanton with it. We observed this word in chapter twenty-three used negatively to describe the evil deeds in which we don't want to become involved.

This powerful image proclaims that God is prodigal with His blessings and benefits. But when we think about our own histories, that seems to be a good description. God is absolutely crazy in how much He loves us. Some people might be offended at the use of such words to portray the holy God, but the poet wants to shock us into the awareness that truly it makes no sense for the LORD to love us with such scandalous generosity.

The second word, translated "miracles" in the TNIV, literally means "extraordinaries" and denotes things hard to comprehend because they fill us with so much awe (see chapter twenty-two).

Only the third word is an ordinary one. It simply means "works" or "doings." In that very simplicity, however, it reminds us that God does everything—even the unadorned little things that we might think were too low for Him. Thus the poet promises, "I will meditate on all your works" (NIV).

"Remember," in this set of four lines about *YHWH*'s works, can also signify causing to be remembered, praising them publicly, mentioning them to others to commemorate them. The poet might gather us to recall with him the ways in which the LORD has acted. "Meditate" and "consider," on the other hand, underscore the value of private musing upon the prodigality of God's works.

Notice all the thinking that is involved. The New Testament similarly emphasizes the renewal of our minds (see, for example, Romans 12:1-2).[1] The poet urges us to be more objective about our troubles so that we can put them into a godly and more comforting perspective.

The psalmist summarizes all his discoveries about the actions of God in the sentence, "Your ways, God, are holy." Our own attitudes sometimes are not. The Hebrew text is a bit more dramatic without a verb—"O God, in holiness your way." The true God's moral administration of the universe is founded in His perfection and sacredness. Consequently, we can all recognize that there is no other god so great as He. When the poet asks, "What god is as great as our God?" this last rhetorical question with the earlier ones brings the sum of seven to completion. All seven of the questions are answered by all the evidence of ancient, past, present, and future history.

After all, God is the one who is doing the wonders, the poet continues. He makes His strength known among all the peoples by taking care of His own children, the descendants of Jacob and Joseph. As we pause at the *Selah* after this strophe, we consider why in this place Israel is referred to as the descendants of Jacob and Joseph. The name *Jacob* records the people's lineage in the covenant relationship of *YHWH* with Abraham, Isaac and Jacob, but perhaps also it is intended here to suggest the deceptiveness of the nation's forebear and remind us that God chose Israel not because they deserved it. *Joseph,* on the other hand, calls to mind God's care for Jacob's son as his brothers sold him into slavery and God's subsequent surprising pro-

---

[1]Also see a deeper explication of this text in chapters one through seven of my book *Truly the Community.*

vision for the Israelites in Egypt as He then used Joseph to save the world through his wise storing of grain for the time of famine.

This designation for the people is a fitting prelude to the next several verses, which recount other deeds as God led His people out of the Egyptian captivity. The poet goes on to hint in vivid terms at the crossing of the Red Sea, the covenant promises of Sinai, the crossing of the Jordan, the leadership of Moses and Aaron. Certainly if God so led His people through all those events of the exodus, He can lead them now—perhaps out of the Babylonian captivity or whatever else might be the occasion for the poet's writing.

Because we do not know the specific historical setting of this poem, we can perhaps more easily transfer its point into our own particular circumstances. Pausing to tell our faith story, to remember how God took care of His people in the past, we immerse ourselves in a historical perspective that enables us to cope with our own griefs and troubles in these times.

When Israel crossed the Jordan River miraculously to enter into the Promised Land, the LORD told the people to gather stones for each tribe and to build an altar as a memorial. Joshua told them to do this "to serve as a sign among you. In the future, when your children ask you, 'What do these stones mean?' tell them that the flow of the Jordan was cut off before the ark of the covenant of the LORD. . . . These stones are to be a memorial to the people of Israel forever" (Joshua 4:6-7).

Because of this and other First Testament stories, we are encouraged to create memorials to help us remember how God has worked on behalf of His people in the past. During my years of grief and intense loneliness, I would sometimes write a poem or learn a song or buy a book and inscribe it with significant events in my spiritual life, physical circumstances, or emotional healing. Whenever I looked at that memorial, I could remember the LORD's deeds of "long ago" and be encouraged for the present. Whenever we review the past, we

have to come to this conclusion: "Your ways, O God, are holy." Grief
put into historical perspective is bearable. When we ask, "How can I
go on?" the answer is the same as the last time: "The LORD will give
you the strength." We know that He will; we have seen it happen time
and again.

For Further Meditation

1. To what events in my life might I build a memorial to remember
   God's deeds? How have I seen God's action in the history of my
   family, nation, people or faith community?

2. What is the importance of my mind in coping with grief or sorrow?

3. How would I answer the seven questions the poet asks?

4. In what ways have God's acts been profligate for me? Do they
   seem *wanton?*

5. What does it mean to call God's ways holy? How are they set
   apart?

6. What stories about Israel appeal to me as good examples of God's
   dealing with His people in their history?

7. What habits of meditation would I like to develop so that my perspective about my life can be more thoroughly grounded in the
   objective truths of many more years?

29

YHWH Will Give Us
the Desires of Our Hearts

Trust in the LORD *and do good;*
dwell in the land and enjoy safe pasture.
Take delight in the LORD
and he will give you the desires of your heart.
Commit your way to the LORD*;*
trust in him and he will do this:
He will make your righteous reward shine like the dawn,
your vindication like the noonday sun.

PSALM 37:3-6

One kind of loneliness strikes when we feel as though we're the only ones trying to bring about justice in a messed-up world. Against the economic chaos and political machinations of our world, we seem to be the only ones trying to remove the causes of poverty and crime, to lessen the gap between the rich and poor, to secure honesty in high office. How will our cause be vindicated? When we get discouraged, everything and everyone around us seem corrupt.

Psalm 37 is a wisdom poem that announces vindication; it is written in the form of an acrostic, in which every verse begins with the next letter of the Hebrew alphabet. We must see the few verses that we are considering here in light of the context of the whole psalm.

Throughout Psalm 37 the phrase *do not fret* occurs frequently. In the introductory verses, the wise poet reminds us that we don't have to fret first of all because the evil ones, like the grass, will soon wither away. (See our study of Psalm 73 in chapter eighteen for related ideas concerning our reactions to those who choose wrong.) As Isaiah 40:6 and 8 insist, all flesh is grass.[1]

After that encouraging reminder to avoid worrying, the poet now turns to the positive side in the verses before us and tells us what to do instead. His plan for action might not change our condition of being alone, but it can turn our painful loneliness into beneficial solitude.

First of all, he urges us to trust in the LORD, a phrase that we have seen often before (in chapter one, for example), and then he exhorts us to do good. The significant order here reminds us that we don't do good out of our ability to accomplish it, but out of our trusting. Our relationship with *YHWH* enables us to produce what is morally good and of benefit to others. Though the Hebrew verb for "doing" basically signifies accomplishing or performing, it sometimes carries added connotations of creating. The phrase "do good," then, implies an invitation to cooperate with the Creator in accomplishing His purposes in the world.

The second poetic line invites us to inhabit the land and enjoy safe pasture. I enjoy the New American Standard Bible's translation of this sentence because it stresses that when we "dwell in the land," we can "cultivate faithfulness," or as the NASB adds in the footnotes, "feed securely" or "feed on His faithfulness." The Hebrew text emphasizes feeding upon faithfulness in the sense of consuming, or taking pleasure in, or nourishing oneself by steadfastness or fidelity.

---

[1]See chapters six through eight of my book *To Walk and Not Faint*.

The TNIV rendering, "safe pasture," gives us a picture of this hope. When the Israelites entered their Promised Land, they were counseled to live within the provisions and principles of the covenant with YHWH that would enable them to be secure in that land. Their pastures would be safe if they continued being faithful to God's call and commands for justice and compassion.

Another implication of the text is that those who dwell in the land are able to observe in the seasons of rain and sunshine and in the harvest the faithfulness of YHWH. Thus, the safety of the pasture is more deeply enjoyed by those who recognize the LORD who makes it secure.

For those of us who read this psalm in the twenty-first century, these words can continue to convey a sense of security. Though few of us live in the countryside where we could know the value of safe pastures, in these days of terrorism and volatile economics we do yearn for the stability that the image offers. We can rely on the fidelity of our God. As long as we are trusting Him and in Him, we will be empowered to do good, to dwell wherever He has called us, and to enjoy being nourished by His steadfastness even as we seek to pass His good gifts on to others.

This ties in very closely with the psalm's next point: that kind of security in the faithfulness of the LORD is much more available to those who supremely delight in Him. We must intensify the NIV rendering, "Delight yourself in the LORD," because the Hebrew accentuates taking *exquisite* delight in Him. The Hebrew word is an intensive reflexive (Hithpael) form of a verb that means "to be of dainty habit." This does not depict believers as effeminate or wishy-washy; rather, the word suggests that their delight is so sensitive that it catches the softest nuances of God's love.

That idea challenges us as Christians to grow so close to the LORD that we would be delicately aware of His presence and guidance and gifting in even the tiniest circumstances of our lives. In this way we would delight in Him much more thoroughly.

Once when I was explaining this notion for a church in Seattle, a participant at the seminar told me of a time during his visit to New Zealand when a very delicate tea was served. Most of the U.S. tourists loaded it with sugar and cream and then complained that it had no flavor. Similarly, he said, many Christians load up their lives with the sugars and creams of luxuries and entertainments and then are unable to see the exquisite ways in which God is working in their lives.

We who live in such a wealthy and wasteful country have so many things and so many varieties of things that we have lost our appreciation for them. We clutter our houses with too many possessions rather than thoroughly enjoying a few. The unsatisfied longing in our lives keeps us thinking we need more; consequently, we don't cherish the finer points of what we have. Even in our accomplishments, we start thinking about greater goals and become dissatisfied.

In our spiritual lives, we frequently do not delight so thoroughly in the LORD that He is the whole focus of our existence. Consequently, we find it difficult to enjoy the present delicacies of His relationship with us.

Notice that when we do delight ourselves in *YHWH,* He will give us the desires of our hearts. That is because our intentional desires will be His. The closer we are to God, the more we will want only what He wants.

We might have to wrestle with this truth, especially when we are lonely. We may believe we want our desires to be *YHWH's* desires, but still we might think, "Why does it have to be this way, LORD? Why can't you give me someone to ease my loneliness?" Perhaps we can't yet accept the brokenness of the present as we learn to await the ultimate fulfillment of what might be His best purposes for us. If we were thoroughly delighted with Him in the first place, our deepest need would be satisfied, and then other supposed needs wouldn't grow so horrendously out of proportion.

We dare not be glib, however, or give merely superficial comfort to others to ease the pain of their lonely longings. The fact that God will give us the desires of our hearts is a truth we might know in our heads, but often don't feel. Nevertheless, to proclaim this truth can encourage us to keep going on in the struggle to believe it. We will come to the point someday of resting in that truth and finding our longings stilled with the deepest *shalom*.

The psalm's next phrase, which the TNIV translates "Commit your way to the LORD," is in the Hebrew a very graphic image—"Roll unto YHWH your way." To roll it as one rolls stones into a groove puts our way firmly into place. Then we can't grab it back and continue to fret about it. If we thoroughly roll our conduct or mode of life or concerns upon YHWH and trust in Him, the poet continues, then He will act. As long as we are hanging on to some things, we are preventing Him from accomplishing His purposes. How much are we holding God up by our stubborn insistence that we know better how to do things?

Most translations conclude verse 5 with a colon, so that the phrase "he will do this" leads directly into the statement that He will make our "righteousness" (NIV) shine like the dawn. That connection is undoubtedly true; one of the things that He will do is make our uprightness gleam. However, I think that we limit the psalm too much if we tie those two poetic lines together insistently. Especially because the verb *to do* is the same one that appeared in the phrase "do good" in verse 3, we could simply say that if we roll our way unto the LORD, then He will act. Not only will He make our righteousness shine like the dawn—although definitely that—but also He will accomplish much more. He will take care of everything that is associated with our "way." When we trust Him, we can "do good" because He is the one doing it through us.

The NASB does not tie the two verses so closely together, but simply states that when we trust in the LORD "He will do it." The word *it* could mean anything, and that is a good ambiguity. God will do whatever our desires require, because when we thoroughly commit everything to Him and are exquisitely delighting in Him, then what we desire will be His good purposes entirely.

Specifically, one of His good purposes will be to make our righteousness shine like the dawn. When we care for the needy, protest military aggression, shelter the homeless, or fight other injustices in our society, our causes will be vindicated. Look at the humble order of sisters of Mother Teresa (I finished proofreading the earlier edition of this chapter the day after she died), or World Vision hospitals that survived the purgings of vicious dictators in such places as Cambodia, or the mission of MAP International to provide equipment and medicines in destitute countries, or the work of the Salvation Army in inner cities. As Isaiah 58:7-8 promises, when you work to "share your food with the hungry and to provide the poor wanderer with shelter—when you see the naked, to clothe them, and not to turn away from your own flesh and blood[,] Then your light will break forth like the dawn, and your healing will quickly appear; then your righteousness will go before you, and the glory of the LORD will be your rear guard."

Moreover, as the parallel poetic line affirms, the justice of our cause will be like the noonday sun. The Hebrew is actually plural, which suggests that the sunshine is intensified so much that its glow seems like "noons." The Jerusalem Bible renders the phrase "making your virtue clear as the light, your integrity as bright as noon." The words *virtue* and *integrity* stress the character, the goodness and wholeness of righteousness and justice. God will certainly vindicate us with the blazing light of justice so that His truth will be clear to everyone.

Notice, finally, that again it is the LORD who accomplishes this, for indeed it is He (emphatic pronoun in the Hebrew) who is doing the acting. He will exhibit our righteousness as a light to the world. The verb in this verse especially underscores that He publishes the justice of our cause or thoroughly vindicates us.

The accent in all this is on the invitation to us to keep on keeping on—doing good, being righteous and just, committing (rolling) our way to YHWH, and trusting that the publishing, the vindicating, the results of all our efforts are up to Him. All we need to be concerned about is that we are thoroughly delighting in the LORD so that the deepest desires of our being are tied in with His faithfulness.

For Further Meditation

1. Why is the order of "Trust in the LORD and do good" so important?

2. How do I nourish myself with faithfulness?

3. What is it like to take exquisite delight in YHWH?

4. What are the deepest desires of my heart?

5. What matters have I "rolled" unto YHWH? What matters have I taken back? Why?

6. How has my righteousness been made by God to shine like the dawn?

7. What do I do if my justice is not vindicated? Has YHWH failed me then?

30

When I Fret and Fall, There Is *Shalom*

Be still before the LORD
   and wait patiently for him;
do not fret when people succeed in their ways,
   when they carry out their wicked schemes. . . .
The LORD makes firm the steps
   of those who delight in him;
though they stumble, they will not fall,
   for the LORD upholds them with his hand. . . .
Consider the blameless, observe the upright;
   a future awaits those who seek peace.

PSALM 37:7, 23-24, 37

Rest in the LORD and wait patiently for Him;
   Fret not yourself because of him who prospers in his way,
   Because of the man who carries out wicked schemes. . . .
The steps of a man are established by the LORD;
   And He delights in his way.
When he falls, he shall not be hurled headlong;
   Because the LORD is the One who holds his hand. . . .
Mark the blameless man, and behold the upright;
   For the man of peace will have a posterity.

PSALM 37:7, 23-24, 37 NASB (1963)

Usually in our agitations it is impossible to be quiet. When we cannot be restful, we are not very able to wait patiently before the LORD. The result is that we miss many of His gifts because we are too frantic to hear His voice.

I like to call my devotional practices "quiet time" to remind me that this block of time is set apart for being still before the LORD in order to hear God, so that my ways are not my own devising. All these verses from scattered parts of Psalm 37 deal with the need for those who are struggling against the wickedness of evil to learn to rest in the LORD. These verses can be especially helpful in coping with loneliness because they bring us the intimate presence of a God who cares enough to sustain us in these tough times. His presence transforms our being alone into a solitude that actively listens, rather than a loneliness that passively suffers.

The first phrase in Hebrew urges us to "be silent to *YHWH*," in the sense of the opposite of activity and motion or speech. Sometimes this happens naturally, as when a person is astounded in amazement or fear and therefore is still before the LORD. The idea is like that of resignation, but without any of its negative connotations. Perhaps "Acceptance-with-Joy" (a phrase in Hannah Hurnard's *Hind's Feet on High Places*) is a better designation.

The verb that the TNIV translates "wait patiently" comes from a Hebrew root that means "to dance or whirl" and is used at times to depict severe pain, as at childbirth. In the form used here, it means "to suffer or writhe in torture" or "to wait with profound longing." Patience is implied in this waiting, but it is also filled with the tension of yearning for release, even as a mother writhes through labor as she awaits the birth of her child.

That image has deep significance for our spiritual lives. We live in the in-between times—days and years between the moment or progression when Christ became the center and focus of our existence and the time when He will come again or we will die and go home to be with Him. So how do we live in the meanwhile?

Christ didn't call us to any easy Christianity, a comfortable "I'm saved" lifestyle that isn't intensely wrapped up in the work of His kingdom. Rather, as we wait for our LORD to come back, we wait with eager longing and anguish, for often what surrounds us is corrupted. Our own loneliness accentuates the brokenness of the world around us. When it is transformed instead into solitude that listens to YHWH, we acquire the courage and power to participate in His present purposes of righteousness and justice as we wait for His final triumph.

Next, the poet encourages us to lay aside our fretting "when people succeed in their ways." The original verb root for "fret" means "to be kindled" and is often used in connection with anger. Thus the phrase encourages us not to burn ourselves out in vexation at the wickedness of human beings. We must, of course, do some careful distinguishing. We *should* be angry—and not just mildly—against injustice, such as world hunger, for example.

Nevertheless, our frustrations with the wickednesses around us must serve only for kindling purposes, to encourage our active involvement in fighting evil, not to start a huge fire of vexation that burns out of control and immobilizes us. Our efforts to combat evil will become overwhelming and hopeless if we forget that ultimately God is in control of the world.

We are not to fret, the poet urges, when people succeed "in their ways, when they carry out their wicked schemes." That depravity seems to triumph is a reality, and a very painful one. However, those who love the LORD know a greater truth, in which we find our composure and are guided to channel our energies constructively. If it seems that the wicked are prospering in their evil ways, it is all the more imperative that we not be immobilized by it. Rather, as we learn to let YHWH establish our steps, they will be more effective in combating injustices.

The word order in the NASB rendition of verse 23 matches more closely the original Hebrew text, which begins with "from *YHWH* the steps of a man are established"; *YHWH*'s name comes first. When we make our relationship with the LORD our top priority, then our course of life is constituted so that we will live out what we know more faithfully. The verb about being established is from a root signifying being firm. In its form here and in the perfect tense (which implies completed action), the word stresses preparation and fixing. If we can learn to be silent before *YHWH,* He will not be thwarted in His purpose to guide us and firmly root our ways.

Once when I was traveling on a ferry, a restful moment of silent contemplation of the sea allowed an organizing principle to surface in my thinking, and the result was that everything I'd been mulling over for days clicked into place. By the time the boat reached its dock, my teaching outline for the next week was prepared. Experiences like this help us see that only in stillness can we receive the guidance the LORD has prepared to give us.

The second half of Psalm 37:23 can be read in two ways as demonstrated by the translations above. One reading promises that *YHWH* will make firm the steps of those who delight in Him. The other promises that the LORD delights in our way because we walk in the steps He has established. Moreover, says the poet, not only do we know the encouragement of His delight in us or the firmness of our steps because we delight in Him, but also we can be sure that we will never be destroyed while seeking to be obedient to God's purposes. The Hebrew text pledges, "Though he fall, never will he be hurled headlong."

A person might fall from weakness or battle wounds, but he or she will not be hurled away like a pot to be shattered. Such protection from utter destruction reminds us of this hopeful sequence from Paul's second letter to the Corinthians:

We are hard pressed on every side, but not crushed; perplexed, but not in despair; persecuted, but not abandoned; struck down, but not destroyed. (2 Corinthians 4:8-9)

J. B. Phillips paraphrases the passage in this way:

We are handicapped on all sides, but we are never frustrated; we are puzzled, but never in despair. We are persecuted, but we never have to stand it alone: we may be knocked down, but we are never knocked out!

The next line of the psalm tells us *why* we can know for sure that we will not be annihilated, though we might have to suffer. *YHWH* upholds with His hand the one whose steps He is establishing. The verb *upholds* encourages us with the promise that we can lean or rest on God, who will always support us; its participial form stresses the continuing nature of *YHWH's* sustaining action.

Since the Hebrew word for "his-hand" has no preposition with it, we cannot be certain whether the word is referring to *YHWH's* hand or to the believers'. The TNIV assumes the former and states that "the LORD upholds them with his hand." The NASB, on the other hand (pun intended), assumes the latter and translates it "the LORD is the one who holds his hand."

With either interpretation the comfort is tender. *YHWH* supports us with His intimate attention. The tangible idea of the hand's anthropomorphic image gives us a human picture to describe an aspect of God who is spirit and therefore doesn't have a hand except metaphorically. This picture conveys an individualized reaching out to hold us personally. God doesn't just dump out a bunch of upholding and hope so that we can catch some for ourselves.

If the hand in the text is our own, the personal touch is still there. God doesn't just drop some support out there under our feet or push us from behind; He takes us by our hand to draw us after

Himself into His purposes and out of dangers.

In these pictures the LORD is both capable of healing us and perfectly willing to do so. This is made explicit in Psalm 62, in which the poet declares this truth:

> One thing God has spoken,
>> two things I have heard:
> "Power belongs to you, God,
>> and with you, Lord, is unfailing love." (Psalm 62:11-12a)

God has both the power to heal and the love to accomplish it.

The poet of Psalm 37 has had ample time to observe these qualities of the LORD. He notes in verse 25, just following our section, that he is now old and has never seen the righteous forsaken. Then in the next several verses he continues his words of wisdom to the young and advises them to turn away from evil and to watch out for the wicked.

The last line of our excerpt, verse 37, summarizes well the message of the psalm. The poet urges us, "Consider the blameless, observe the upright; a future awaits those who seek peace" *(shalom)*. Rather than to warriors, there will be a future to those who seek peace instead.

Remember from chapter twenty-six that a person of *shalom* lives in right relationship with God and, therefore, in right relationship with himself or herself and with others. That kind of person—one who is tranquil and contented and fulfilled and whole—does indeed have a "posterity." That last word could refer either specifically to children, as the New English Bible and the Jerusalem Bible translate it, or simply to a future. The word is used sometimes as a poetic parallel to the word *hope,* so it emphasizes that all dimensions of the future will eventually turn into good for the person of *shalom*.

For this reason the poet urges his listeners to "consider the blameless." The NASB challenges us to "mark" such a one. We should use our intelligence to observe what happens to such persons of God so that we might be inspired by their example. The ones we are to watch are those who are complete—the morally innocent, the ones having integrity.

Similarly, we are to "behold the upright" (NASB), in the sense of perceiving or understanding those who are virtuous. This same word, *upright,* has been used in verse 14 to signify those who are being persecuted by the wicked, but this psalm emphasizes that they are afflicted only for a little while. These troubles will soon be over, for there is a future, ultimately, for the person of *shalom.*

These verses invite us to be a part of that future, to steady ourselves by listening to *YHWH.* When we are silent before Him, He is not hindered. Our own solitude can help us learn to be still and listen. The more we observe those who have integrity, the more we will follow their example and rest in the wholeness that *YHWH* delights to establish for us.

For Further Meditation

1. When during the day am I silent before *YHWH*? What could I do to make my "quiet time" more a time of genuine listening?

2. Do I wait longingly for God's purposes to be fulfilled? Why or why not?

3. When have I experienced burnout because of vexation? How could I avoid that problem?

4. How have I seen that *YHWH* has established my steps?

5. How have I experienced the fact that, though I might fall, I will not be hurled headlong—or, as Paul says, that I might be struck down, but never struck out?

6. What have I learned from the models of persons of integrity?

7. What does the term *posterity* mean for me as it is promised to the person of *shalom*? Why is *shalom* such an important aspect of God's promise?

31

So Now I Can't Keep It to Myself

I waited patiently for the LORD;
*   he turned to me and heard my cry. . . .*
He put a new song in my mouth,
*   a hymn of praise to our God.*
Many will see and fear the LORD
*   and put their trust in him.*
Blessed are those
*   who make the LORD their trust,*
who do not look to the proud,
*   to those who turn aside to false gods.*
Many, LORD my God,
*   are the wonders you have done.*
*   the things you planned for us.*
None can compare with you;
*   were I to speak and tell of your deeds,*
*   they would be too many to declare.*
Sacrifice and offering you did not desire—
*   but my ears you have opened—*
*   burnt offerings and sin offerings you did not require. . . .*
"I desire to do your will, my God;
*   your law is within my heart."*
I proclaim your saving acts in the great assembly;
*   I do not seal my lips, LORD,*

as you know.
I do not hide your righteousness in my heart;
  I speak of your faithfulness and your saving help.
I do not conceal your love and your faithfulness
  from the great assembly.

PSALM 40:1, 3-6, 8-10

In funny ways the LORD uses the circumstances of our lives to speak of His love to others! After ten months of morning devotions in which I studied the Psalms as a source for healing, I finally knew roughly the general content of each of them enough to think about all 150 of them one at a time while I swam lengths in the pool. On the Tuesday before Thanksgiving, I "swam through" the whole book of Psalms twice. Though a bit more than four and a quarter miles was an exercise record for me then, the greater value lay in meditating on the Psalms, once to review their content and once as a vehicle for prayer. When I finished, I felt so exhilarated by the Joy of that meditation time that I kidded with friends about trying to swim seven miles in May—since seven is the biblical number for perfection.

Suddenly it seemed silly to wait until May when I was already in shape for it, so two weeks later, meditating on the Psalms gave me strength to do seven miles. My swimming partner had (to my great dismay) told the local newspaper about my attempt, and they decided, because of my multiple handicaps, to do a special-interest story. Consequently, when I finished five hundred lengths, I was greeted not only by a few friends, but also by a photographer from the paper and a reporter, who asked me first why I had done it. That opened up the opportunity for witness.

My goals in the swim had been to know God better, to challenge my memory in meditating on the Psalms, and to use the Scriptures for emotional healing, as well as to prove to myself my own physical fitness in spite of debilitating handicaps. When the story appeared in the newspaper two days later, the swim also became a wonderful means for speaking to my home community about the love of God. Four months later I did a ten-mile swim to raise money to pay heating bills for the unemployed, and it was an even greater opportunity to bring God's love to bear on a particular problem in our society.

Out of my loneliness and the gift of the Psalms came ministry. That had been the story all along. God kept turning around things that caused me pain and continued to use them as vehicles for witness and service. That is also the message of Psalm 40. This psalm includes a lament—in fact, the lament is repeated almost exactly as the seventieth poem in the Psalter. But Psalm 40 also begins with a hymn of praise as the poet's response to all the good things that God has brought out of his trouble. When David declares that he had waited patiently for the LORD and that YHWH had turned to him, heard his cry, and lifted him out of the pit, he sets the scene for the praises that follow.

I am ashamed, however, when I read the opening phrase of the psalm, since I've never been very able to accept waiting. After all he went through, how could David say, "I waited patiently"? Yet the literal Hebrew idiom reads, "To wait for, I waited for YHWH." Its special infinitive absolute form stresses the hope and patience involved until the waiting ended in deliverance. The result of that deliverance, in turn, was witness, which is recorded in several ways that we will consider here.

The first expression of witness comes immediately after the poet's description of God's deliverance. He declares that YHWH "put a new song in my mouth, a hymn of praise to our God." Notice that YHWH places the song in his mouth. That correlates with several New Tes-

tament passages that promise us that we do not need to worry about
what we will say, for the Holy Spirit will give us the what and the how ·
(see, for example, Matthew 10:19-20). God is in charge of creating
our songs; He enables us to praise and witness.

God did indeed put new songs in my mouth when the reporter
asked me why I had swum seven miles. Praise came easily because so
very obviously the whole situation had been created by God. He had
given me the strength to swim through the Psalms on which I meditated—and thus God was the Giver of both the words to contemplate
for empowerment and the words to describe it.

Next, David tells us that from a new song of praise "many will see
and fear the LORD and put their trust in him." After the newspaper
article on my swim appeared, a few lonely people called for support.
(I had mentioned that I was working on this book on the Psalms.)
Various friends told me how the story had encouraged them and
stimulated their faith. A pastor in town referred to the article in his
sermon the next Sunday in order to urge his parishioners to study the
Scriptures. In so many ways God can use things we would never expect as vehicles of praise to draw people closer to Himself. Some of
the new songs He creates might seem odd to us, but He has good pur- .
poses behind them.

The fourth verse adds a necessary warning: blessedness, it declares, lies in making the LORD one's trust, not in turning to the
proud or to those falling away to a lie. This is accentuated by the
use here of the gendered word for "strong man" rather than the generic "person." Those who are more likely to rely on themselves will
indeed be blessed when instead they recognize the illusion of such
dependency. Some scholars think that the word for "proud" is a
scribal error and should read "the Baalim," the name for the false
gods of the cultures surrounding Israel. This passage does later contain a specific warning against idolatry, but at this point let's not
miss its warning to seek humility.

How easily we forget our proper place! The incident of the newspaper story forced me to recognize the danger of pride when people commented to me about the "great feat" of swimming so far. I was constantly grateful for this psalm's reminder that blessedness lies in making the LORD our trust. My "swimming the Psalms" project had been intended from the beginning as a way to learn to know the LORD better, both intellectually and spiritually, and to receive His healing for my physical and emotional being. Consequently, I wanted to make sure that credit went where credit was due.

The LORD is always to be our confidence. We dare never let ourselves get caught up in complacent pride and must be wary always of that temptation. I want to be sure that even my motives in telling you about the swimming incident are to illustrate the ideas of witness in this psalm and not to make you think well of me. See what a subtle danger there always is? Our human nature of self-centeredness would certainly like to corrupt everything if it could.

The psalm's second warning is against trusting in those "who turn aside to false gods," or as the TNIV footnote says, "to lies." Manuscript evidence seems to favor the second interpretation. Either way, the warning is necessary.

Our culture surrounds us with temptations everywhere to turn to lies. For example, since our society places so much emphasis on physical beauty, the spiritual benefits of my swimming meditation times could get lost if I got caught up in the advantages for my fitness instead. We dare not trust in our physical strength instead of in the LORD.

Psalm 147:10-11 is a good caution against that. Those verses remind us that the LORD's "pleasure is not in the strength of the horse, nor his delight in the power of human legs; the LORD delights in those who fear him, who put their hope in his unfailing love." Of course, we are healthier if we stay in shape as much as possible, and God is glorified when we take good care of our bodies, which are His temple. Ultimately, however, physical well-being could hardly be what pleases God about us. The LORD wants us to fear Him, to hope in His *chesedh* (defined in chapter one) and to trust in Him rather than in ourselves.

I couldn't rely on my own strength once I had "proved" it. In fact, as I was thinking through the Psalms the day of the long swim, I realized more than ever how dependent everything in life is upon the gracious provision of our Father, whose care we can't live without. I became more grateful for all the medicines that remind me constantly that my life is totally dependent.

Many other lies in the world tempt us to turn away from trusting in *YHWH*. We easily get swept into political illusions, the deceptions of Mammon, the fascinating promises of newer technologies.[1] However, the poet shows us that a genuine reflection upon God's works will soon turn us back to recognizing His supremacy and the emptiness of the world's deceits. In the process we are also taken back again to the theme of witness, of evangelism.

When the poet assesses what God has done, he realizes that the latter has accomplished many wonders. We encountered this noun in Psalm 139 (see chapter twenty-two). It describes those deeds that fill a person with awe because they are so extraordinary. God's works appear impossible to us, so we are filled with amazement. The things that *YHWH* has planned for us "no one can recount" (NIV). The LORD's marvels are so astounding that we realize that "none can compare" with *YHWH*, the only true God.

God's gifts and wonders are too many for us to proclaim. His plans

---

[1]See especially the books of Jacques Ellul on these subjects, including *The Political Illusion,* trans. Konrad Kellen (New York: Knopf, 1967); *Money and Power,* trans. LaVonne Neff (Downers Grove, Ill.: InterVarsity Press, 1984); and *The Technological Bluff,* trans. Joyce Main Hanks (Grand Rapids, Mich.: Eerdmans, 1990). See also my books *Sources and Trajectories* and *Unfettered Hope: A Call to Faithful Living in an Affluent Society* (Louisville: Westminster John Knox, 2003).

are too great for us to comprehend (compare Isaiah 55:8-9). We cannot adequately understand them, nor can we thoroughly announce them to the world. His deeds are simply too colossal.

This gives us tremendous confidence as we seek to share with others the good news of faith. We know how easy it is to talk when we have too much to say. If we see a friend after being apart for a long time and have to catch up on everything, words just come pouring out. In the same way, our witness to the wonders of the LORD's doing comes out of the overflow of our lives. As we observe His glorious works, with Joy we proclaim them because their magnificence overwhelms us.

I was exclaiming about that with one of my newest friends on Thanksgiving, two days after the swim. As we discussed God's loving action in our situations, we anticipated using the rest of our lives to keep on learning and sharing such things, yet we will still need all of eternity to comprehend the Joy of it all.

Once again the poet moves to the negative side as he reminds himself and us that *YHWH* does not really desire sacrifices and offerings. The second Hebrew word specifically refers to grain offerings, as opposed to the burnt and sin offerings that are mentioned next. All of these were useful tools for God's chosen people to reenact for them the sacrifices made when God established the covenant with them (see Exodus 24). As we New Testament people look back, we recognize that the sacrifices also pictured the coming of the One who would be the perfect sacrifice, but these offerings served only as tools. The sacrifices themselves could not save the people. Animals and harvests were not really what the LORD wanted from them.

What He wants is still the same today as in the First Testament times. God longs for us to desire to do His will (v. 8). He wants His instruction to be so important to us that we eagerly hold it within our hearts. Though the TNIV uses the translation "heart," the original Hebrew uses a word that we could translate "bowels," signifying the

very midst of a person, in the inward part. This word choice emphasizes that God wants us to hold His instruction in that which is the
source of our emotions. We will not be guided purely subjectively, by
our emotions themselves, but our feelings will be tempered by His
instruction.

When David declares that the training of *YHWH* is at the very core
of his being, I realize how far from that goal I am. God doesn't want
our sacrifices. After all, he owns the cattle on a thousand hills, so why
would he need our extra bullock (as we are told in Psalm 50:7-10)?
YHWH doesn't want our burnt offerings. He wants us. Therefore,
Paul urges us to "offer [our] bodies as a living sacrifice, holy and
pleasing to God—this is true worship" (Romans 12:1).

David announces in the middle of verse 6, "But my ears you have
opened." God has made it possible for us to hear His perfect will.
Some other translations, including the NIV, say, "My ears you have
pierced." When slaves were set free, yet chose to stay with their masters and serve them, their ears were pierced with an awl to signify
their devotion. God would have us choose to serve Him gladly, even
though His love has set us free. The apostle Paul uses somewhat this
same image in the many places of his letters where he calls himself
the slave of Christ.

Finally in the section of Psalm 40 we are considering, the poet
moves back to a statement about his witness: he continually proclaims *YHWH's* righteousness in the great assembly. As the LORD
knows, he does not seal his lips. The psalmist does not hide *YHWH's*
goodness, but rather speaks of His faithfulness, His salvation, His
steadfast love, His truth. All these themes that we have seen throughout the Psalms are the subject of the poet's praise in the great assembly. He is "not ashamed of the gospel," as Paul would say, for the good
news of God's mercy "is the power of God that brings salvation to everyone who believes" (Romans 1:16).

Notice all the poetic repetitions in these last two verses. The poet's

witness before the worshiping throng both begins and ends the sequence. Several similar verbs repeat the idea of not concealing, not hid-
ing, not suppressing. Once we grasp the immensity of the righteousness and steadfast love and faithfulness and salvation of our God,
it is impossible for us to keep silent about those things. We can't hide
them. They must spring forth and become apparent to those around
us.

This has been my prayer for you throughout this book. Not only
have I wanted to bring God's comfort into your particular life situation against whatever sadness or grief or loneliness oppresses you,
but beyond that my deeper goal is that the comfort of the Psalms be
passed on through you to others. Many around you suffer from the
same kinds of loneliness or sorrow that you are experiencing. If God
has here used the Psalms to touch you with peace and healing, then
let me encourage you to proclaim in the great assembly what He has
done. His wonders are, after all, too many to recount.

If we all get started now telling others about His wonderful works
on our behalf, we won't be finished by the time we get to heaven. And
there we will perfectly praise Him, even as there we will perfectly
know His comfort and hope and peace. Then we will proclaim and
dwell in His truth and faithfulness and righteousness and salvation
and steadfast love into all eternity. There in Joy we will never be
lonely again, and the LORD Himself will wipe away all the tears from
our eyes.

For Further Meditation

1. What new songs has the LORD given me to sing lately? What new
   songs have I discovered since I started reading this book?

2. How have others come to know the LORD more deeply through
   the new songs in my heart?

3. How have I experienced loss of blessedness when I have become

proud?

4. How have I experienced loss of blessedness when I have turned to the deceptions or lies of the world around me or to the false gods that can't give me the security for which I am longing?

5. What happens to my feelings and attitudes when I realize that God's blessings are too many to count or to begin to declare to others?

6. If God does not desire sacrifice and offerings, what is the place for them in our Christian lives? How do they fit in with what He does want—for us to want His will?

7. What opportunities do I have to speak *YHWH's* praises in the great assembly or in daily life? How might I create new ways to do so?

Appendix A

Swimming the Psalms

My best meditation on the Word happens in the swimming pool.[1] Now don't immediately stop reading this article because you're thinking, "But I don't like to swim" or "On what verses do I meditate while I'm drowning?" The point is that I have found great value in linking together my spiritual and physical disciplines. My desire for both is strengthened, and the benefits of both seem to be increased.

I pray that this description of personal Bible study habits that have been helpful to me will stimulate your own thinking, that perhaps you might get some new ideas for your own quiet times. I don't share my experience as an expert, however; in fact, my very need to link Scripture meditation with a physical discipline is probably a sign of my own weakness—I'm not sure. In any case, such a connection works for me.

As a freelance Bible teacher, I became very frustrated that I often said to people, "Turn to the Psalms; they include every human emotion and can be vastly comforting in every situation," but I did not know various psalms well enough to be able to suggest in particular circumstances which specific psalms might be suitable. At the same time, I was bored with lap swimming. It is necessary for my health for me to work out vigorously several times each week, but the miles of laps back and forth in the same water dragged on interminably. After thinking about the idea only superficially for several months, I fi-

---

nally took the plunge and began to be serious about learning to know the Psalms better. The methods that have evolved over half a year have brought such Joy to me that I'm eager to tell you about them.

My morning quiet times at home begin with the reading of the next psalm, after which I read about that psalm in *The Layman's Bible Commentary* [vol. 9 (Richmond, Va.: John Knox Press, 1960)]. Then I read the psalm again to follow its structure and to pick out a few key verses or ones that particularly strike me. At scattered moments throughout the day and in the weeks to come, I work on memorizing these verses. All of this information is gathered in a meditation notebook. For each psalm I record a title and the kind of psalm that it is, such as an individual or community thanksgiving or lament, a hymn of praise, an affirmation of faith, and so forth. These classifications are well introduced and listed in the commentary. Next in my notebook I put an outline of the psalm and then the verses that I have selected to memorize. This is the material for the pool meditation.

The importance of the notebook emphasizes a significant distinction between two elements that have greatly deepened my growth in the Scriptures. The morning time of writing in the notebook is *study*. When I am swimming and thinking, that study provides the basis for my *meditation*. During the first half-lap, I think about the first psalm. That happens to be one that I have memorized entirely, so I usually recite it as I stroke down the lane, but sometimes I think about ways in which I have fallen into the company of the godless or how blessed it is to delight in the instruction of the LORD. On the second length I think about the second psalm, and so on.

For some of the psalms I have learned songs. To sing those songs while I swim is a good way for me to spend time simply praising God in His own words. Other psalms touch off prayers for particular people. For example, Psalms 14 and 52, which are almost exactly alike, speak of fools who say there is no God. Usually those two lengths are filled with prayers for people, especially some friends of mine, who haven't yet come to know Christ. Length twenty-two, which uses a slower, resting backstroke in my warm-up routine, gives me extra time to think about all the images of the passion of Christ in Psalm 22.

I have been adding a psalm each day for several months, so now it takes more than a mile and a quarter to think about them all. I have seen that my body is getting stronger even as is my spirit. My goal is to be ready to swim the whole book of Psalms by Thanksgiving.

All sorts of exciting results have come out of studying the Psalms in this way. First of all, I really am learning them better, and that has been helpful for my own times of discouragement, as well as for counseling. Now, instead of paging through the Bible trying to find something that is comforting, I know better which of the psalms are appropriate to whatever I might be encountering.

Also, I am amazed by the constant newness of the Scriptures. It astounds me that a psalm that I've been meditating upon for several months yields new insights at each fresh approach. One delightful experience of that freshness happened the day I'd come to Psalm 90. I was so thrilled by what I'd learned in my meditations that morning that I swam through all ninety again, and then I was filled with such wonder that I'd learned even more new things on the second time through that I did them all a third time. Once again the Psalms spoke to me in yet more new ways. I was so excited that I wasn't even tired, though I had swum four miles for the first time in my life. God's Word is indeed a treasure chest.

It is essential for me to look over my notebook frequently, because verses that I have chosen get forgotten after many weeks. I try to keep refreshing my memory so that the Spirit has plenty of material to work with as He nudges my thoughts in various directions proceeding from those things that He brings to my mind.

Another benefit of studying the Psalms in this way has been a deepened appreciation of the Word in formal worship settings. I be-

long to a Lutheran church, which frequently uses psalms in the structured services. When a psalm is simply read or a section of one is
chanted as part of the liturgy, I experience it much more deeply because I have spent many laps thinking about the meanings and ap-
plications of that psalm.

A new benefit of such meditation just opened up for me two days
ago. A dear friend, whose kidneys failed several years ago, met with
his doctor to discuss the advantages and disadvantages of changing
to a new method of dialysis. The decision that my friend had to make
between his present treatment and a new type of treatment would
greatly affect his time, appearance, and potential for work and ministry. I promised Tim that I would support him in prayer all the while
he was at the doctor's office.

At first I thought that I would have to skip my Psalms meditations
for the day, but those very excerpts from the Psalms proved to be
magnificent vehicles for my prayers. I have never prayed for one person for two hours before, and it was a Joy-filled experience! For example, as I swam the fourth length, I thought of the verse, "Know
that the LORD has set apart the godly for himself; the LORD will hear
when I call to him" (4:3 NIV). That led me to thank God that He has
set Tim apart as a sacred vessel and that I could trust Him to guide
Tim's decision so that he would choose the best means of treatment
for God's purposes.

Suddenly, in connection with one of the psalms, it hit me that I had
been praying for Tim to choose the treatment that would best affect his
ministry to his family and friends and in his church, but I had not at
all prayed about which treatment would be best for his own personal
growth in relationship with the LORD. Then, Psalm 81 led me to think
about the various false gods that could affect his decision—idols of appearance or security or our culture's valuing of people according to the
status of their jobs. It took me several laps to pray through all that I discovered about idolatry, and that led to some serious thinking later that

afternoon about the false gods in my own life.

The whole process gave me many new insights into my friend's situation and caused me to praise God in so many new ways for who He is, for God's actions in His people's lives, and for the gift of Tim. I don't think I had ever realized so powerfully before how directly connected to our present-day experiences and twentieth-century decisions the words of the Scriptures are. Finally, one of the greatest Joys for me was that Tim felt thoroughly enfolded in an assurance of truth and the love of God the whole time that he weighed the decision. The Word had been the vehicle for my prayers and his trust.

You might be wondering how any of this could be applied to your own devotional life. Perhaps the following principles drawn from the illustrations above will suggest some ideas for you to try:

1. Times of physical exercise—such solo activities as jogging, calisthenics, isometrics, walking, bicycling, housecleaning, or swimming—can be good times for thinking about the Scriptures.

2. Time spent in study prior to the opportunity for meditation provides food for your thoughts.

3. It is spiritually enriching simply to praise God in His own words, to reflect on His character and its meaning for our lives.

4. The better we know the Scriptures, the more use we can make of them for comfort and sustenance in the tough times.

5. An open mind allows God constantly to be teaching us new things from the passages of His Word upon which we meditate.

6. Meditation on passages of the Scriptures that are used in liturgical services makes them more significant in our worship experiences.

7. Meditation on the Word is an excellent basis for our prayers. The Scriptures reveal to us the character of God and teach us how we can turn to Him. They enable us to be specific about our requests.

Appendix B

When Is a Rut Not a Rut?

Hidden Promise in Psalm 23

There is more than one way to be in a rut.[1]

As I rode my bike through the woods, I kept trying to stay out of the deep rut made, I suppose, by a motorcycle. Frustration mounted as I continued to lose my balance, to get my tires stuck, and to waste a lot of energy trying to make progress. But when I finally gave up fighting that awful rut and chose instead to ride along in it, I was amazed at the ease and pleasure that resulted. As long as I was careful to stay in the midst of what had now become a "track" to me, I didn't get mired in mud or snagged by dead branches. I was more free to enjoy the scenery and to pedal with more power. Whether the path was a "rut" or a "track" depended upon my choice and the perspective that resulted.

So it is with the way of the LORD. I was excited to learn recently that the Hebrew word that we translate "paths" in Psalm 23:3 ("He guides me in the paths of righteousness / For His name's sake") could be rendered "tracks." The word comes from a Hebrew verb root that means "to roll" something that is round. From this verb is derived the noun that signifies a "cart" and, consequently, the word used in Psalms 23:3 for an "entrenchment" or "wagon-track."

The term is used figuratively in the Scriptures to mean both "the

---

[1]Reprinted by permission of *Eternity,* copyright ©1980, Evangelical Ministries, Inc., 1716 Spruce St., Philadelphia, PA, 19103. Psalm 23 in this article is cited from the New American Standard Bible.

snares of the wicked" (Psalm 140:6) and "a course of action or life" (Proverbs 4:26). Since in Psalm 23:3 the word occurs together with the noun for "that which is right," we know that the tracks meant in this verse are a positive course of action.

Psalm 23 begins, of course, with the assurance that the LORD is a faithful Shepherd, who feeds and provides rest and refreshment for His flock. But He doesn't carry the sheep in the path that they should travel. He *leads* them. They could choose not to follow if they wanted. The parable of Jesus about the one who goes astray (Matthew 18:12-14) indicates that even some who are members of the flock might wander away. We each must choose what we want to do about our Shepherd's leading.

Two other phrases in the psalm add insight to our comprehension of the meaning of the LORD's leading us in the tracks of righteousness. The one I want to study with you first was a surprising discovery for me because of the misunderstanding created by a romanticized interpretation of this psalm. In verse 4, the phrase, "Thy rod and Thy staff, they comfort me," is usually thought of in soft and gentle terms. We like to hear the word *comfort* as if it were meant to make us comfortable. Recently the Navigators' *Daily Walk* Bible-reading program offered this arresting sentence: "God does not comfort us to make us comfortable, but to make us comforters."

When we read this phrase in Psalm 23, we must remember that the rod was used by the shepherd for beating or smiting—for chastisement. It was a club, not a feather! (And the staff was a pole ending in a crook to grab a sheep by the neck to keep it, perhaps, from falling over a cliff!) The implication is that sometimes the sheep need to be dealt with sternly to keep them in the tracks of righteousness.

We might wonder how that could be comforting. The Hebrew construction of the phrase almost seems to be directed toward our doubts. It adds an extra pronoun *they* in order to say, "Thy rod and Thy staff—*they* are comforting me." David seems to be assuring us,

"Yes, indeed! What actually appears to be painful to you is in reality the source of comfort."

That makes a lot of sense to me! Recently my life was being torn up by great turmoil and personal crisis. Some days the stress seemed too great as I moved into new work outside of the parish I had been serving and as I battled several dimensions of deterioration in my health. Yet above all the anguish came this promise: the rod is a source of comfort! Sufferings are meant to help me follow the Shepherd in the tracks of righteousness. Yes, indeed! It was good to know that my wise Shepherd loved me so much that He allowed those dimensions of difficulty to keep me in the right tracks.

Just as the jarring of the rough edge reminded me I needed to concentrate on keeping my bicycle in the center of the tracks, so I needed the discipline of the Shepherd's rod and staff to remind me to watch carefully how He leads and to keep me from falling over cliffs. I don't want to wander from the tracks of His righteousness. I want Him to change me, to conform me to the image of the perfect Lamb.

The other phrase that further defines the nature of this entrenchment is this final thought from verse 3: "for His name's sake." The phrase suggests that God guides us into paths of righteousness "for the purpose of vindicating the LORD's name, of maintaining His reputation or character consistently."

What a privilege! Our Shepherd leads us in tracks that will show His character to be consistent. If His people stay in the tracks of His right ways of behaving, they will be witnesses to dimensions of this Shepherd's character. If they remain loving in the face of brutal opposition or persecution, they will maintain the reputation of a God of love. If they suffer calamity with calmness and trust, they will reveal their Shepherd to be a God of strength and grace. Again I say, what a privilege!

Our God has been revealed to us as such a God—of love and strength and grace. In our times of discipline we have the honor of passing that revelation on to those around us. Surely His goodness and mercy will follow us if that is the choice of our life! We will indeed dwell in the LORD's house forever because He has kept us in His path. And we will have invited others to join us in His house because we have revealed the goodness of His tracks to them by our choosing to remain in them.

There is more than one way to be in a rut. To be in the rut of sin, despair, and rebellion against the purposes of God leads to death. In contrast, our Shepherd calls us to follow Him in the tracks of righteousness. We are guided and comforted there by the rod of His chastisement and the staff of His rescue. The results of staying in those tracks are glory to Him, as His character is shown to be consistent, and Joy to us, as we experience the consequent freedom, power, and blessings of pasture and eternal rest.

Resources

Works on the Psalms

Since many new volumes on the Psalms appear every year and since *My Soul Waits* was written many years ago, it would be impossible to give a complete bibliography of works consulted at that time and resources on the Psalms that I have found since then. Instead, I will simply list a few older works that are especially helpful to parishioners and might be missed in the abundance of new material, as well as a sampling of some excellent works by two of my favorite authors.

Also, many topics in the areas of Bible study, Christian community and the culture are introduced only briefly in this book, so I will list other books of mine that delve into these subjects more deeply.

Older Helpful Works on the Psalms

Brandt, Leslie F. *Psalms/Now.* St. Louis: Concordia, 1973.

Kidner, Derek. *Psalms 1—72* and *Psalms 73—150. Tyndale Old Testament Commentaries* vols. 14a and 14b. D. J. Wiseman, gen. ed. Downers Grove, Ill.: InterVarsity Press, 1973.

Leupold, H. C. *Exposition of Psalms.* Reprint. Grand Rapids, Mich.: Baker, 1969.

Lewis, C. S. *Reflections on the Psalms.* New York: Harcourt Brace & World, 1958.

Marty, Martin E. *A Cry of Absence: Reflections for the Winter of the Heart.* San Francisco: Harper and Row, 1983.

Rhodes, Arnold B. *The Book of Psalms.* Vol. 9 of *The Layman's Bible*

Commentary. Balmer H. Kelly, ed. Richmond, VA: John Knox Press, 1960.

Spurgeon, C. H. *The Treasury of David: An Expository and Devotional Commentary on the Psalms*. 7 vols. Grand Rapids, Mich.: Baker, 1977.

Westermann, Claus. *The Living Psalms*. Translated by J. R. Porter. Grand Rapids, Mich.: Eerdmans, 1989.

Books on the Psalms by Two Superb Scholars

Brueggemann, Walter. *Abiding Astonishment: Psalms, Modernity and the Making of History*. Louisville: Westminster John Knox, 1991.

————. *Israel's Praise: Doxology Against Idolatry and Ideology*. Philadelphia: Fortress, 1988.

————. *The Message of the Psalms: A Theological Commentary*. Minneapolis: Augsburg-Fortress, 1984.

————. *The Psalms and the Life of Faith*. Edited by Patrick D. Miller. Minneapolis: Augsburg-Fortress, 1995.

Peterson, Eugene H. *Answering God: The Psalms as Tools for Prayer*. San Francisco: HarperSanFrancisco, 1992.

————. *A Long Obedience in the Same Direction: Discipleship in an Instant Society*. Downers Grove, Ill.: InterVarsity Press, 1980.

————. *Psalms. The Message: The Bible in Contemporary Language*. Colorado Springs: NavPress, 2002.

————. *Praying with the Psalms: A Year of Daily Prayers and Reflections on the Words of David*. San Francisco: HarperSanFrancisco, 1993.

————. *Psalms: Prayers of the Heart*. Downers Grove, Ill.: InterVarsity Press, 1987.

————. *Where Your Treasure Is: Psalms That Summon You from Self to Community*. 2nd ed. Grand Rapids, Mich.: Eerdmans, 1993.

Selected Books by Marva Dawn

How Shall We Worship? Biblical Guidelines for the Worship Wars. Wheaton, Ill.: Tyndale House, 2003.

Is It a Lost Cause? Having the Heart of God for the Church's Children. Grand Rapids, Mich.: Eerdmans, 1997.

Joy in Divine Wisdom: Practices of Discernment from Other Cultures and Christian Traditions. San Francisco: Jossey-Bass, 2006.

Joy in Our Weakness: A Gift of Hope from the Book of Revelation. Rev. ed. Grand Rapids, Mich.: Eerdmans, 2002.

Keeping the Sabbath Wholly: Ceasing, Resting, Embracing, Feasting. Grand Rapids, Mich.: Eerdmans, 1989.

Morning by Morning: Daily Meditations from the Writings of Marva J. Dawn. Edited by Karen Dismer. Grand Rapids, Mich.: Eerdmans, 2001.

Powers, Weakness and the Tabernacling of God. Grand Rapids, Mich.: Eerdmans, 2001.

Reaching Out Without Dumbing Down: A Theology of Worship for This Urgent Time. Grand Rapids, Mich.: Eerdmans, 1995.

A Royal "Waste" of Time: The Splendor of Worshiping God and Being Church for the World. Grand Rapids, Mich.: Eerdmans, 1999.

The Sense of the Call: A Sabbath Way of Life for Those Who Serve God, the Church and the World. Grand Rapids, Mich.: Eerdmans, 2006.

Sexual Character: Beyond Technique to Intimacy. Grand Rapids, Mich.: Eerdmans, 1993.

Sources and Trajectories: Eight Early Articles by Jacques Ellul That Set the Stage. Translated and edited by Marva J. Dawn. Grand Rapids, Mich.: Eerdmans, 1997.

Talking the Walk: Letting the Christian Language Live Again. Grand Rapids, Mich.: Brazos Press, 2005.

To Walk and Not Faint: A Month of Meditations on Isaiah 40. 2nd ed. Grand Rapids, Mich.: Eerdmans, 1997.

Truly the Community: Romans 12 and How to Be the Church. Grand Rapids, Mich.: Eerdmans, 1992; reissued 1997.

Unfettered Hope: A Call to Faithful Living in an Affluent Society. Louisville: Westminster John Knox, 2003.

The Unnecessary Pastor: Rediscovering the Call. With Eugene H. Peterson. Grand Rapids, Mich.: Eerdmans, 1999.